SUBSTANTIVE LAW

Resources Workbook

CHRIS TURNER

Hodder & Stoughton
A MEMBER OF THE HODDER HEADLINE GROUP

Orders: please contact Bookpoint Ltd, 78 Milton Park, Abingdon, Oxon OX14 4TD. Telephone: (44) 01235 827720, Fax: (44) 01235 400454. Lines are open from 9.00–6.00, Monday to Saturday, with a 24 hour message answering service. Email address: orders@bookpoint.co.uk

British Library Cataloguing in Publication Data
A catalogue record for this title is available from The British Library

ISBN 0 340 753 390

First published 2000

Impression number	10 9 8 7 6 5 4 3 2 1
Year	2005 2004 2003 2002 2001 2000

Typeset by Fakenham Photosetting Limited, Fakenham, Norfolk NR21 8NN.
Printed in Great Britain for Hodder & Stoughton Educational, a division of Hodder Headline Plc, 338 Euston Road, London NW1 3BH by J. W. Arrowsmith, Bristol.

CONTENTS

PREFACE

As an examiner of many years' experience, I often receive 'letters' at the end of exam papers beginning 'Dear examiner...'. This seems to put the relationship with the candidate on quite a personal footing, so I hope you will not mind me beginning 'Dear reader' (whether it be 'Dear student' or 'Dear teacher', and I hope that it is both).

This book of resources and exercises is aimed primarily at students on A Level Law courses, of whatever examining board, but there is no reason why it should not be used by any first-time student of criminal law, contract law or tort.

The book is made up of a variety of resources, materials, exercises and other learning aids on the three substantive areas of law contained in the A Level Law syllabuses of the various examining boards. It is broken down into sections roughly representing the sorts of chapters that you will find in the textbooks on the same areas, each of which is preceded by a brief overview of the area outlining the sorts of points that may be raised in the source material.

This book is obviously designed to be a companion to the textbook on *Criminal Law* by Diana Roe and the textbook on *Contract Law and Tort* written by myself. It can also be a companion to the *English Legal System* textbook and *English Legal System Resource Book*, both by Jacqueline Martin. Alternatively it could be used to supplement any textbook on the three substantive areas of law included.

The materials in the book include:

- extracts from reported cases (sometimes from the law reports themselves and sometimes from other sources such as the NLJ reports);
- extracts from Acts of Parliament or from delegated legislation;
- articles from newspapers, legal journals, books and even reports of law reform bodies.

These extracts vary in size, but they all represent only small parts of the whole from which they are drawn, so that they are introducing you, the reader, to actual primary sources of law, but in manageable proportions. Inevitably they only touch the surface of the materials that could be included and represent no more than a selection of relevant materials.

As with Jacqueline Martin's *English Legal System Resource Book*, all the extracts here are accompanied by questions to test your comprehension of the material. Some of these questions can be answered very briefly, while others are more thought-provoking and similar to questions that you might be set in exams. In some cases where it seemed appropriate there are also some small exercises or activities allowing for a different, often more practical, way of testing your understanding.

The last but one chapter of the book is made up of some revision aids and a number of different exercises in the form of crosswords, quizzes, wordsearches, etc., all of these being ways I have used over the years in an effort to give my own students a more light-hearted alternative to the slog of revision, but hopefully helping to make a few more case names stick before the exam.

The final chapter is an examiner's view of how to cope with the different types of testing that you may come across during exams, whether they be traditional essay questions, problem solving or the more recent data response-type questions.

One of the key aims of the book is that it should be an accessible and lively alternative to other learning methods. I hope you will find it so. Above all I hope that you will enjoy the law as I do. The law is ultimately about people and the often strange things that happen to them. All of the reported cases here involve real events, and as you read many of the reports you will realise the reality of the old maxim that the truth is stranger than fiction. I hope that you will find also that the law is in fact as entertaining and interesting as any work of fiction.

ACKNOWLEDGMENTS

The author and publisher would like to thank the following for permission to reproduce copyright material:

Extracts reproduced by kind permission of *The Legal Executive Journal*, pp. 12, 46, 77, 86, 106, 123.
© *The Times*, p. 48.
Parliamentary copyright material from 'Violence: Reforming the Offences Against the Person Act, 1981, Draft Offences Against the Person Bill 1998' is reproduced with the permission of the Controller of Her Majesty's Stationery Office on behalf of Parliament, p. 31.
Justice of the Peace, pp. 160–161.
New Law Journal, pp. 16, 25, 28, 33, 66, 107, 115.
Brenda Barrett in *The Law Teacher*, (1999) 33 *Law Teach* 94, p. 138.
Crown Copyright material from The Law Commission No. 160, reproduced by permission of the Controller of Her Majesty's Stationery Office on behalf of Parliament, p. 73.
Criminal Law Review, pp. 21–23.

Every effort has been made to trace copyright holders but this has not always been possible in all cases; any omissions brought to our attention will be corrected in future printings.

Table of Statutes and Statutory Instruments

TABLE OF CASES

Elliott v C (a Minor) [1983] 77 Cr App R 103
Esso Petroleum Ltd v Commissioners of Customs and Excise [1976] 1 WLR 1
Fagan v Metropolitan Police Commissioner [1969] 1 QB 439
Felthouse v Bindley [1862] 11 CB (NS) 869; 142 ER 1037
Fibrosa Spolka Akcyjna v Fairbairn Lawson Combe Barbour Ltd [1943] AC 32, HL
Fisher v Bell [1961] 1 QB 394
Fitch v Dewes [1921] AC 158, HL
Froom v Butcher [1976] QB 286, CA
Gibson v Manchester City Council
Gifford v Dent [1926] 1 WN 336
Glasgow Corporation v Taylor [1922] 1 AC 44
Goldman v Hargrave [1967] 1 AC 645
Goldsoll v Goldman [1915] 1 Ch 292, CA
Guthing v Lynn [1831] 2 B & Ad 232
Harris v Nickerson [1873] LR. 8 QB 286
Harvela Investments Ltd v Royal Trust Co of Canada [1988] 3 WLR 276
Harvey v Facey [1893] Ac 552
Haseldine v Daw [1941] 2 KB 343
Haughton v Smith [1975] AC 476
Haynes v Harwood [1935] 1 KB 146
Hedley Byrne & Co Ltd v Heller & Partners Ltd [1964] AC 465, HL
Herd v Weardale Steel, Coal and Coke Co [1915] AC 67, HL
Herrington v BR Board [1972] Ac 877
Hoenig v Isaacs [1952] 2 All ER 176
Household Fire Insurance Co v Grant [1879] 4 Ex D 216
Howard Marine & Dredging Co Ltd v A Ogden & Sons (Excavations) Ltd [1978] 2 WLR 515, CA
Hunter and Others v Canary Wharf Ltd [1997] 2 All ER 426
Hyde v Wrench [1840] 3 Beav 334
Jarvis v Sawn Tours Ltd [1973] QB 233, CA
JCC (a minor) v Eisenhower [1983] 3 All ER 230, QBD
Jolley v London Borough of Sutton, NLJ 19 June 1998
Jones v Padavattor [1969] 1 WLR 328
Jones v Tower Boot Co Ltd [1997] IRLR 168
Junior Books Ltd v Veitchi Co Ltd [1983] AC 520, HL
Kelsen v Imperial Tobacco Co Ltd [1957] 2 QB 334
Khorasandjian v Bush [1993] 3 WLR 476
Kings Norton Metal Co Ltd v Edridge, Merrett & Co Ltd [1897] 14 TLR 98, CA
Krell v Henry [1903] 2 KB 740 CA
Lampleigh v Braithwaite [1615] Hob 105
Leslie (R) Ltd v Sheill [1914] 3 KB 607, CA
L'Estrange v Graucob (F) Ltd [1934] 2 KB 394, CA
Lewis v Averay [1971] 3 All ER 907, CA
Liesborch v Edison [1933] Ac 449
Lloyd v Grace, Smith & Co
Lumley v Wagner [1852] 1 De GM & G 604
McCutcheon v David MacBrayne Ltd [1964] 1 WLR 125, HL
McKew v Holland & Hannen & Cubitts (Scotland) Ltd [1969] 3 All ER 1621, HL
McLoughlin v O'Brian [1982] 2 All ER 298
Mahmoud and Ispahani, Re [1921] 2 KB 716 CA
Maritime National Fish Ltd v Ocean Trawlers Ltd [1935] AC 524, PC
Merritt v Merritt [1970] 1 WLR 1211
Miller v Jackson [1977] QB 966, CA
Moynes v Cooper [1956] 1 QB 439
Murphy v Brentwood District Council [1991] AC 398, HL
Nash v Sheen [1953] *The Times* 13 March 1953
Nettleship v Weston [1971] 2 QB 691
North Ocean Shipping Co v Hyundai Construction Co (The Atlantic Baron) [1978] 3 All ER 1170
North Western Railway Co v M'Michael [1851] 5 Exch 114
Olley v Marlborough Court Hotel Ltd [1949] 1 KB 532, CA
Oscar Chess v Williams [1957] 1 WLR 370, CA
Overseas Tankship (UK) Ltd v Mort's Dock and Engineering Co Ltd (The Wagon Mound (No 1)) [1961] AC 388
Oxford v Moss [1978] 68 Cr App R 183, QBD

TABLE OF EXTRACTS FROM BOOKS, ARTICLES AND REPORTS

'Abolition of privity', Richard Hudson, *New Law Journal*, 22 January 1999

'Battered Women and Provocation: The Implications of *R v Ahluwhalia*', Donald Nicolson and Robert Sanghvi, *Criminal Law Review*, October 1993, 728–738

'Bolam and Bolitho: A new standard of care for doctors?', Dr Walter Scott, *New Law Journal*, 16 January, 1998, p 64

'Consent: public policy or legal moralism?' Susan Nash, *New Law Journal*, 15 March 1996

'Damages for psychiatric injuries', Andrew Ritchie, *New Law Journal*, 9 December 1994

'Exposing the flaws in Britain's libel laws', David Pannick, QC, *The Times*, 20 April 1999

'Foresight and foreseeability', Sean Enright, *New Law Journal*, 6 November 1998, 1636–1637

'*Gomez* revisited', Richard Akinjide, *New Law Journal*, 10 June 1994

Home Office, 'Violence: Reforming the Offences Against the Person Act 1861, Draft Offences Against the Person Bill 1998'

'Inflicting injuries for sexual pleasure illegal, Lords rule', Frances Gibb, *The Times*, 12 March 1993

'Intention and recklessness', Denis Lanser, *The Legal Executives Journal*, November 1995

'Involuntary intoxication', Nicholas Reville, *The Legal Executives Journal*, January 1995

Law Commission Report No 160, *Sale and Supply of Goods* (Cm 137 (1987)), paragraphs 3.5, 3.11 and 3.12

'Limitation Clauses in Standard Term Contracts—are they ever enforceable?', Sylvia Elwes, *The Legal Executives Journal*, September 1995

'Mad or bad—the dilemma of insanity', Dr Gary Slapper, *The Times*, 8 December 1998

'Manslaughter: *Dalby* Revisited' Stephen O'Doherty, *Justice of the Peace*, Vol 163 8/5/1999, pp 368–371

'Manslaughter, *mens rea* and medicine', Gary Slapper, *New Law Journal*, 8 July 1994

Privity of Contract: Contracts for the Benefit of Third Parties (Law Commission No 242)

'Right, Privilege or Pastime?', Bill Thomas, *The Legal Executives Journal*, July 1997

'The Creditor, the House, the Misled and her Lover', Simon Brooman, *The Legal Executives Journal*, October 1995

'*Trotman v North Yorkshire County Council* [1998] (CRTF 97/1273/3) The Limits of Vicarious Liability', Brenda Barrett (1999), *The Law Teacher*, Vol 3 No 1

'When the Pitch becomes a Battle Ground ...', Sarah Philbrook, *The Legal Executives Journal*, June 1997

CHAPTER 1

CRIMINAL LAW

SECTION 1: THE ELEMENTS OF A CRIME: *ACTUS REUS*

Most crimes require both conduct which is criminal and the necessary criminal intent. The conduct element and the circumstances surrounding it are known as the '*actus reus*'. The key aspects of the *actus reus* are that it should involve voluntary conduct, and that it should be the cause of the consequence which the law sees as unacceptable, and therefore criminal. Sometimes an omission rather than a deed can be the *actus reus*. On rare occasions a mere state of affairs is criminal.

EXTRACT ADAPTED FROM THE JUDGMENT IN *R V LARSONNEUR* [1933] 97 JP 206, COURT OF CRIMINAL APPEAL

Larsonneur, a French woman, landed in England with an endorsement for a temporary stay only on her passport. This was later revoked and she was required to leave by a certain date. She then went to Ireland where she was deported and transported back to England. She was arrested and charged for being in breach of the Aliens Order 1920. She had no choice about returning to England, and had no control over her presence here but she was still guilty of the offence.

LORD HEWART CJ

The appellant ... was at Holyhead on 21 April 1933, practically a month after the day limited by the condition on her passport.

In these circumstances it seems quite clear that the Aliens Order 1920 applies. The appellant was in the position she would have been in if she had been prohibited from landing by the Secretary of State. She was found here and was, therefore, deemed to be in the class of persons whose landing had been prohibited by the Secretary of State, by reason of the fact that she had violated the condition on her passport.

Questions

1. Why does the case appear to be at odds with the normal requirement that *actus reus* involves voluntary conduct?
2. How would you usually define voluntary conduct?

EXTRACT ADAPTED FROM THE JUDGMENT IN *R V STONE AND DOBINSON* [1977] 1 QB 354, CA

A very inadequate couple, one aged 67, partially deaf, almost blind and of low intelligence, and the other aged 43 and described as ineffectual, took into their home the younger one's sister. She was suffering from anorexia nervosa. The couple were incapable of looking after her, failed at first to get her a doctor and eventually she died. The couple were convicted of manslaughter and appealed unsuccessfully.

GEOFFREY LANE LJ

There is no dispute as to the matters on which the jury must be satisfied before they can convict of manslaughter in circumstances such as the present. They are (1) that the defendant undertook the care of a person who by reason of age or infirmity was unable to care for himself; (2) that the defendant was grossly negligent in regard to his duty of care; (3) that by reason of such negligence the person died.

[Counsel for the appellants] submitted that the evidence that might support the assumption of a duty by the appellants does not, when examined, succeed in doing so. Fanny came to this house as a lodger. Largely if not entirely due to her own eccentricity and failure to look after herself or feed herself properly, she became increasingly infirm and immobile and eventually unable to look after herself. The suggestion is that, heartless though it may seem, this is one of those situations where the appellants were entitled to do nothing; where no duty was cast upon them to help, any more than it is cast upon a man to rescue a stranger from drowning, however easy such a rescue might be.

This was not a situation analogous to the drowning stranger. They did make efforts to care. They tried to get a doctor; they tried to discover the previous doctor. The appellant Dobson helped with the washing and the provision of food. All these matters were put before the jury in terms which we find it impossible to fault. They were entitled to find that the duty had been assumed. They were entitled to conclude that once Fanny became helplessly infirm the appellants were, in the circumstances, obliged either to summon help or else to care for Fanny themselves.

Questions

1. What basic test does Geoffrey Lane LJ suggest enables a jury to determine that a defendant is guilty of manslaughter in the circumstances?
2. What in the defendants' behaviour does he suggest imposed a duty on them to care for Fanny?
3. What principle does the case demonstrate?

EXTRACT ADAPTED FROM THE JUDGMENT IN *R V BLAUE* [1975] 1 WLR 1411

Blaue stabbed a woman and perforated her lung. The woman was told at hospital that she needed a blood transfusion, but she refused this because of her beliefs as a Jehovah's Witness and she then died. The medical treatment would have saved the woman's life but Blaue was still convicted of murder and appealed, unsuccessfully, on the ground that there was a break in the chain of causation.

LAWTON LJ

Counsel for the defendant invited the judge to direct the jury to acquit. His argument was that her refusal to have a blood transfusion had broken the chain of causation between the stabbing and her death.

When the judge came to direct the jury on this issue he did so by telling them that they should apply their common sense . . . He placed particular reliance on what Maule J had said in *R v Holland* . . . 'the real question is, whether in the end the wound inflicted by the prisoner was the cause of death.' That distinguished judge left the jury to decide that question as did the judge in this case. They had to decide it as juries always do, by pooling their experience of life and using their common sense.

Maule J's direction to the jury reflected the common law's answer to the problem. He who inflicted an injury which resulted in death could not excuse himself by pleading that his victim could have avoided death by taking greater care of himself.

Mr Comyn tried to overcome this line of reasoning by submitting that the jury should have been directed that if they thought the deceased's decision not to have a blood transfusion was an unreasonable one, then the chain of causation would have been broken. At once the question arises—reasonable by whose standards?

... It has long been the policy of the law that those who use violence on other people must take their victims as they find them. It does not lie in the mouth of the assailant to say that the victim's religious beliefs which inhibited him from accepting certain kinds of treatment were unreasonable. The question for decision is what caused her death. The answer is the stab wound. The fact that the victim refused to stop this end coming about did not break the causal connection between the act and the death.

Questions

1. What is a 'break in the chain of causation'?
2. Why, according to Lawton LJ, is there no break in the chain of causation in *Blaue*?
3. What do you think of the defence argument that there should be no conviction because the refusal to have a blood transfusion was unreasonable?

SECTION 2: THE ELEMENTS OF A CRIME: *MENS REA*

With the exception of 'strict liability' offences all crimes require criminal intent, known as the '*mens rea*'. In general three states of mind can lead to criminal liability. The first is intention. This is not always easy to show and sometimes has to be inferred, so one problem is the part played by foresight of consequences. The second is recklessness. This is of two types: subjective, which is appreciating the existence of an unjustified risk but still taking it; and objective, which is the taking of an obvious risk. The third type is gross negligence. This applies to man-slaughter and involves falling so far below the standards of a duty that is owed that it amounts to a crime.

EXTRACT ADAPTED FROM 'INTENTION AND RECKLESSNESS', DENIS LANSER, *THE LEGAL EXECUTIVE JOURNAL*, NOVEMBER 1995

Though liability in criminal law is generally incurred by those who act either intentionally or recklessly, there are some offences for which only intention will suffice.

Examples include murder, wounding and causing grievous bodily harm with intent under the Offences Against the Person Act 1861 section 18 and attempts, at any rate, so as to any consequences in the *actus reus* of the full offence.

... the trilogy of cases, *Moloney, Hancock and Shankland* and *Nedrick* seem to have established the current approach ... The key features ... are:

- the absence of any clear definition of intention;
- the assertion that little guidance on the meaning of intention need be given to the jury in the ordinary run of cases because the jury can be expected to recognise it when they see it;
- insistence that foresight of consequences alone is not the same thing as intention, though it can be evidence of intention ... if it amounts to foresight of virtual certainty that the consequences will occur.

Guidance on the latter aspect should only be given to juries in cases where it is clearly necessary.

In most cases, where the issue of intention is raised, there will be no need for the judge to complicate matters by trying to define it. This approach has considerable limitations and the disadvantages of any clear definition of intention are all too evident when the case is not ... simple .... Thus a common sense approach does not yield an obvious answer to the question 'did Hancock and Shankland intend death or serious injury?', since they could claim to have been intent merely on blocking the road and disrupting the convoy.

In such cases our perception of the blameworthiness of the conduct is very much bound up with our perception of the likelihood that the consequences will occur and with our views as to the *accused's* perception of that likelihood.

In other words, if we are satisfied that the accused foresaw the consequences as virtually certain or very highly probable, we may wish to conclude that he *should* be guilty because, in terms of blameworthiness, that state of mind is indistinguishable from intention.

Nevertheless, the current approach would deny the simple equating of the one state of mind with the other. Instead, the jury is required to take a further step in any offence requiring proof of intention. That step is to *draw the inference* that the accused *intended* the consequence from proof that he foresaw it.

The jury is invited somehow to infer from one state of mind (foresight), a qualitatively different state of mind (intention) despite the fact that they have been given no guidance as to what intention means. . . .

In attempting to escape from the uncertainties of the approach adopted in *Hyam* where, as a matter of law, foresight of any degree of probability (as distinct from possibility) of death or serious injury would have sufficed, the courts have established a clear rule that mere foresight is not enough and promptly obscured it by opening up an alternative route through 'inference' from foresight.

If the Law Commission's proposals on intention in non-fatal offences were ... adopted and applied to all offences, these . . . difficulties would . . . be reduced, if not eliminated . . . . Intention would be defined *and* that definition would include not only having the purpose of causing a consequence but also, though not having that purpose, being aware that it will occur in the ordinary course of events if the accused were to succeed in his purpose of causing some other consequence.

The Law Commission's commentary makes it plain that 'in the ordinary course of events' . . . covers only consequences recognised by the accused as 'near inevitable' and cites as . . . example an explosion designed to destroy an aeroplane in mid-air . . . to claim insurance on the cargo but which will inevitably kill the crew and passengers.

If the 'virtual certainty' which *Nedrick* demands must be proved to have been foreseen before the jury is entitled (but not bound) to infer intention is co-extensive with 'aware that it would occur in the ordinary course of events', then this change would eliminate the requirement for the jury to *infer* the intention. That awareness would *be* intention.

Questions

1. In his article what does Denis Lanser suggest are the three main strands to the courts' approach to intention?
2. How does Denis Lanser suggest that our perception of intention is tied in with our own perception of blameworthiness?
3. What were the 'uncertainties in *Hyam*' identified in the source?
4. What does the Law Commission's definition of intention include, according to the article?

EXTRACT ADAPTED FROM THE JUDGMENT IN *R V CUNNINGHAM* [1957] 2 QB 396, CA

Cunningham ripped a coin-operated gas meter from the basement wall of a house in order to take the money in it. As the result of this gas then leaked from the pipes into the adjoining property. He was convicted of maliciously administering a noxious substance contrary to s23 Offences Against the Person Act 1861 on the trial judge's direction that the jury could convict if satisfied that his actions were 'wicked'. He appealed successfully on this interpretation of malice.

BYRNE J

The following principle was propounded by the late Professor CS Kenny ... 'In any statutory definition of a crime, malice must be taken not in the old vague sense of wickedness ... but as requiring either (1) ... actual intention to do the particular kind of harm ... in fact ... done; or (2) recklessness as to whether such harm should occur ... (i.e. the accused has foreseen that the particular kind of harm might be done and yet ... gone on to take the risk ...). It is neither limited to nor does it indeed require any ill will towards the person injured' ... We think that this is an accurate statement of the law ... the word 'maliciously' in a statutory crime postulates foresight of the consequences.

... we think that it is incorrect to say that the word 'malicious' in a statutory offence merely means wicked. We think the judge was, in effect, telling the jury that if they were satisfied that the appellant had acted wickedly—and he had clearly acted wickedly in stealing the gas meter and its contents—they ought to find that he had acted maliciously in causing the gas to be taken by Mrs Wade so as to thereby endanger her life.

... it should have been left to the jury to decide whether, even if the appellant did not intend to injure Mrs Wade, he foresaw that the removal of the gas meter might cause injury to someone but nevertheless removed it.

EXTRACT ADAPTED FROM THE JUDGMENT IN *ELLIOTT V C (A MINOR)* [1983] 77 CR APP R 103

A 14-year-old girl of low intelligence and in a remedial class at school stayed out all night without sleep in a garden shed. She poured some white spirit on to carpet and threw matches on it to light it. The shed was destroyed and she was charged under the Criminal Damage Act 1971. Magistrates acquitted because they believed that, owing to her age, lack of intelligence and lack of sleep there would not have been an obvious risk of the damage to her. The prosecution appealed by way of case stated and the divisional court, applying *R v Caldwell*, felt compelled to allow the appeal.

GLIDEWELL J

Mr Moses submits that the phrase 'creates an obvious risk' means that the risk must be one which must have been obvious to a reasonably prudent man, not necessarily to the particular defendant if he or she had given thought to it.

It follows, says Mr Moses, that if the risk is one which would have been obvious to a reasonably prudent person, once it has also been proved that the particular defendant gave no thought to the possibility of there being such a risk, it is not a defence that because of limited intelligence or exhaustion she would not have appreciated the risk even if she had thought about it

... we are in my judgment bound to hold that the word 'reckless' in section 1 of the Criminal Damage Act 1971 has the meaning ascribed to it by Mr Moses.

ROBERT GOFF LJ

I agree with the conclusion reached by Glidewell J but I do so simply because I believe myself constrained to do so by authority.

This is not a case where there was a deliberate disregard of a known risk of damage or injury of a certain type or degree; nor is it a case where there was a mindless indifference to a risk of such damage or injury; nor is it even a case where failure to give thought to the possibility of the risk was due to some blameworthy cause such as intoxication. This is a case where it appears that the only basis upon which the accused might be held to have been reckless would be if the appropriate test to be applied was purely objective—a test which in some circumstances might be thought justifiable. But such a test does not appear at first sight to be appropriate to a crime such as that under consideration in the present case.

Questions

Read the two extracts above and answer the questions.

1. What definition of the word 'maliciously' is identified in the case of *Cunningham*?
2. How is 'recklessness' defined in the same case?
3. Why was the appeal successful in the case?
4. What different definition of recklessness is apparent from the judgment of Glidewell J in *Elliott v C*?
5. On what basis did Robert Goff LJ agree with the conclusion in *Elliott v C*?

SECTION 3: UNLAWFUL KILLING: MURDER

Murder is the most serious crime. It involves an unlawful killing which is intended. Problems associated with murder usually involve proving the necessary intention, in which the relevance of foresight of consequences is always prominent.

EXTRACT ADAPTED FROM THE JUDGMENT IN *R V HANCOCK AND SHANKLAND* [1986] AC 455 HL

Two striking miners during the miners' strike of 1984 pushed a heavy concrete block off a bridge into the path of a taxi taking another miner to work, in order to frighten him. The block went through the windscreen, killing the taxi driver. The miners denied that they had intended any harm, claiming that they only intended to block the road. The Crown rejected a plea of guilty to manslaughter and the miners were convicted of murder. The House of Lords had to consider whether there was sufficient *mens rea.*

LORD SCARMAN

First the House cleared away the confusions which had obscured the law during the last 25 years, laying down authoritatively that the mental element of murder is a specific intent, the intent to kill or to inflict serious bodily harm. Nothing less suffices: and the jury must be sure that the intent existed when the act was done which resulted in death before they can return a verdict of murder.

Secondly the House made it absolutely clear that foresight of consequences is no more than evidence of the existence of ... intent; it must be considered, and its weight assessed, together with all the evidence in the case. Foresight does not necessarily imply the existence of intention, though it may be a fact from which when considered with all ... other evidence a jury may think it right to infer the necessary intent.

Thirdly, the House emphasised that the probability of the result of an act is an important matter for the jury to consider and can be critical in their determining whether the result was intended.

Questions

1. How is the necessary mental element for murder defined in the case?
2. How does Lord Scarman describe the nature of foresight?

Extract adapted from 'Foresight and foreseeability', Sean Enright, *New Law Journal*, 6 November 1998, 1636–1637

'Foresight and foreseeability are not the same thing as intention although either may give rise to an irresistible inference of such ...' (*R v Hyam* [1985]). Difficult legal concepts neatly expressed. The wonder is that the common law is still grappling with the relationship between foresight and intention and the directions to be given to a jury in such circumstances. The latest attempt to resolve the issue in *Woollin* [1998] is likely to create as many problems as it solves.

The issue surfaced as long ago as *DPP v Smith* [1961] ... the defendant killed a policeman by driving from the scene while the officer was hanging onto the car. The Lords ruled that the defendant was guilty of murder because death was foreseen by him as a likely result of his act and that he was deemed to have foreseen the risk a reasonable person in his position would have foreseen.

... that *mens rea* could be imputed to a defendant facing a murder charge was bound to be unpopular. With hindsight the test was always likely to prove unworkable.

In fact *DPP v Smith* was soon overruled by Parliament implementing s8 of the Criminal Justice Act 1967 which provides:

'A court or jury in determining whether a person has committed an offence, shall not be bound by law to infer that he intended or foresaw a result of his actions by reason only of its being a natural and probable consequence of those actions; but shall decide whether he did intend or foresaw that result by reference to all the evidence, drawing such inferences from the evidence as appear proper in the circumstances.'

The intervention ... failed to resolve matters. In the great majority of cases there was no difficulty. Juries were directed that before convicting it was necessary to be sure that the defendant intended to kill or cause serious harm. The continuing difficulty related to that class of case where such a simple direction did not fit the facts ... —where, for instance, a defendant's intent was not readily apparent ....

The next opportunity for the Lords to resolve the difficulty arose in *Hyam* [1975] which split the Lords three/two. Almost uniquely, the speeches of the three Law Lords who prevailed gave different tests to be applied on the question of intent.

Their Lordships had another bite of the cherry in *Moloney* [1985] ... [and issued] guidelines on what constituted the necessary mental intent in murder ...

- [In] a crime of specific intent ... the probability of consequences taken to have been foreseen must be little short of overwhelming before it will suffice to establish the necessary intent.
- In directing the jury, the judge should avoid any elaboration or paraphrase of what is meant by intent, and leave it to the jury's good sense to decide whether the accused acted with the necessary intent, unless the judge is convinced ... some further explanation or elaboration is strictly necessary to avoid misunderstanding.
- Foresight of consequences, as an element of bearing on the issue of intention in murder or any other crime of specific intent, belongs not to the substantive law but to the law of evidence. In the rare cases in which it is necessary for the judge to direct a jury by reference to foresight ... he should direct the jury to answer two questions: first, was the death or really serious injury a natural consequence of the defendant's voluntary act? Secondly, did the defendant foresee that consequence as being a natural consequence of that act? If the jury answer yes to both questions it is ... proper [to infer] that he intended that consequence.

Did this settle the law? Sadly not. Further trips were made to the Lords in *Hancock and Shankland*... the Lords ... held that where it was necessary to direct the jury on the issue of intent by reference to foresight ..., the judges should refer to probability and explain ... that the greater the probability of the consequence the more likely that it was foreseen, and that if it was foreseen the more likely it was that it was intended.

If anyone thought that this would unscramble the mess they were sadly mistaken. *Nedrick* [1986] was another arson case which raised the same old difficulties of proving intent from actions. The Court of Appeal created complications by adding words of advice to trial judges: '... the jury should be directed that a person may intend a certain result while not desiring it to come about; in determining whether the defendant had the necessary intent, they may find it helpful to ask themselves, first how probable was the consequence that resulted from his voluntary act and, secondly, whether he foresaw that consequence; he could not have intended to bring death or serious harm about if he did not appreciate that death or serious harm was likely to result from his act. If he thought that the risk to which he was exposing the deceased was only slight the jury may easily conclude that he did not intend to bring about the death; the jury should be directed that they are not entitled to infer the necessary intention unless they feel sure that death or serious harm was a virtual certainty and that he appreciated that was the case.

Nedrick at last brings us to *Woollin* [who] lost his temper and threw his three-month old son onto a hard surface. The son sustained a fractured skull and died. At the trial, the prosecution did not contend that the appellant had desired to kill his son or to cause him serious injury. The issue was whether the appellant had the intent to cause serious harm.

Subject to one qualification the trial judge had summed up in accordance with guidance given by Lane CJ in *Nedrick* and gave the jury what has become known as the 'virtual certainty' direction. ... the judge diluted the test by directing the jury that it was open to them to convict if they found that the appellant must have realised and appreciated when he threw the child that there was a substantial risk that he would cause the child serious injury. The jury convicted of murder.

Following an unsuccessful appearance before the Court of Appeal the following questions of public importance were certified:

'In murder, where there is no direct evidence that the purpose of the defendant was to kill or inflict serious harm on the victim, is it necessary to direct a jury that they may only infer an intent to do serious injury if they are satisfied

- That serious bodily harm was a virtually certain consequence of the defendant's voluntary act and
- That the defendant appreciated that fact. If the answer to question 1 is 'yes' is such a direction necessary in all cases or is it only necessary in cases where the sole evidence of the defendant's intention is to be found in his actions and their consequences to the victim?'

Their Lordships declined to answer the certified question ... It is plain [they] ... found that the direction by the trial judge diluted the *Nedrick* direction to such an extent that the distinction between recklessness and murder was blurred.

On ... whether *Nedrick* was correctly decided, the Lords approved the ... test ... describing it as 'a tried and tested formula. Trial judges ought to continue to use it'. ... the ... test continues to apply to that class of murder case where exceptionally, the usual direction on intention to kill or cause serious harm is thought to be insufficient.

Lord Steyn and Lord Hope observed that the two subsidiary questions posed by the Court of Appeal in *Nedrick*: 'how probable was the consequence? Did he foresee that consequence?' ought never be put to a jury.

Woollin raised some important difficulties. At the heart of the debate lies the notion of 'intent', a concept quite different from motive, desire or foresight ... academics and judges tend to fight shy of definitions of intent. Instead, the debate has focused on the means by which intent can be proved or inferred.

The direction in *Woollin* comes perilously close to implementing the imputed knowledge test in *DPP v Smith.* Equally a direction given pursuant to *Woollin* would appear to prevent the jury construing intent in accordance with s8 of the Criminal Justice Act 1967.

EXTRACT ADAPTED FROM THE JUDGMENT IN *R V WOOLLIN* [1998] 3 WLR 382

The facts appear in the previous source.

LORD STEYN

In *Hancock* Lord Scarman did not express disagreement with the test of foresight of a probability which is 'little short of overwhelming' as enunciated in *Moloney.* ... Lord Scarman merely said that model directions were generally undesirable. ... The manner in which trial judges were to direct juries was left unclear. Moreover, in practice juries sometimes ask probing questions which cannot easily be ignored by trial judges. For example, imagine that in a case such as *Hancock* the jury sent a note to the judge to the following effect: 'We are satisfied that the defendant, though he did not want to cause serious harm, knew that it was probable that his act would cause serious bodily harm. We are not sure whether a probability is enough for murder. Please explain.'

One may alter the question by substituting 'highly probable' for 'probable'. Or one may imagine the jury asking whether a foresight of a 'substantial risk' that the defendant's act would cause serious injury was enough. What is the judge to say to the jury? *Hancock* does not rule out an answer by the judge but it certainly does not explain how such questions are to be answered. ... judges were sometimes advised to deflect such questions by the statement that 'intention' is an ordinary word in the English language. That is surely an unhelpful response to what may be a sensible question. In these circumstances it is not ... surprising that in *Nedrick* the Court of Appeal felt compelled to provide a model direction for the assistance of trial judges.

Questions

Read the two extracts above and answer the questions

1. In Sean Enright's article what problem does he identify in *DPP v Smith*?
2. How far do you think s8 of the Criminal Justice Act 1967 overcame that problem?
3. Following *Moloney* when, according to the article, will a judge need to direct a jury on the issue of intention?
4. How, according to the article, does the judgment in *Hancock and Shankland* elaborate on the issue of foresight of consequences?
5. What extra point was added by *Nedrick*?
6. In *Woollin* why do you think Sean Enright suggests that 'their Lordships found that the direction by the trial judge diluted the *Nedrick* direction to such an extent that the distinction between recklessness and murder was blurred'?
7. In the extract from *Woollin* how does Lord Steyn justify the 'model direction' in *Nedrick*?
8. In what ways is Sean Enright's comment that the judgment in *Woollin* 'comes perilously close to implementing the imputed knowledge test in *DPP v Smith*' accurate?

SECTION 4: UNLAWFUL KILLING: VOLUNTARY MANSLAUGHTER

Voluntary manslaughter occurs where the defendant has both the *actus reus* and the necessary *mens rea* for murder. The defendant pleads one of three partial defences in the Homicide Act 1957 which if successful have the effect of reducing the charge to manslaughter and remove the mandatory life sentence. Diminished responsibility involves an 'abnormality of the mind'. Provocation involves conduct by the victim which has caused the defendant to lose self-control where reasonable people would have reacted similarly. Interesting features of provocation are the characteristics of the defendant that can be taken into account, and the difficulties faced by battered women who try to use the plea.

Diminished Responsibility

EXTRACT FROM S2 HOMICIDE ACT 1957

2. Persons suffering from diminished responsibility

(1) Where a person kills or is party to the killing of another, he shall not be convicted of murder if he was suffering from such abnormality of mind (whether arising from a condition of arrested or retarded development of mind or any inherent causes or induced by disease or injury) as substantially impaired his mental responsibility for his acts and omissions in doing or being a party to the killing.

(3) A person who but for this section would be liable, whether as principal or as accessory, to be convicted of murder shall be liable instead to be convicted of manslaughter.

EXTRACT ADAPTED FROM THE JUDGMENT IN *R V BYRNE* [1960] 2 QB 396

Byrne was convicted of the murder of a young girl who he had strangled, afterwards horribly mutilating her body. His defence was diminished responsibility. Evidence given by psychologists at the trial showed that he was a 'sexual psychopath', driven by uncontrollable and perverted sexual desires. His appeal was allowed and a verdict of manslaughter substituted, although his life sentence was not altered.

LORD PARKER CJ

'Abnormality of mind', which has to be contrasted with the time-honoured expression in the M'Naghten Rules 'defect of reason', means a state of mind so different from that of ordinary human beings that the reasonable man would term it abnormal. It appears ... enough to cover the mind's activities in all its aspects, not only the perception of physical acts and matters, and the ability to form a rational judgment as to whether an act is right or wrong, but also the ability to exercise will power to control physical acts in accordance with that rational judgment. The expression 'mental responsibility for his acts' points to a consideration of the extent to which the accused's mind is answerable for his physical acts which must include a consideration of the extent of his ability to exercise will power to control his physical acts.

Whether the accused was at the time of the killing suffering from any 'abnormality of the mind' in the broad sense which we have indicated is a question for the jury. On this question medical evidence is no doubt important, but the jury are entitled to take into consideration all the evidence, including the acts or statements of the accused and his demeanour.

Assuming that the jury are satisfied that the accused was suffering from 'abnormality of mind' from one of the causes specified in the parenthesis of the subsection, the crucial question nevertheless arises: was the abnormality such as substantially impaired his mental responsibility for his acts in doing or being a party to the killing? This is a question of degree and essentially one for the jury.

Furthermore, in a case where the abnormality of mind is one which affects the accused's self-control the step between 'he did not resist his impulse' and 'he could not resist his impulse' is ... one which is incapable of scientific proof.

Inability to exercise willpower to control physical acts, provided that is due to abnormality of mind from one of the causes specified in the parenthesis in the subsection is ... sufficient to entitle the accused to the benefit of the section; difficulty in controlling his physical acts, depending on the degree of difficulty it may be. It is for the jury to decide on the whole of the evidence whether such inability or difficulty has, not as a matter of scientific certainty but on the balance of probabilities, been established, and in the case of difficulty whether the difficulty is so great as to amount ... to a substantial impairment of the accused's mental responsibility for his acts.

Questions

1. What, according to the Act, will be the consequences of a successful plea of diminished responsibility?
2. How does Lord Parker explain the expression 'abnormality of mind' from s2 of the Act, and do you think that this fully explains it?
3. What part does Lord Parker think medical evidence should play in determining whether or not a plea of diminished responsibility succeeds?
4. What are the causes of the abnormality of mind 'specified in the parenthesis of the subsection' and what do they refer to?
5. In what way was Byrne suffering from diminished responsibility?

Provocation

EXTRACT FROM S3 HOMICIDE ACT 1957

3. Provocation

Where on a charge of murder there is evidence on which the jury can find that the person charged was provoked (whether by things done or by things said or by both together) to lose his self-control, the question whether the provocation was enough to make a reasonable man do as he did shall be left to be determined by the jury; and in determining that question the jury shall take into account everything both done and said according to the effect which in their opinion, it would have on a reasonable man.

EXTRACT ADAPTED FROM THE JUDGMENT IN *R V CAMPLIN* [1978] AC 705, HL

Camplin, who was aged 15 at the time, was buggered and then mocked about the incident by an old man with whom he was alone in the old man's flat. Camplin killed the old man by splitting his skull with a large frying pan. He was convicted of murder but on appeal a verdict of manslaughter by reason of provocation was substituted.

LORD DIPLOCK

The public policy that underlay the adoption of the 'reasonable man' test in the common law doctrine of provocation was to reduce the incidence of fatal violence by preventing a person relying upon his own exceptional pugnacity or excitability as an excuse for loss of self-control. ...

Although it is now for the jury to apply the 'reasonable man' test, it still remains for the judge to direct them what ... is the meaning of this apparently inapt expression ... the 'reasonable man' has never been confined to the adult male. It means an ordinary person of either sex, not exceptionally excitable or pugnacious, but possessed of such powers of self-control as everyone is entitled to expect that his fellow citizens will exercise in society as it is today.

... now that the law has been changed ... to permit ... words being treated as provocation, even though unaccompanied by any other acts, the gravity of verbal provocation may well depend upon the particular characteristics or circumstances of the person to whom a taunt or insult is addressed. It would stultify much of the mitigation of the previous harshness of the common law in ruling out verbal provocation as capable of reducing murder to manslaughter if the jury could not take into consideration all those factors which in their opinion would affect the gravity of taunts or insults when applied to the person to whom they are addressed ... to this extent ... the unqualified proposition ... in *Bedder v DPP* [1954] that for the purposes of the 'reasonable man' test any unusual physical characteristics of the accused must be ignored requires revision as a result of the passing of the Act of 1957.

That he was only 15 years of age at the time of the killing is the relevant characteristic ... in the instant case. It is a characteristic which may have its effects on temperament as well as physique. If the jury think that the same power of self-control is not to be expected in an ordinary, average or normal boy of 15 as in an older person, are they to treat the lesser powers of self-control possessed by an ordinary, average or normal boy of 15 as the standard of self-control with which the conduct of the accused is to be compared?

... a proper direction to the jury on the question left to their exclusive determination by section 3 of the Act of 1957 would be on the following lines. The judge should state what the question is to them using the very words of the section. He should then explain ... that the reasonable man referred to in the question is a person having the power of self-control to be expected of an ordinary person of the sex and age of the accused, but in other respects sharing such of the accused's characteristics as they think would affect the gravity of the provocation to him; and that the question is not merely whether such a person would in like circumstances be provoked to lose self-control but also whether he would react to the provocation as the accused did.

It seems to me that as a result of the changes effected by s3, a jury is entitled to consider whether an accused person, placed as he was, only acted as even a reasonable man might have acted if he had been in the accused's situation.

Questions

1. What are the three essential elements of a plea of provocation identified in s3 of the Homicide Act 1957?
2. What does Lord Diplock suggest was the reason for including a 'reasonable man' test in the law on provocation?
3. Why does Lord Diplock say that the jury should be entitled to take into account characteristics of the accused?
4. In what way does Lord Diplock suggest that *Bedder* is wrong?
5. What is the appropriate test identified by Lord Diplock in *Camplin*?

EXTRACT ADAPTED FROM 'BATTERED WOMEN AND PROVOCATION: THE IMPLICATIONS OF *R V AHLUWHALIA*', DONALD NICOLSON AND ROBERT SANGHVI, *CRIMINAL LAW REVIEW*, OCTOBER 1993, 728–738.

Deepak Ahluwhalia began beating Kiranjit only days after their arranged marriage. Over the next decade, despite two restraining injunctions, his violence continued to increase in frequency and ferocity until it occurred almost daily. Kiranjit was slapped, punched, pushed when pregnant, beaten with hard objects, sexually abused and raped. Her many injuries included persistent bruising, broken bones and teeth, split and swollen lips, scalding and being knocked unconscious. Frequent death threats by Deepak, sometimes made while holding a foot-long screwdriver close to her, were lent credence by attempts at strangulation and running down.

From January 1989 the violence intensified. In March Kiranjit discovered Deepak was having an affair, exacerbating her worries over the future of their marriage. But when he left her for a few days, she abjectly pleaded for his return, making a number of self-denying promises. On his return the beatings continued.

On the night of May 8/9, 1989, Kiranjit begged Deepak not to desert the family, but he refused to talk to her, declaring ... their relationship ... over. He demanded money for a telephone bill and threatened to beat her the next morning if it was not forthcoming. Later he put a hot clothes iron against her face, threatening to burn her if she did not leave him alone. Deepak then went to bed. After brooding for about two-and-a-half hours, Kiranjit went outside, fetched some petrol, lit a candle, poured the petrol over Deepak and ignited it. She then calmly collected her son and left the house. Alerted neighbours reported her to be in a shocked state. Six days later, Deepak died ...

At her trial for murder, Mrs Ahluwhalia denied having the requisite *mens rea* and pleaded provocation ... The jury was unimpressed and she began a life sentence ... she eventually obtained leave to appeal. Three grounds ... were argued ... two alleged jury misdirections on the subjective and objective conditions of provocation, respectively, and the third that there was fresh evidence of diminished responsibility. On the latter ground alone, the Court of Appeal set aside Mrs Ahluwhalia's conviction as unsafe and unsatisfactory and ordered a retrial.

The treatment of the first ground of appeal has gone largely unnoticed, yet is perhaps the most important aspect of the case in challenging the law's maleness ... the subjective condition requires a 'sudden and temporary loss of self-control.'

Designation of the existence of a 'cooling time', not simply as evidence of cooled passion, but as legally precluding the provocation defence, was clearly premised upon a male-oriented view of behaviour and significantly prejudiced battered women.

On the objective condition of provocation, the trial judge had directed the jury to consider how a reasonable, educated, Asian woman would have responded to the provocation. The appellant argued that this wrongly omitted to mention that being a battered woman was also a relevant characteristic.

The decision in *Ahluwhalia* ... provide[s] some assistance to battered women who kill, but in a way ... likely to push them down the medical paths of diminished responsibility and Battered Woman Syndrome, both of which have invidious consequences for battered women and for women in general. Nevertheless, the decision does leave openings which can be exploited in less harmful ways.

First, ... by arguing for jury directions which do not treat a 'cooling time' as legally precluding the defence. This will obviously help battered defendants avoid life sentences. It should also encourage prosecutors to accept manslaughter pleas, thus sparing the battered women the murder trial—an experience which could be described as the bruising which follows the battering. In addition, if the police learn ... to investigate not just the moment of the killing, but also its history, the credibility of a battered woman's evidence in her defence or mitigation will be bolstered by the spontaneity of her original confession.

... the biggest obstacle to battered women posed by provocation's subjective condition remains: the need to show that self-control was in fact lost. The man who 'snaps' following provocation can show that homicide was demonstrably a result of a sudden loss of self-control. Like Kiranjit ..., battered women frequently behave in an outwardly calm manner, suggesting revenge rather than rage. The next step is ... to persuade the courts to accept that an outwardly calm killing by a battered woman is legally and morally the equivalent to the ... male 'snapping' since in neither case has reason 'dominion over the mind.'

Finally, the Court of Appeal's recognition of the relevance to provocation of the battered women context can be exploited in a way which avoids the problems ... Instead of expecting jury members to consider how reasonable sufferers would have reacted ... —itself absurdly unrealistic— judges can be asked to direct juries to simply consider how a reasonable person in the shoes of the defendant, having suffered the same level of violence and abuse, might have been expected to act.

Questions

1. Why would Kiranjit Ahluwhalia's plea of provocation have failed?
2. Why is a 'cooling off period' or 'cooling time' so important in deciding whether there has been provocation?
3. Why do the authors suggest that the way in which a battered woman reacts to a provocation is the same as men 'snapping'?
4. What are the possible dangers in accepting this reasoning?
5. Is the attitude that the law on provocation is fairer to men than women justified?
6. Why is a battered woman like Kiranjit Ahluwhalia succeeding under diminished responsibility but not under provocation unsatisfactory?

SECTION 5: UNLAWFUL KILLING: INVOLUNTARY MANSLAUGHTER

Involuntary manslaughter involves any killing falling between murder and an accidental killing. The problems are easy to imagine with such a vast area. Constructive manslaughter involves an unlawful act which is dangerous and which inadvertently causes death. It is also possible to have reckless manslaughter and in situations where a duty is owed gross negligence manslaughter is possible.

Constructive manslaughter

EXTRACT ADAPTED FROM THE JUDGMENT IN *DPP V NEWBURY AND JONES* [1977] AC 500, HL

Two 15-year-old boys pushed a piece of concrete paving slab off a bridge, into the path of an oncoming train. The guard was killed when the concrete slab hit him. The boys were convicted and appealed unsuccessfully to the Court of Appeal who certified the following point of general public importance: 'Can a defendant be properly convicted of manslaughter, when his mind is not affected by drink or drugs, if he did not foresee that his act might cause harm to another?'

LORD SALMON

The learned judge did not direct the jury that they should acquit the appellants unless they were satisfied beyond a reasonable doubt that the appellants had foreseen that they might cause harm to someone by pushing the piece of paving stone off the parapet into the path of the approaching train. In my view the learned judge was quite right not to give such a direction ... The direction which he gave is completely in accordance with established law ... In *Larkin* Humphreys J said: 'Where the act which a person is engaged in performing is unlawful, then if at the same time it is a dangerous act, that is, an act which is likely to injure another person, and quite inadvertently he causes the death of that other person by that act, then he is guilty of manslaughter.'

I agree entirely with Lawton LJ that that is an admirably clear statement of the law which has been applied many times. It makes it plain (a) that an accused is guilty of manslaughter if it is proved that he intentionally did an act which was unlawful and dangerous and that that act inadvertently caused death and (b) that it is unnecessary to prove that the accused knew that the act was unlawful or dangerous. This is one of the reasons why cases of manslaughter vary so infinitely in their gravity. They may amount to little more than pure inadvertence and sometimes to little less than murder. The test is still the objective test. In judging whether the act was dangerous, the test is not did the accused recognise that it was dangerous but would all sober and reasonable people recognise its danger.

EXTRACT ADAPTED FROM THE JUDGMENT IN *R V SCARLETT, NEW LAW JOURNAL,* 30 JULY 1993

The appellant was licencee of a public house. Ten minutes after closing time one evening a heavily built man the worse for drink entered the public house. The appellant told him that he would not serve him and told him to get out or he would put him out. The deceased then indicated that he was not going to leave voluntarily, the appellant then pinned his arms and bundled him to the door. He got the deceased as far as the lobby, the deceased fell backwards down a flight of five steps ... struck his head when he fell and received injuries from which he later died. The appellant was charged with manslaughter. The prosecution case was that he had used excessive force and thus committed an unlawful act and his death was consequently manslaughter. The appellant was convicted. He appealed successfully.

LORD BELDAM

This unfortunate miscarriage ... might have been avoided if the clear advice of the Criminal Law Revision Committee in 1980 had been implemented. ... [It] recommended abolition of the antiquated relic of involuntary manslaughter based on the commission of an unlawful act and the adoption of the more rational and systematic approach to the law of manslaughter ... The present law is in urgent need of reform.

The judge began his summing up by telling [the jury] that the case boiled down to one fairly short question which they would have to ask themselves: 'Am I sure that [the appellant] used unnecessary and unreasonable and therefore unlawful force in ejecting [the deceased] and did that force actually cause his fall?' The whole tenor of the judge's directions was that if the jury concluded that the appellant used more force than was necessary in the circumstances, and if they were satisfied that that caused the deceased to fall and strike his head, he was guilty of manslaughter. His exposition that in law manslaughter was made out 'if the killing was the result of the accused man's unlawful act, like an assault which all reasonable people would inevitably realise must subject the victim to some form of harm even if not serious' was founded on the statement of the law in *DPP v Newbury*. The conduct of the accused in that case was clearly both unlawful and dangerous.

Where one of the issues for the jury is whether the accused is guilty of the unlawful act of assault in circumstances in which he is entitled to use reasonable force either in self-defence or for the purpose of preventing crime, or as here in removing a trespasser, the need for a careful direction was stressed by Lord Lane in *R v Gladstone Williams*: 'One starts off with the meaning of the word "assault". "Assault" in the context of this case, that is to say using the word as a convenient abbreviation for assault and battery, is an act by which the defendant intentionally or recklessly applies unlawful force to the complainant.'

The issue in *R v Williams* was whether the accused was entitled to be acquitted if he mistakenly believed that he was justified in using force. The court held that, even if the jury came to the conclusion that the mistake was an unreasonable one, if the defendant may genuinely have been labouring under it, he was entitled to rely upon it ... because he did not intend to apply unlawful force.

Where, as in the present case, an accused is justified in using some force and can only be guilty of an assault if the force used is excessive, the jury ought to be directed that he cannot be guilty of an assault unless the prosecution proved that he acted with the mental element necessary to constitute his action an assault, that is: 'that the defendant intentionally or recklessly applied force to the person of another.'

Further they should be directed that he is not to be found guilty merely because he intentionally or recklessly used force which they consider to have been excessive. They ought not to convict him unless they are satisfied that the degree of force used was plainly more than was called for by the circumstances as he believed them to be and, provided the circumstances called for the degree of force used, he was not to be convicted even if his belief was unreasonable.

The expression used by the witnesses that the appellant 'bundled' the deceased towards the door certainly provided no basis for saying the appellant was reckless, nor by itself did it imply that the force used was excessive in the circumstances. It is important to emphasise that the question whether the action of the appellant was unlawful and whether it was dangerous have to be considered separately.

Questions

1. According to Lord Salmon in *Newbury and Jones*, then, what are the three necessary ingredients that must be proved in order to establish this type of manslaughter?
2. How should the dangerousness of the unlawful act be measured, according to Lord Salmon?
3. Why, according to Lord Beldam in *Scarlett*, should a jury not convict merely because they think that the defendant 'intentionally or recklessly used force that they consider to be excessive'?

Gross negligence manslaughter

EXTRACT ADAPTED FROM THE JUDGMENT IN *R V ADOMAKO* [1995] 1 AC 171, HL

An anaesthetist was convicted when the patient in his care became disconnected from the oxygen supply during an operation and he failed to notice it for ten minutes so that the patient suffered a cardiac arrest and died.

LORD MACKAY LC

... the ordinary principles of ... negligence apply to ascertain whether or not the defendant has been in breach of a duty of care towards the victim who has died. If such a breach of duty is established the next question is whether that breach of duty has caused the death of the victim. If so, the jury must ... consider whether that breach ... should be categorised as gross negligence and therefore as a crime. This will depend on the seriousness of the breach of duty committed by the defendant in all the circumstances in which the defendant was placed when it occurred. The jury will have to consider whether the extent to which the defendant's conduct departed from the proper standard of care incumbent upon him, involving as it must have done a risk of death to the patient, was such that it should be judged criminal. ... The essence of the matter which is supremely a jury question is whether having regard to the risk of death involved, the conduct of the defendant was so bad in all the circumstances as to amount in their judgment to a criminal act or omission.

EXTRACT ADAPTED FROM 'MANSLAUGHTER, *MENS REA* AND MEDICINE', GARY SLAPPER, *NEW LAW JOURNAL*, 8 JULY 1994

The combined effect of two recent developments may ... halt the apparently growing trend to prosecute negligent doctors for manslaughter when death results from their serious errors. The first development was the publication by the Crown Prosecution Service of its revised code, . . . the second . . . the House of Lords decision in *R v Adomako.*

It has been historically rare for doctors to be prosecuted for manslaughter following the death of a patient under their care, although, strangely, one of the main authorities on manslaughter is *R v Bateman.* Here a doctor performing a manual version (turning the baby's head downwards) during childbirth mistakenly removed a portion of the patient's uterus, ruptured her bladder and caused other internal injuries from which the patient died the following week.

The key change in the new code is the inclusion of public interest factors which may militate against a prosecution. In cases which pass the evidential test (that is, that there is sufficient admissible evidence to give the case a 'realistic prospect of conviction'), prosecutors must weigh up whether the public interest is best served by a prosecution.

Doctors are trained for and dedicated to preserving and improving life. The decision to spend thousands of pounds on prosecuting one for manslaughter should clearly be a very rare event. Doctors are increasingly working over-long hours and under huge, often unmanageable stress. Yet the Government has secured the exclusion of hospital doctors from the European Union's Working Time Directive, designed to prevent unhealthy working practices.

The House of Lords decision in *R v Adomako* should be seen as a clarification of law which lessens the likelihood of doctors being convicted of manslaughter. . . . The defendant's conviction for manslaughter was upheld but the test of 'gross negligence' was confirmed to be something, effectively, in the hands of the jury. Lord Mackay stated that the test of how far conduct must depart from accepted standards to be characterised as criminal was necessarily a question of degree. Any attempt to specify that degree more closely was likely to achieve only a spurious precision. The essence of the matter was 'supremely a jury question'; it was, whether, having regard to the risk involved, the conduct of the defendant was so bad in all the circumstances as to amount in their judgment to a criminal act or omission.

In the wake of the hospital league tables, and the current concern to evaluate medical care in a corporate way, it is to be hoped that jurors asked to decide whether a doctor has been criminally negligent will take into account the whole context including the situation in which the doctor was put to work by the employer.

Questions

1. According to Lord Mackay, who should decide the test of whether the defendant's conduct amounted to gross negligence?
2. What does Lord Mackay think that the presence of gross negligence depends on?
3. In what way is the Crown Prosecution Service Code of Practice likely to affect prosecutions of doctors for manslaughter?
4. Why do you think that Gary Slapper thinks that to prosecute doctors for manslaughter is a bad thing?
5. In what way do you think that the case of *Adomako* will 'clarify' the law on manslaughter and make prosecution of doctors less likely?

SECTION 6: NON-FATAL OFFENCES AGAINST THE PERSON: ASSAULT

Assaults are to be found under the Criminal Justice Act 1988 and also under the Offences Against the Person Act 1861. The law is very inconsistent and in need of reform. Particular problems concern the necessary *mens rea* for the offence and the situations in which consent is available as a defence.

EXTRACT ADAPTED FROM THE JUDGMENT IN *R V VENNA* [1975] 3 WLR 737, CA

Venna was convicted of an assault contrary to s47 Offences Against the Person Act 1861. He had struggled with policemen trying to arrest him and kicked one of them, fracturing that officer's hand. He appealed unsuccessfully on the trial judge's direction that he could be convicted if he intentionally kicked out or did so recklessly.

JAMES LJ

In *Fagan v Metropolitan Police Commissioner*, it was said: 'An assault is any act which intentionally or ... recklessly causes another person to apprehend immediate and unlawful personal violence'. In *Fagan* it was not necessary to decide the question whether proof of recklessness is sufficient to establish the *mens rea* ... of assault. That question falls for decision in the present case. Why ... the Crown put the case forward on the alternative bases of 'intention' and 'recklessness' is not clear to us.

On the evidence of the appellant himself, one would have thought that the inescapable inference was that the appellant intended to make physical contact with whoever might try to restrain him. Be that as it may, in the light of the direction given, the verdict may have been arrived at on the basis of 'recklessness'. Counsel for the appellant cited *Ackroyd v Barett* in support of his argument that recklessness, which falls short of intention, is not enough to support a charge of battery.

We see no reason in logic or ... law why a person who recklessly applies physical force to ... another should be outside the criminal law of assault. In many cases the dividing line between recklessness and intention is barely distinguishable. This is such a case.

EXTRACT ADAPTED FROM THE JUDGMENT IN *R V IRELAND; R V BURSTOW*, HOUSE OF LORDS, *NEW LAW JOURNAL*, 5 SEPTEMBER 1997

I appealed from the dismissal of his appeal from the Court of Appeal against conviction of three counts of assault occasioning actual bodily harm contrary to s47 of the Offences against the Person Act 1861. The Court of Appeal certified as being a point of law of general public importance the question 'as to whether the making of a series of silent telephone calls can amount in law to an assault'. [This was the behaviour that led to I's conviction.]

B appealed against the dismissal by the Court of Appeal of his appeal against conviction [of] unlawfully and maliciously inflicting grievous bodily harm contrary to s20 of the 1861 Act following a ruling by the judge that an offence might be committed where no physical violence had been applied directly or indirectly to the body of the victim. [B had carried out an eight-month campaign of harassment against a woman, including both silent and abusive phone calls.]

LORD STEYN

Harassment of women by repeated silent telephone calls, accompanied on occasions by heavy breathing, is apparently a significant social problem. That the criminal law should be able to deal with this problem and, so far as is practicable, afford effective protection to victims is self evident.

It is to the provisions of the Offences against the Person Act 1861 that one must turn to examine whether our law provides effective criminal sanctions for this type of case. An ingredient of each of the offences is 'bodily harm' to a person. In respect of each section the threshold question is therefore whether a psychiatric illness, as testified to by a psychiatrist, can amount to 'bodily harm'.

If ... the answer ... is yes, it will be necessary to consider whether the persistent silent caller, who terrifies his victim and causes her to suffer a psychiatric illness, can be criminally liable ...

The correct approach is simply to consider whether the words of the ... Act considered in the light of contemporary knowledge cover a recognisable psychiatric injury ...

The proposition that the Victorian legislator when enacting ss 18, 20 and 47 of the 1861 Act, would not have had in mind psychiatric illness is no doubt correct. Psychiatry was in its infancy. But the subjective intention of the draftsman is immaterial. The only relevant inquiry is as to the sense of the words in the context in which they are used.

[Accordingly] 'bodily harm' must be interpreted so as to include recognisable psychiatric illness.

[In] *Burstow* ... counsel laid stress on the difference between 'causing' grievous bodily harm in s18 and 'inflicting' grievous bodily harm in s20 [and] submitted that it is inherent in the word 'inflict' that there must be a direct or indirect application of force to the body ...

The question is whether as a matter of current usage ... 'inflict' can embrace the idea of one person inflicting psychiatric injury on another. One can without straining the language in any way answer ... in the affirmative ...

It is now necessary to consider whether the making of silent telephone calls causing psychiatric injury is capable of constituting an assault under s47 ...

It is necessary to consider the two forms which an assault may take. The first is battery, which involves the unlawful application of force ... The second form ... is an act causing the victim to apprehend an immediate application of force upon her ...

The proposition that a gesture may amount to an assault, but that words can never suffice, is unrealistic and indefensible ... There is no reason why something said should be incapable of causing an apprehension of immediate personal violence ... I would, therefore, reject the proposition that an assault can never be committed by words.

... to the critical question whether a silent caller may be guilty of an assault. The answer ... seems ... to be 'yes, depending on the facts'. It depends on questions of fact within the province of the jury. After all, there is no reason why a telephone caller who says to a woman in a menacing way 'I will be at your door in a minute or two' may not be guilty of an assault if he causes his victim to apprehend immediate personal violence. Take now the case of the silent caller. He intends by his silence to cause fear and so he is understood. The victim ... may fear the *possibility* of immediate personal violence. As a matter of law the caller may be guilty of an assault, whether he is or not will depend on the circumstance and in particular on the impact of the caller's potentially menacing call or calls on the victim. Such a prosecution case under s47 may be fit to leave to the jury. I conclude that an assault may be committed in the particular factual circumstances which I have envisaged. For this reason I reject the submission that as a matter of law a silent telephone caller cannot ever be guilty of an offence under s47.

EXTRACT ADAPTED FROM 'CONSENT: PUBLIC POLICY OR LEGAL MORALISM?', SUSAN NASH, *NEW LAW JOURNAL*, 15 MARCH 1996

In *R v Wilson* the Court of Appeal held that consensual activity between a husband and wife in the privacy of the matrimonial home was not a proper matter for a criminal prosecution. The defendant had been charged with assault occasioning actual bodily harm contrary to s47 of the Offences Against the Person Act 1861. The 'activity' involved the defendant burning his initials onto his wife's right buttock with a hot knife because 'she had wanted his name on her body'. This decision rekindles the debate regarding the extent to which the criminal law should be concerned with the consensual activities of adults in private. In *R v Brown* the House of Lords upheld convictions under ss20 and 47 of the Offences Against the Person Act notwithstanding that the victims had given their consent. This decision has been described as 'unprincipled and incoherent'.

The trial judge in *Wilson* ... ruled that consent was no defence to ... assault occasioning actual bodily harm. In arriving at this conclusion he stated that he felt bound by *R v Donovan* and *R v Brown*. The Court of Appeal considered it misdirection for the judge to say these cases constrained him to rule that consent was no defence.

The majority of the House of Lords in *Brown* held that it was not in the public interest that a person should wound or cause actual bodily harm to another for no good reason. Thus, in the absence of a good reason the victim's consent would not amount to a defence to a charge under s47 or s20 of the 1861 Act.

The defendants had taken part in consensual acts of violence for the purpose of sexual gratification which had resulted in varying degrees of injury. The court was of the opinion that the satisfying of sado-masochistic desires could not be classed as a good reason and dismissed the appeals. Lord Templeman considered that in some circumstances the accused would be entitled to an acquittal although the activity resulted in the infliction of some injury.

'Surgery involves intentional violence resulting in actual or sometimes serious bodily harm but surgery is ... lawful ... Other activities carried on with consent by or on behalf of the injured person have been accepted as lawful notwithstanding that they involve actual bodily harm or may cause serious harm. Ritual circumcision, tattooing, ear-piercing and violent sports including boxing are lawful ...'. This reference to tattooing has now assumed significance. Lords Templeman and Jauncy referred to it as being an activity which, if carried out with the consent of an adult, did not involve an offence under s47. Wilson ... engaged in an activity which in principle was no more dangerous than professional tattooing. Thus, the Court of Appeal was of the opinion that it was not in the public interest that his activities should amount to criminal behaviour.

Questions

1. According to Lord Justice James in *Venna*, what does an accused have to do to commit assault?
2. Why is recklessness sufficient *mens rea* for assault?
3. In *Ireland and Burstow* how does Lord Steyn suggest that the accused were able to be convicted for causing 'actual bodily harm'?
4. Also in *Ireland and Burstow* what justification does Lord Steyn give for holding that words alone or even silence are sufficient for an assault?
5. According to Susan Nash's article, when will consent be a defence to charges of assault and when will it not?
6. To what extent are these differences sensible or justifiable?

SECTION 7: NON-FATAL OFFENCES AGAINST THE PERSON: WOUNDING

Wounding offences are found in the Offences Against the Person Act 1861. They are even more in need of reform than assault offences. Inconsistencies include the use of different words in the different offences, 'cause' and 'inflict', which make it hard to differentiate a proper hierarchical structure to the offences. Problems also surround what *mens rea* is appropriate. There is also the problem of whether the offences must involve assaults or not.

EXTRACT FROM S18 OFFENCES AGAINST THE PERSON ACT 1861

18. Shooting or attempting to shoot, or wounding, with intent to do grievous bodily harm, or to resist apprehension

Whosoever shall unlawfully and maliciously by any means whatsoever wound or cause grievous bodily harm to any person with intent to do some grievous bodily harm to any person, or with intent to resist or prevent the lawful apprehension or detainer of any person, shall be guilty of felony, and being convicted thereof shall be liable to be kept in penal servitude for life.

EXTRACT FROM S20 OFFENCES AGAINST THE PERSON ACT 1861

20. Inflicting bodily injury, with or without weapon

Whosoever shall unlawfully and maliciously wound or inflict any grievous bodily harm upon any other person, either with or without any weapon or instrument, shall be guilty of a misdemeanour, and being convicted thereof shall be liable to be kept in penal servitude [for not more than five years].

EXTRACT ADAPTED FROM *R V MARTIN* [1881] 8 QBD 54

Martin barred the exits to a theatre and then turned lights off in a staircase where people would be exiting at the end of a performance. He did so with the purpose of causing terror in the minds of the audience, and succeeded. Many people were injured as a result. He was convicted under s20 of unlawfully and maliciously inflicting grievous bodily harm and his appeal on the meaning of 'malicious' was unsuccessful.

LORD COLERIDGE CJ

Upon these facts the prisoner was convicted and the jury found all that was necessary to sustain the conviction. The prisoner must be taken to have intended the natural consequences of that which he did. He acted 'unlawfully and maliciously', not that he had any personal malice against the particular individuals injured, but in the sense of doing an unlawful act calculated to injure, and by which others were in fact injured. Just as in the case of a man who unlawfully fires a gun among a crowd, it is murder if one of the crowd is thereby killed.

EXTRACT ADAPTED FROM THE JUDGMENT IN *JCC (A MINOR) V EISENHOWER* [1983] 3 ALL ER 230, QBD

The appellant fired an air gun at the victim who was struck in the area of the left eye, causing a bruise under the eyebrow and bleeding behind the eye. He was convicted under s20 Offences Against the Person Act 1861, and appealed successfully on the ground that the injuries were insufficient to amount to a 'wounding'.

ROBERT GOFF LJ

In my judgment, that conclusion [of the magistrates] was not in accordance with the law. It is not enough that there has been a rupturing of blood vessels internally for there to be a wound under the statute because it is impossible for a court to conclude from that evidence alone whether or not there has been any break in the continuity of the whole skin. There may have simply been internal bleeding of some kind or another, the cause of which is not established. Furthermore, even if there had been a break in some internal skin, there may not have been a break in the whole skin.

... the evidence is not enough ... to establish a wound within the statute. In my judgment, the magistrates erred in their conclusion on the evidence before them.

EXTRACT ADAPTED FROM THE JUDGMENT IN *R V MOWATT* [1967] 3 WLR 1192, CA

The defendant or his friend had stolen £5 from the victim's pocket. The victim seized hold of him and Mowatt then struck the victim, arguing that he was acting in self-defence. The defendant punched the victim and pulled him up from the ground, hitting him repeatedly until he nearly lost consciousness. He was charged with wounding with intent under s18 Offences Against the Person Act 1861 and convicted of s20 malicious wounding. He appealed unsuccessfully on the ground that the jury had not been properly directed on the meaning of the word 'maliciously'.

DIPLOCK LJ

In s18 the word 'maliciously' adds nothing. The intent expressly required by that section is more specific than such element of foresight of consequences as is implicit in the word 'maliciously' and in directing a jury about an offence under this section the word 'maliciously' is best ignored. In the offence under s20 and in the alternative verdict which may be given on a charge under s18—for neither of which is any specific intent required—the word 'maliciously' does import on the part of the person who unlawfully inflicts the wound or other grievous bodily harm an awareness that his act may have the consequences of causing some physical harm to some other person. That is what is meant by 'the particular kind of harm' in the citation from Professor Kenny's *Outlines of Criminal Law.* It is quite unnecessary that the accused should have foreseen that his unlawful act might cause physical harm of the gravity described in the section i.e. a wound or serious physical injury. It is enough that he should have foreseen that some physical harm to some person, albeit of a minor character, might result.

EXTRACT ADAPTED FROM HOME OFFICE, 'VIOLENCE: REFORMING THE OFFENCES AGAINST THE PERSON ACT 1861, DRAFT OFFENCES AGAINST THE PERSON BILL 1998'

1(1) A person is guilty of an offence if he intentionally causes serious injury to another. (Max: life imprisonment)

2(1) A person is guilty of an offence if he recklessly causes serious injury to another. (Max: seven years' imprisonment)

3(1) A person is guilty of an offence if he intentionally or recklessly causes injury to another. (Max: five years' imprisonment)

4(1) A person is guilty of an offence if—

(a) he intentionally or recklessly applies force to or causes an impact on the body of another, or

(b) he intentionally or recklessly causes the other to believe that any such force or impact is imminent.

(2) No such offence is committed if the force or impact, not being intended or likely to cause injury, is in the circumstances such as is generally acceptable in the ordinary conduct of daily life and the defendant does not know or believe that it is in fact unacceptable to the other person. (Max: six months' imprisonment)

15(1) In this Act 'injury' means—

(a) physical injury, or

(b) mental injury.

(2) Physical injury does not include anything caused by disease but (subject to that) it includes pain, unconsciousness and any other impairment of a person's physical condition.

(3) Mental injury does not include anything caused by disease but (subject to that) it includes any impairment of a person's mental health.

Questions

1. On reading s18 and s20, what appear to be the significant differences between them?
2. According to Lord Coleridge in *Martin*, to what do the words 'unlawfully and maliciously' refer in s20?
3. What will and will not amount to a wound according to the judgment in *JCC v Eisenhower*?
4. How does Diplock LJ explain the different applications of the word 'malicious' in s18 and s20?
5. In what ways do you think that the wording in the offences identified in the Draft Offences Against the Person Bill 1998 will improve on the wording in the existing offences in the 1861 Act?

SECTION 8: PROPERTY OFFENCES: THEFT

Theft was codified in the 1968 Act but problems of interpretation meant that Parliament had to go back and pass a further Act in 1978. There are still problems of interpretation particularly with the meaning of 'appropriates'. There is an apparent overlap with the offence of deception in s15. The way that dishonesty is measured is also less than satisfactory.

EXTRACT FROM S2 THEFT ACT 1968

2. 'Dishonesty'

(1) A person's appropriation of property belonging to another is not to be regarded as dishonest—

(a) if he appropriates the property in the belief that he has in law the right to deprive the other of it, on behalf of himself or of a third person; or

(b) if he appropriates the property in the belief that he would have the other's consent if the other knew of the appropriation and the circumstances of it; or

(c) (except where the property came to him as trustee or personal representative) if he appropriates the property in the belief that the person to whom the property belongs cannot be discovered by taking reasonable steps.

(2) A person's appropriation of property belonging to another may be dishonest notwithstanding that he is willing to pay for the property.

EXTRACT ADAPTED FROM THE JUDGMENT IN *R V GHOSH* [1982] 3 WLR 110

The defendant, a surgeon acting as a *locum,* was convicted of deception for falsely claiming money for an operation, when it had been carried out by another doctor under the National Health Service. He argued that the fees were in any case owing to him as consultancy fees and that, therefore, his actions were not dishonest. He appealed unsuccessfully on a misdirection on the meaning of dishonesty.

LORD LANE CJ

Is 'dishonesty' in s1 of the Theft Act 1968 intended to characterise a course of conduct? Or is it intended to describe a state of mind? If the former, then ... it could be established independently of the knowledge or belief of the accused. But if ... it is the latter, then the knowledge and belief of the accused are at the root of the problem.

Take ... a man who comes from a country where public transport is free. On his first day here he travels on a bus. He gets off without paying. He never had any intention of paying. His mind is clearly honest; but his conduct, judged objectively by what he has done, is dishonest. It seems to us that in using the word 'dishonesty' in the

Theft Act, Parliament cannot have intended to catch dishonest conduct in this sense . . .

If . . . dishonesty is something in the mind of the accused, then if the mind of the accused is honest, it cannot be deemed dishonest merely because members of the jury would have regarded it as dishonest to embark on that course of conduct.

There remains the objection that to adopt a subjective test is to abandon all standards but that of the accused himself, and to bring about a state of affairs in which 'Robin Hood would be no robber'. This misunderstands the nature of the subjective test. [The defendant] is entitled to say ' I did not know that anybody would regard what I was doing as dishonest.' He may not be believed . . . But if he is believed, the jury cannot be sure that he was dishonest.

In determining whether the prosecution has proved that the defendant was acting dishonestly, a jury must first of all decide whether according to the ordinary standards of reasonable and honest people what was done was dishonest. If it was not dishonest by those standards, that is the end of the matter and the prosecution fails.

If it was dishonest by those standards, then the jury must consider whether the defendant himself must have realised that what he was doing was by those standards dishonest.

Questions

1. What is the objective part of Lord Lane's test in *Ghosh*?
2. What is the subjective part of the test in *Ghosh*?
3. What problems is the test likely to cause?

Activity

Using the test in *Ghosh* and the tests of dishonesty in s2, consider whether there is dishonesty in the following situations:

1. John gets on a train and picks up and starts to read a newspaper that has been left on the seat he occupies. After the train moves off Reginald returns from the buffet and demands to know what John is doing with his newspaper.
2. Aaron regularly borrows his next door neighbour's lawnmower. He takes it when his neighbour is on holiday and uses it but forgets to put it back.
3. As a hard-working law lecturer, I take books from the college library to help with my preparation and with no intention of returning them because I honestly believe that the college should supply me with books.
4. The garage has repaired Jim's car. Jim does not like the bill and refuses to pay so the garage will not let him take the car back. He returns when the garage is shut, with his spare keys, and takes the car back, believing that the garage had no right to keep the car.

EXTRACT FROM S3 THEFT ACT 1968

3. 'Appropriates'

(1) Any assumption by a person of the rights of an owner amounts to an appropriation, and this includes, where he has come by the property (innocently or not) without stealing it, any later assumption of a right to it by keeping or dealing with it as owner.

EXTRACT ADAPTED FROM '*GOMEZ* REVISITED', RICHARD AKINJIDE, *NEW LAW JOURNAL*, 10 JUNE 1994

In *R v Gomez*, the House of Lords finally decided that *Lawrence* was rightly decided and that *Morris* was wrongly decided.

Both were previous decisions of the House of Lords. The resolution, at last, is therefore of great importance ...

The Court of Appeal ... granted a certificate that a point of law of general public importance was involved ... to wit:

'When theft is alleged and that which is alleged to be stolen passes to the defendant with the consent of the owner, but that consent has been obtained by a false representation, has: (a) an appropriation within the meaning of s1(1) of the Theft Act 1968 taken place, or (b) must such passing of property necessarily involve an element of adverse interference with or usurpation of some right of the owner?'

The House of Lords allowed the appeal by the Crown and restored the conviction of Gomez after answering the two questions as follows: (a) Yes, and (b) No

Gomez, an assistant ... manager of a shop, induced his manager to sell goods worth over £16,000 to a customer and to accept for their payment two cheques which Gomez knew were stolen and worthless. Gomez assured his manager that he had found out about the cheques from the bank and the cheques were 'as good as cash'. The cheques were dishonoured on presentation. Gomez was later jointly charged with ... theft under s1(1) of the Theft Act 1968. He was convicted ... The Court of Appeal ... allowed Gomez's appeal and quashed his conviction. The Crown's appeal to the House of Lords was on the ground that the Court of Appeal was wrong in holding that there was no 'appropriation' within s1(1) of the Theft Act 1968. ...

The net result of *Gomez* is that it is irrelevant for the purpose of theft that the act, with or without deception, was done with the authority or consent of the owner.

EXTRACT FROM S4 THEFT ACT 1968

4. 'Property'

(1) 'Property' includes money and all other property, real or personal, including things in action and other intangible property

EXTRACT ADAPTED FROM THE JUDGMENT IN *OXFORD V MOSS* [1978] 68 CR APP R 183, QBD

An engineering student at Liverpool University stole the proof of an exam paper he was due to sit the following month. The stipendiary magistrate dismissed the case on the basis that the exam paper was not intangible property within the meaning of s4 Theft Act 1968. The prosecution appealed unsuccessfully by way of case stated.

SMITH J

The question for this court is whether confidential information of this sort falls within that definition contained in s4(1). We have been referred to a number of authorities emanating from the area of trade secrets and matrimonial secrets.

Those are cases concerned with what is described as the duty to be of good faith. They are clear illustrations of the proposition that, if a person obtains information which is given to him in confidence and then sets out to take an unfair advantage of it, the courts will restrain him by way of an order of injunction or will condemn him in damages if an injunction is found to be inappropriate. It seems to me ... that they are of little assistance in the present situation in which we have to consider whether there is property in the information which is capable of being the subject of a charge of theft. In my judgment, it is clear that the answer to that question must be no.

Questions

1. What, according to s4 and *Oxford v Moss*, will the term 'intangible property' include and what will it not include?
2. What is Smith J suggesting would have been a better course of action in respect of the exam papers?

EXTRACT FROM S5 THEFT ACT 1968

5. 'Belonging to another'

(1) Property shall be regarded as belonging to any person having possession or control of it, or having in it any proprietary right or interest (not being an equitable interest arising only from an agreement to transfer or grant an interest).

(3) Where a person receives property from or on account of another, and is under an obligation to the other to retain and deal with that property or its proceeds in a particular way, the property or proceeds shall be regarded (as against him) as belonging to the other.

(4) Where a person gets property by another's mistake, and is under an obligation to make restoration (in whole or in part) of the property or its proceeds or of the value thereof, then to the extent of that obligation the property or proceeds shall be regarded (as against him) as belonging to the person entitled to restoration, and an intention not to make restoration shall be regarded accordingly as an intention to deprive that person of the property or proceeds.

EXTRACT ADAPTED FROM THE JUDGMENT IN *R V TURNER (NO 2)* [1971] 1 WLR 901

Turner took his car to Brown's garage for repair. When it was ready he promised to return for the car and to pay the bill. Instead he went that night with his spare keys and took the car. After the garage owner had located the car Turner was then convicted of its theft. He appealed unsuccessfully on the ground that within the meaning of s5 Theft Act 1968 it was not property 'belonging to another'.

LORD PARKER CJ

The words 'belonging to another' are specifically defined in section 5 of the Act ... The sole question is whether Mr Brown had possession or control.

This court is satisfied that there is no ground whatever for qualifying the words 'possession or control' in any way. It is sufficient if it is found that the person from whom the property is taken, or to use the words of the Act, appropriated, was at the time in fact in possession or control. At the trial there was a long argument as to whether that possession or control must be lawful, it being said that by reason of the fact that this car was subject to a hire-purchase agreement, Mr Brown could never even as against the defendant obtain lawful possession or control. ... this court is quite satisfied that the judge was quite correct in telling the jury they need not bother about lien, and that they need not bother about hire-purchase agreements. The only question was whether Mr Brown was in fact in possession or control.

EXTRACT ADAPTED FROM THE JUDGMENT IN *R V HALL* [1973] 1 QB 126

Hall was a travel agent. He received money from clients as deposits for holidays. This money was put into the firm's general account. When certain holidays were not forthcoming, not only were the clients deeply upset but Hall was convicted of theft of the money. He appealed successfully on the ground that, under s5(3) Theft Act 1968, he had not been placed under any obligation to retain or deal with the money in any particular way.

EDMUND DAVIES LJ

Counsel for the appellant submitted that in the circumstances ... there arose no such 'obligation' on the appellant. He referred us to the Eighth Report of the Criminal Law Revision Committee: 'Subsection (3) provides for the special case where property is transferred to a person to retain and deal with for a particular purpose and he misapplies it or its proceeds. An example would be the treasurer of a holiday fund. The person in question is in law the owner of the property; but the subsection treats the property, as against him, as belonging to the persons to whom he owes the duty to retain and deal with the property as agreed. He will therefore be guilty of stealing from them if he misapplies the property or its proceeds.' What counsel for the appellant resists is that in such circumstances the travel agent 'is under an obligation' to the client 'to retain and deal with ... in a particular way' sums paid to him in such circumstances.

Nevertheless, when a client goes to ... travel agents and pays them money, he expects that in return he will, in due course, receive the tickets and other documents necessary ... to accomplish the trip which he is paying for, and the firm are 'under an obligation' to perform their part to fulfil his expectation and are liable to pay him damages if they do not. But ... what was not here established was that these clients expected him to 'retain and deal with that property or its proceeds in a particular way,' and that an 'obligation' to do so was undertaken by the appellant. ... Cases could ... conceivably arise where by some special arrangement, the client could impose on the travel agent an 'obligation' falling within section 5(3). But no such special arrangement was made in any of the seven cases here being considered.

It follows from this that, despite what on any view must be condemned as scandalous conduct by the appellant, in our judgment on this ground alone this appeal must be allowed and the conviction quashed.

EXTRACT ADAPTED FROM THE JUDGMENT IN *R V GILKS* [1971] 1 WLR 1341, CA

A betting shop clerk mistakenly paid Gilks winnings on a horse that had in fact lost. Gilks realised the mistake but kept the money anyway. He was convicted of theft and appealed unsuccessfully. The court considered also s5(4) Theft Act 1968 which the court had said had no application to the case or if it did then s5(4) included an obligation which was not a legal obligation. Gilks had appealed that these directions to the jury were wrong.

CAIRNS LJ

The gap in the law which section 5(4) of the Theft Act 1968 was designed to fill was, as the deputy chairman rightly held, that which is illustrated by *Moynes v Cooper*. There a workman received a pay packet containing £7 more than was due to him but did not become aware of the overpayment until he opened the envelope some time later. He then kept the £7. This was held not to be theft ...

An alternative ground on which the deputy chairman held that the money should be regarded as belonging to Ladbrokes was that 'obligation' in section 5(4) meant an obligation whether a legal one or not. In the opinion of this court that was an incorrect ruling. In a criminal statute, where a person's criminal liability is made dependent on his having an obligation, it would be quite wrong to construe that word so as to cover a moral or social obligation as distinct from a legal one.

Questions

1. How could *Turner* steal his own car?
2. Why was it impossible to convict *Hall* under the meaning of s5(3) despite the fact that his behaviour was described as 'scandalous'?

3. Why is a defendant guilty of theft under s5(4) when (s)he has only come by the property by mistake?

Activity

Suggest whether there is 'property belonging to another' sufficient for a conviction of theft in the following situations:

1. My flat mate gives me money to pay the gas bill. I spend it on law books.
2. Hodder give me two cheques for royalties by mistake. I refuse to return one.
3. I take a law book belonging to the college library from the house of a student who has had it for some years but I do not take it back to the library.

EXTRACT FROM S6 THEFT ACT 1968

6. 'With the intention of permanently depriving the other of it'

(1) A person appropriating property belonging to another without meaning the other permanently to lose the thing itself is nevertheless to be regarded as having the intention of permanently depriving the other of it if his intention is to treat the thing as his own to dispose of regardless of the other's rights; and a borrowing or lending of it may amount to so treating it if, but only if, the borrowing or lending is for a period and in circumstances making it equivalent to an outright taking or disposal.

EXTRACT ADAPTED FROM THE JUDGMENT IN *R V LLOYD & OTHERS* [1985] QB 829, CA

Lloyd was a projectionist at a cinema. With two others he arranged to take films in order to copy them and then to put them back. They were convicted of a conspiracy to steal but on appeal the convictions were quashed since no intention to permanently deprive could be shown.

LORD LANE CJ

... in this case we are concerned with the second part of s 6(1), the words after the semi-colon.

These films, it could be said, were borrowed by Lloyd from his employers in order to enable him and the others to carry out their 'piracy' exercise.

Borrowing is ex hypothesi not something which is done with an intention to permanently deprive. This half of the subsection, we believe, is intended to make it clear that a mere borrowing is never enough to constitute the necessary guilty mind unless the intention is to return the 'thing' in such a changed state that it can truly be said that all its goodness or virtue has gone.

That being the case, we turn to inquire whether the feature films in this case fall within this category. Our view is that they cannot.

Questions

1. Why could it not be proved that the projectionist in *Lowe* intended to permanently deprive the cinema of the film?
2. If my son borrowed my Wolverhampton Wanderers FC season ticket ten matches before the end of the season, went to the matches, then give me the season ticket back after the final game would he be guilty of theft, and if so why?

SECTION 9: PROPERTY OFFENCES: ROBBERY

A robbery is a theft accompanied by some force. Problems usually concern what level of force must be applied and at what point.

EXTRACT FROM S8 THEFT ACT 1968

8. Robbery

(1) A person is guilty of robbery if he steals, and immediately before or at the time of doing so, and in order to do so, he uses force on any person or puts or seeks to put any person in fear of being then and there subjected to force.

EXTRACT ADAPTED FROM THE JUDGMENT IN *R V DAWSON* [1976] 64 CR APP R 170

Three men jostled a sailor and while he struggled to keep his balance one of the three stole the sailor's wallet. They were convicted of robbery and appealed unsuccessfully on the issue of whether their actions could amount to 'force'.

LAWTON LJ

Mr Locke had submitted at the end of the prosecution's case that what had happened could not in law amount to the use of force. . . .

The choice of the word 'force' is not without interest because under the Larceny Act 1916 the word 'violence' had been used, but Parliament deliberately on the advice of the Criminal Law Revision Committee changed that word to 'force'. Whether there is any difference between 'violence' or 'force' is not relevant for . . . this case; but the word is 'force'. It is a word in ordinary use. It is a word . . . juries understand. The learned judge left it to say whether jostling a man in the way which the victim described to such an extent that he had difficulty in keeping his balance could be said to be the use of force. The learned judge, because of the argument put forward by Mr Locke, went out of his way to explain to the jury that force in these sort of circumstances must be substantial to justify a verdict.

Whether it was right for him to put that adjective before the word 'force' when Parliament had not done so we will not discuss for the purposes of this case. It was a matter for the jury. They were there to use their common sense and knowledge of the world. We cannot say that their decision as to whether force was used was wrong. They were entitled to the view that force was used.

EXTRACT ADAPTED FROM THE JUDGMENT IN *R V HALE* [1978] 68 CR APP R 415

Two men entered the victim's house wearing stockings over their faces as masks. Hale put his hand over the victim's mouth to stop her screaming while the other man went upstairs and took jewellery. They then tied her up and threatened that they would harm her child if she phoned the police within five minutes of them leaving. Hale was convicted of robbery and appealed unsuccessfully on the basis that any force used did not come before or at the time of the theft.

EVELEIGH LJ

In so far as the facts of the present case are concerned, counsel submitted that the theft was completed when the jewellery box was first seized and any force thereafter could not have been 'immediately before or at the time of stealing' and certainly not 'in order to steal'. The essence of the submission was that the theft was completed as soon as the jewellery box was seized. . . .

In the present case there can be little doubt that if the appellant had been interrupted after the seizure of the jewellery box the jury would have been entitled to find that the appellant and his accomplice were assuming the rights of an owner at the time when the jewellery box was seized. However, the act of appropriation does not suddenly cease. It is a continuous act and it is a matter for the jury to decide whether or not the act of appropriation has finished. Moreover, it is . . . clear that the intention to deprive the owner permanently, which accompanied the assumption of the owner's rights, was a continuing one at all material times. This Court therefore rejects the contention that the theft had ceased by the time the lady was tied up. As a matter of common-sense the appellant was in the course of committing the theft; he was stealing.

There remains the question whether there was robbery. ... the jury were at liberty to find the appellant guilty of robbery relying upon the force used when he put his hand over Mrs Carrett's mouth to restrain her from calling for help. ... they were also entitled to rely upon the act of tying her up provided they were satisfied (and it is difficult to see how they could not be ...) that the force so used was to enable them to steal.

EXTRACT ADAPTED FROM THE JUDGMENT IN *CORCORAN V ANDERTON* [1980] 71 CR APP R 104

The defendants accosted their victim with a view to snatching her handbag. One struck her in the back from behind and a struggle ensued for control of the handbag. The struggle caused the victim to release the bag, which fell to the floor, but the man ran away to avoid capture. His accomplice was convicted of robbery. In his appeal he argued that there could be no robbery since control of the bag was never gained at any time, so there was no appropriation. His appeal failed.

WATKINS J

... I think that an 'appropriation' takes place when an accused snatches a woman's handbag completely from her grasp, so that she no longer has physical control of it because it has fallen to the ground. What has been involved in such activity as that, bearing in mind the dishonest state of mind of the accused, is an assumption of the rights of the owner, a taking of the property of another. ... In my judgment there cannot possibly be, save for the instance where a handbag is carried away from the scene ... a clearer instance of robbery than that which these justices found was committed.

Turning to the actual question ... 'Could the tugging at the handbag, accompanied by force, amount to robbery, notwithstanding that the co-accused did not have sole control of the bag at any time?' in my opinion, which may be contrary to some notions of what constitutes a sufficient appropriation to satisfy the definition of that word in section 3(1) of the Theft Act, the forcible tugging of the handbag of itself could in the circumstances be a sufficient exercise of control by the accused person so as to amount to an assumption by him of the rights of the owner, and therefore an appropriation ...

Questions

1. What particular feature distinguishes a robbery from any other theft?
2. In *Dawson* what definition of the word 'force' does Lord Justice Lawton give?
3. In the light of the result of the case what difference do you think there is between the words 'force' and 'violence'?
4. What degree of 'force' is sufficient according to the judgment in *Hale*?
5. What difficulty is presented in the case of *Hale* and how did Eveleigh LJ see it being overcome?
6. Based on the extracts, does an accused actually have to get away with the property in order for his actions to amount to robbery?

SECTION 10: PROPERTY OFFENCES: BURGLARY

There are separate offences of burglary both of which involve trespassing on to premises. One set of offences involves entering with intent to commit one of four further offences. The other type involves one of two offences being carried out after the entry. The obvious question is whether the law needs to be so complex. Problems in the past have concerned the trespass and what it will comprise.

EXTRACT FROM S9 THEFT ACT 1968

9. Burglary

(1) A person is guilty of burglary if—

(a) he enters any building or part of a building as a trespasser and with intent to commit any such offence as is mentioned in subsection (2) below; or

(b) having entered any building or part of a building as a trespasser he steals or attempts to steal anything in the building or that part of it or inflicts or attempts to inflict on any person therein any grievous bodily harm.

(2) The offences referred to in subsection (1)(a) above are offences of stealing anything in the building or art of a building in question, of inflicting on any person therein any grievous bodily harm or raping any person therein, and of doing unlawful damage to the building or anything therein.

EXTRACT ADAPTED FROM THE JUDGMENT IN *R V COLLINS* [1973] 1 Q.B. 100, CA

Collins was convicted of burglary with intent to rape under s9 (1)(a) Theft Act 1968. He appealed successfully. The facts are dealt with in detail in the judgment.

EDMUND DAVIES LJ

Let me relate the facts. Were they put into a novel or portrayed on the stage, they would be regarded as being so improbable as to be unworthy of serious consideration and as at times verging on farce. At about 2 o'clock in the early morning ... a young lady of 18 went to bed at her mother's home ... She had taken a certain amount of drink ...

She has the habit of sleeping without wearing night apparel in a bed which is very near the lattice type window of her room.

At about 3.30 she awoke and ... saw in the moonlight a vague form crouched in the open window. She was unable to remember, and this is important, whether the form was on the outside of the window sill or on that part of the sill which was inside the room, and ... that seemingly narrow point is of crucial importance.

The young lady then realised several things: first ... that the form in the window was that of a male; secondly that he was a naked male; and thirdly, that he was a naked male with an erect penis. She also saw in the moonlight that his hair was blonde. She thereupon leapt to the conclusion that her boyfriend, with whom for some time she had been on terms of regular and frequent sexual intimacy, was paying her an ardent nocturnal visit. She promptly sat up in bed, ... the man descended from the sill and joined her ... and they had full sexual intercourse. But there was something about him that made her think that things were not as they usually were between her and her boyfriend. So she turned on the bedside light, saw that her companion was not her boyfriend and slapped the face of the intruder. ... he promptly vanished.

The complainant said that she would not have agreed to intercourse if she had known that the person entering her room was not her boyfriend. But there was no suggestion of any force having being used upon her, and the intercourse which took place was undoubtedly effected with no resistance on her part.

The defendant was seen by the police [and] the conversation which took place elicited these points: He was very lustful the previous night. He had taken a lot of drink ... he knew the complainant because he had worked around her house. On this occasion, desiring sexual intercourse ... he walked around the house saw a light in an upstairs bedroom, and he knew that this was the girl's bedroom. He found a step ladder, leaned it against the wall and climbed up and looked into the bedroom. He could see through the wide-open window a girl who was naked and asleep. So he descended the ladder and stripped off all his clothes, with the exception of his socks, because apparently he took the view that if the girl's mother entered the bedroom it would be easier to effect a rapid escape if he had his socks on ...

Having undressed, he then climbed the ladder and pulled himself up on to the window sill. ... he was pulling himself in when she awoke. She then got up, knelt on the bed, ... put her arms around his neck and body, and ... seemed to pull him into the bed.

Now one feature of the case which remained at the conclusion of the evidence in great obscurity is where exactly Collins was at the moment when, according to him, the girl manifested that she was welcoming him. Was he kneeling on the sill outside the window or was he already in the room, having climbed through the window frame, and kneeling upon the inner sill? It was a crucial matter, for there were certainly three ingredients that it was incumbent upon the Crown to establish ... the entry of the accused into the building must first be proved. Secondly, it must be proved that he entered as a trespasser. Thirdly, it must be proved that he entered as a trespasser with intent at the time of entry to commit rape therein.

The second ingredient of the offence—the entry must be as a trespasser—is one which has not ... been previously canvassed in the courts. What does that involve? ...

A view ... was expressed by Professor Smith's book on *The Law of Theft* 'D should be acquitted on the ground of lack of *mens rea*. Though, under the civil law, he entered as a trespasser, ... he cannot be convicted of the criminal offence unless he knew of the facts which caused him to be a trespasser or, at least, was reckless'.

The matter has also been dealt with by Professor Griew ... 'What if D wrongly believes that he is not trespassing ... for the purpose of criminal liability a man should be judged on the basis of the facts as he believed them to be ... D should be liable ... only if he knowingly trespasses or is reckless as to whether he trespasses or not'.

We prefer [these views] ... there cannot be a conviction for entering premises 'as a trespasser' within the meaning of section 9 ... unless the person entering does so knowing that he is a trespasser and nevertheless deliberately enters, or, at the very least, is reckless as to whether or not he is entering ... without the other party's consent.

... the pivotal point of this appeal is whether the Crown established that this defendant at the moment he entered the bedroom knew perfectly well that he was not welcome there, or being reckless as to whether he was welcome or not, was nevertheless determined to enter. That in turn involves consideration as to where he was at the time the complainant indicated that she was welcoming him into the bedroom.

Unless the jury were entirely satisfied that the defendant made an effective and substantial entry into the bedroom without the complainant doing or saying anything to cause him to believe that she was consenting to his entering it, he ought not to be convicted of the offence charged.

EXTRACT ADAPTED FROM THE JUDGMENT IN *R V WALKINGTON* [1979] 1WLR 1169

The defendant was seen loitering near tills in Debenhams in Oxford Street while cashing-up was in process. He then went into a till area, which was for staff only, and which was unattended. He looked into the partly open cash drawer and then slammed it shut when he saw that it was empty. He was convicted of burglary with intent to steal, contrary to s9(1)(a) Theft Act 1968 and appealed unsuccessfully.

GEOFFREY LANE LJ

It seems to this court that in the end one simply has to go back to the words of the Act itself and if the jury are satisfied so as to feel sure that the defendant had entered any building or part of a building as a trespasser, and are satisfied that at the moment of entering he intended to steal anything in the building or that part of the building, the fact that there was nothing in the building worth while to steal seems to us to be immaterial. He nevertheless had the intent to steal. As we see, to hold otherwise would be to make a nonsense of this part of the Act and cannot have been the intention of the legislature at the time when the Theft Act 1968 was passed. Nearly every prospective burglar could no doubt truthfully say that he only intended to steal if he found something in the building worth stealing.

Questions

1. How many different offences of burglary are there?
2. What is the basic difference between s9(1)(a) and s9(1)(b)?
3. According to Edmund Davies LJ in *Collins* what are the necessary features of a trespass in order for there to be a burglary?
4. What effect does the defendant's state of mind have on the trespass?
5. What does the case of *Walkington* reveal about the meaning of 'part of a building'?

Activity

Consider which of the following could be a burglary and suggest whether under s9(1)(a) or s9(1)(b):

1. Jerry, a known drug abuser, is found at 2 o'clock in the morning, having broken into a chemist shop. He has no drugs on him.
2. Jerry is caught with his arm reaching inside a jeweller's window, with his hand full of rings, having been seen smashing the window first with a brick.
3. Jerry, a known drug abuser, is found by police in the back yard of a chemist shop after closing hours.
4. Jerry has been caught by store detectives in a store room, access to which is prohibited to the public.
5. Jerry stole a tray of apple pies resting on Mavis's window sill cooling.

SECTION 11: PROPERTY OFFENCES: DECEPTION

Deception offences have caused many problems of interpretation and led to further enactment and there are a great number of different offences. There is a confusing overlap between theft under s1 and obtaining property by deception under s15.

EXTRACT FROM S15(4) THEFT ACT 1968

(4) For purposes of this section 'deception' means any deception (whether deliberate or reckless) by words or conduct as to fact or as to law, including a deception as to the present intentions of the party using the deception or any other person.

EXTRACT ADAPTED FROM THE JUDGMENT IN *R V CHARLES* [1977] AC 171, HL

Charles had a bank account and was given a cheque book and a cheque guarantee card with a limit of £30 per cheque. The bank manager had previously told him that he was not to use the cheque card more than once in a day. Charles used a complete book of 25 cheques, written for £30 each, to buy chips at a gambling club, knowing that he had insufficient funds in the bank but that each cheque would be honoured by the bank because it was within the limit of the cheque guarantee card. He was convicted of deception and his appeal in the House of Lords failed.

LORD DIPLOCK

The whole foundation of liability under the doctrine of ostensible authority is a representation, believed by the person to whom it is made, that the person claiming to contract as agent for a principal has the actual authority of the principal to enter the contract on his behalf.

That is the representation that the drawer makes to the payee when he uses a cheque card to back a cheque which he draws in compliance with the conditions endorsed on the card. That in the instant case Mr Cersell, the manager of the gaming club, so understood it is implicit from the passage in his evidence ... Mr Cersell ... would not have taken the accused's cheques had he not believed that the accused was authorised by the bank to use the cheque card to back them.

Questions

Read the two extracts above and answer the questions.

1. What is a deception, according to the sources?
2. In what circumstances might a deception 'by conduct' occur?
3. What was the deception in *Charles*?
4. Give an example of a deception as to law.
5. Give an example of a deception as to fact.
6. Give an example of a deception as to the present intentions of the party making the deception.

SECTION 12: PROPERTY OFFENCES: CRIMINAL DAMAGE

Criminal damage offences are offences against property. They involve damage or destruction rather than an interference with rights of ownership. They can be very serious if the damage is caused by fire (arson) or if done with the purpose of endangering life or reckless as to that possibility.

EXTRACT FROM S1 CRIMINAL DAMAGE ACT 1971

1. Destroying or damaging property

(1) A person who without lawful excuse destroys or damages any property belonging to another intending to destroy or damage any such property or being reckless as to whether any such property would be destroyed or damaged shall be guilty of an offence.

(2) A person who without lawful excuse destroys or damages any property, whether belonging to himself or another—

(a) intending to destroy or damage any property or being reckless as to whether any property would be destroyed or damaged; and

(b) intending by the destruction or damage to endanger the life of another or being reckless as to whether the life of another would be thereby endangered;

shall be guilty of an offence.

(3) An offence committed under this section by destroying or damaging property by fire shall be charged as arson.

EXTRACT ADAPTED FROM THE JUDGMENT IN *R V CALDWELL* [1981] 1 ALL ER 961

Caldwell felt that he had a legitimate grievance against the owner of a hotel. Caldwell then set fire to the hotel. While there were ten guests staying in the hotel at the time of the fire, it was quickly put out without any serious damage being caused. Caldwell was convicted of arson and recklessly endangering life under the Criminal Damage Act 1971 and failed in his appeal.

LORD DIPLOCK

As respects the charge under section 1(2) the prosecution did not rely upon an actual intent of the respondent to endanger the lives of the residents but relied upon his having been reckless whether the lives of any of them would be endangered. His act of setting fire to it was one which the jury were entitled to think created an obvious risk that the lives of the residents would be endangered; and the only defence with which your Lordships are concerned is that the respondent had made himself so drunk as to render him oblivious of that risk.

If the only mental state capable of constituting the necessary *mens* ... were that expressed in the words 'intending by the destruction or damage to endanger the life of another', it would have been necessary to consider whether the offence was to be classified as one of 'specific' intent for the purpose of the rule of law which this House affirmed and applied in *R v Majewski*, and this it plainly is. But this is not in my view a relevant enquiry where 'being reckless as to whether the life of another would be thereby endangered' is an alternative mental state ...

Reducing oneself by drink or drugs to a condition in which the restraints of reason and conscience are cast off was held to be a reckless course of conduct and an integral part of the crime.

So ..., the fact that the respondent was unaware of the risk of endangering the lives of the residents in the hotel owing to his self-induced intoxication, would be no defence if that risk would have been obvious to him had he been sober.

Questions

Read the two extracts above and answer the questions.

1. What is the necessary mental intent for criminal damage under s1(1) of the Act?
2. What are the essential differences in the offence under s1(2)?
3. Why do you think that there is a separate offence of arson?
4. How was the mental element in *Caldwell* described?
5. Why was the defendant's drunken state no defence in the case?

SECTION 13: DEFENCES

There are a variety of defences to crimes. Some, such as insanity, operate because they prevent the defendant from forming the necessary intent. Some, like automatism, operate because they also mean that conduct is involuntary so the *actus reus* is not made out either. Intoxication, on the other hand, if it is self-induced begins with voluntary actions so that the defence is harder to use. Others, such as duress and necessity, do not operate in this way but are rather excuses made for a particular class of conduct.

Insanity

EXTRACT ADAPTED FROM 'MAD OR BAD— THE DILEMMA OF INSANITY', DR GARY SLAPPER, *THE TIMES*, 8 DECEMBER 1998

... Only last month the stabbing of a social worker at a South London hostel for psychiatric patients raised the issue of how the law should deal with people who commit crimes while suffering from clinical mental conditions.

Nowhere is the 'mad or bad' dichotomy reflected in a more confused way than in the criminal law's approach to insanity. For some people it is curious that the perpetrators of terrible crimes can be seen as anything other than psychotic and in need of treatment. In what circumstances can a deranged and savage person be judged as 'normal' then simply thrown in front of a judge and jury in an ordinary criminal trial, and convicted and punished?

Mental illness is a huge social problem. One in ten us will at some time suffer a mental disorder. More than 50 people in Britain have been murdered by the mentally ill since 1993.

Kenneth McCaskill thought that he was the devil when he killed his father with a 12-inch kitchen knife, and then stabbed his mother. Yet in Edinburgh last month, McCaskill, whose condition was diagnosed as schizophrenia, was acquitted by a jury on the basis that he was 'not guilty by reason of insanity'. He will thus be sent to a secure mental institution.

By contrast, Michael Stone was last month jailed for life for the murders of Lin and Megan Russell. Stone had a history of mental illness, and before the killings had requested hospital treatment (which had been denied).

Criminal law on insanity is based on 19th century legal and medical assumptions. There have been calls for radical change of the rule but the law is still in a mould of outdated thinking. At the core of the problems are the different criteria of madness preferred in law and psychiatry.

Lord Lloyd recently highlighted the awkward relationship between the law and psychiatry. Sometimes, Parliament can legislate without envisaging that 'an existing psychiatric disorder might be regarded as treatable today and untreatable tomorrow owing to a change in psychiatric thinking'.

The basis of the law on insanity, which permits the insane to be found not guilty of any crime because of their condition, is that such people are not responsible for their actions. If a toddler pushes a brick out of a window and it kills someone, we do not presume to prosecute the child because it is not responsible for its actions or their consequences. The same reasoning applies to acquit the insane.

The guiding principles of insanity in law are found in the M'Naghten Rules, which arose from a case in 1843. M'Naghten had shot and killed a man whom he believed was Robert Peel, the Home Secretary. He had acted under a 'morbid delusion' that he was being persecuted by the police at the Government's behest.

There was political disquiet at his acquittal. The judges formulated a new set of rules starting with the proposition that every man is presumed to be sane and responsible for his crimes. The defence of insanity would only be open to someone who, at the time of a crime was 'labouring under such a defect of reason, from disease of the mind, as not to know the nature and quality of his act; or if he did know it, that he did not know that what he was doing was wrong'. . . .

. . .

It is remarkable that, at a time when so many patients are receiving 'care in the community', insanity (the only appropriate defence they can use if accused of a crime), is successfully used . . . less than 20 times a year. A Royal Commission on capital punishment in 1953 deemed the M'Naghten Rules 'obsolete and misleading'. Unfortunately, nothing fundamental in the insanity laws has changed since.

Questions

1. What is the effect of a successful plea of 'insanity'?
2. What does Dr Slapper say is the major problem in the law's treatment of insanity?
3. Why is an insane person who kills to be considered in the same way as a very young child who kills might be?
4. What sorts of defects can you identify in the basic M'Naghten Rules?
5. What possible alternatives could be used instead of the present test?

Intoxication

EXTRACT ADAPTED FROM THE JUDGMENT IN *DPP V MAJEWSKI* [1976] 2 WLR 623, HL

The defendant was convicted for assault, having attacked people in a public house and then the police officers who tried to arrest him. He had consumed large quantities of alcohol and drugs. His appeal, on the ground that his intoxication prevented him from forming the necessary *mens rea,* was also unsuccessful.

LORD ELWYN-JONES LC

Self-induced intoxication has been a factor in crimes of violence, like assault, throughout the history of crime in this country. But voluntary drug taking with the potential and actual dangers to others it may cause has added a new dimension to the old problem . . .

Originally the common law would not and did not recognise voluntary intoxication as an excuse.

The authority which for the last half century has been relied on in this context has been the speech of Lord Birkenhead LC in *DPP v Beard*: Under the law of England as it prevailed until early in the nineteenth century voluntary drunkenness was never an excuse for criminal misconduct; and indeed the classic authorities broadly assert that voluntary drunkenness must be considered rather an aggravation than a defence.

From this it seemed clear that it is only in the limited class of cases requiring proof of specific intent that drunkenness can exculpate. Otherwise in no case can it exempt completely from criminal liability.

I do not . . . regard that general principle as either unethical or contrary to the principles of natural justice. If a man of his own volition takes a substance which causes him to cast off the restraints of reason and conscience, no wrong is done to him by holding him answerable criminally for any injury he may do while in that condition. His course of conduct in reducing himself by drugs and drink to that condition in my view supplies the evidence of mens rea, of guilty mind certainly sufficient for crimes of basic intent. It is a reckless course of conduct and recklessness is enough to constitute the necessary mens rea in assault cases . . .

EXTRACT ADAPTED FROM 'INVOLUNTARY INTOXICATION', NICHOLAS REVILLE, *THE LEGAL EXECUTIVE JOURNAL*, JANUARY 1995

The recent unanimous House of Lords ruling . . . in *Kingston*, that the absence of moral fault on the part of the accused is not sufficient . . . to negative the necessary mental elements of a crime, has important practical implications for legal advisers.

In *Kingston* it was held that . . . intent to commit an indecent assault is a 'criminal' intent even though it is formed in circumstances of loss of self control induced by a third party surreptitiously administering soporific drugs.

. . . Kingston had paedophiliac homosexual tendencies. Another man, P, arranged to blackmail him by photographing and audio-taping him in a compromising situation with a boy. P lured a boy of 15 to his flat, where he gave him what seemed an innocuous drink and some cannabis. The boy fell asleep and remembered nothing until he woke the next morning.

While the boy was in this state, P invited Mr Kingston to abuse the boy sexually. He did so, and was photographed and taped doing it. Both Mr Kingston and P were charged with indecent assault on the boy.

Mr Kingston's defence was that P had laced his drink [and] had no recollection of events that night and had woken in his own home the next morning.

The House of Lords found that the induced mental condition on which Mr Kingston relied was disinhibition. . . .

The taking of the drug lowered his ability to resist temptation, in that his desires overrode his ability to control them. The drug was not alleged to have created the desire but rather to have enabled it to be released.

The proposition that criminal liability should not be imposed on conduct which is the ultimate consequence of an event outside the defendant's volition is appealing. However, the harshness of the *Kingston* principle can be explained.

It would be difficult to reconcile a defence of irresistible impulse derived from a combination of innate drives and external disinhibition with the rule that irresistible impulse of a solely internal origin does not in itself excuse.

Equally, the state of mind which founds such a defence superficially resembles diminished responsibility. The effect in law is quite different.

There are also serious practical problems. Before a jury could form an opinion on whether the drug might have turned the scale, witnesses would have to give a picture of the defendant's personality.

More significant than this, the House of Lords felt in *Kingston*, would be the opportunities for a spurious defence.

The defendant would only have to assert, and support by the evidence of well wishers, that he was not the sort of person to have done this kind of thing.

In *Kingston*, the House of Lords felt that disinhibition should be a mitigating factor and not a defence. This best recognised the interplay between the wrong done to the victim, the individual characteristics of the defendant and the pharmacological effects of whatever drug may be potentially involved.

Clearly a loss of self control through the acts of a third party do not now generally constitute a defence.

Consequently, provided the intoxication is not such as to cause automatism or temporary insanity, involuntary intoxication or disinhibition is not a defence to a criminal charge if it is proved that the defendant had the necessary intent when the necessary act was done by him. It is immaterial that the intent arose out of circumstances for which he was not to blame.

If, however, the defendant was so intoxicated that he could not form . . . intent, he has a defence.

Questions

1. In what way would we expect a defence of intoxication to work?
2. How does Lord Elwyn-Jones in *Majewski* suggest that the defence of intoxication differs between crimes of specific intent and crimes of basic intent?
3. In what way does he also suggest that voluntary intoxication supplies sufficient *mens rea* for a crime?
4. What in the article on *Kingston* is said to have been the basis of *Kingston's* argument why he should not be convicted?
5. Why did this argument not succeed?
6. According to the article, when will a plea of involuntary intoxication be successful?

Consent

EXTRACT ADAPTED FROM THE JUDGMENT IN *R v DONOVAN* [1934] 2 KB 498, COURT OF CRIMINAL APPEAL

Donovan was convicted of common assault after caning a 17-year-old girl for sexual gratification. His defence that she consented was rejected. The conviction was quashed on appeal for a misdirection that it was for the Crown to disprove consent.

SWIFT J

If an act is unlawful in the sense of being in itself a criminal act, it ... cannot be rendered lawful because the person to whose detriment it is done consents ... No person can licence another to commit a crime. So far as ... criminal law is concerned, therefore, where the act charged is in itself unlawful, it can never be necessary to prove absence of consent on the part of the person wronged ... to obtain the conviction of the wrongdoer. There are, however, many acts in themselves harmless and lawful which become unlawful only if ... done without ... consent of the person affected. What is, in one case, an innocent act of familiarity or affection, may, in another, be an assault, for no other reason than that, in the one case there is consent, and in the other consent is absent. As a general rule, although ... there are well-established exceptions, it is an unlawful act to beat another person with such a degree of violence that the infliction of bodily harm is a probable consequence, and when such an act is proved consent is immaterial.

EXTRACT ADAPTED FROM 'INFLICTING INJURIES FOR SEXUAL PLEASURE ILLEGAL, LORDS RULE', FRANCES GIBB, *THE TIMES*, 12 MARCH 1993

People who inflict sado-masochistic injuries on each other for sexual pleasure are guilty of criminal assault even though they consent to what happens, the law lords held yesterday.

In a landmark ruling ... immediately attacked by civil libertarians, the law lords held that consent to such practices was no defence to charges of wounding or causing actual bodily harm.

Lord Templeman said: 'Society is entitled and bound to protect itself against a cult of violence. Pleasure derived from the infliction of pain is an evil thing. Cruelty is uncivilised.'

The ruling prompted calls for a law on privacy. Andrew Puddephatt, general secretary of Liberty, said the ruling had 'potentially criminalised a whole range of perfectly harmless activities'.

Nicki Wolf, of Feminists Against Censorship, said the ruling showed 'Despite 30 years of campaigning to have domestic violence put on the political agenda, it seems legal condemnation is reserved for men who mutually consent to sado-masochistic sex.' She said the ruling was 'an insult to all women and we condemn it both for its removal of rights over our own bodies and the failure of the law to recognise the true nature of sexual violence.'

Lord Templeman said some consensual activities which involved actual bodily harm—such as ritual circumcision, tattooing, ear-piercing and violent sports like boxing—were lawful. But duelling and fighting were both unlawful and the consent of the protagonists afforded no defence.

He said there was a difference between violence which was incidental and violence which was inflicted for the indulgence of cruelty.

Questions

Read the two extracts above and answer the questions.

1. In what circumstances does the judge in *Donovan* suggest that consent cannot be available as a defence?
2. In what ways does the judgment in *Donovan* suggest that it is possible legally to inflict some physical harm on another person?
3. What different viewpoints are expressed in Frances Gibb's article regarding the inflicting of harm on other people?
4. In what circumstances do you think that a defence of consent can be justified in relation to assaults and wounding?

Duress

EXTRACT ADAPTED FROM THE JUDGMENT IN *R V HOWE* [1987] 1 AC 417, HL

Howe and another man, Bannister, took part in the torturing and abusing of another man who was then strangled by a further man. Following the torture of another man on another occasion they this time strangled and killed the victim. They did so, they said, because they acted under threats of violence, duress. They were convicted of the second murder though the defence of duress was allowed in respect of the first murder where they were accessories. In their failed House of Lords appeal it was considered that duress should not be available to an accessory to murder either.

LORD HAILSHAM LC

A long line of cases establish duress as . . . defence in a wide range of crimes.

. . . some degree of proportionality between the threat and the offence must, at least to some extent, be a prerequisite of the defence under existing law. Few would resist threats to the life of a loved one if the alternative were driving across the red lights or in excess of 70 m.p.h. on the motorway. But it would take rather more than the threat of a slap on the wrist or even moderate pain or injury to discharge the evidential burden even in the case of a fairly serious assault. In such a case the 'concession to human frailty' is no more than to say that in such circumstances a reasonable man of average courage is entitled to embrace as a matter of choice the alternative which a reasonable man could regard as the lesser of two evils. Other considerations necessarily arise where the choice is between the threat of death or . . . serious injury and deliberately taking an innocent life. In such a case a reasonable man might reflect that one innocent human life is at least as valuable as his own or that of his loved one. In such a case a man cannot claim that he is choosing the lesser of two evils. Instead he is embracing the cognate but morally disreputable principle that the end justifies the means.

LORD GRIFFITHS

As I can find no fair and certain basis on which to differentiate between participants to a murder and as I am firmly convinced that the law should not be extended to the killer, I would depart from the decision of this House in *Director of Public Prosecutions for Northern Ireland v Lynch* and declare the law to be that duress is not available as a defence to a charge of murder, or to attempted murder.

Necessity (duress of circumstances)

EXTRACT ADAPTED FROM THE JUDGMENT IN *R V MARTIN* [1989] 88 CR APP R 343, CA

Martin was convicted of driving while disqualified. He claimed as his defence that his wife had suicidal tendencies and, on the occasion in question had threatened to commit suicide unless he drove his stepson to work. The boy had overslept and would be late otherwise. There was evidence of his wife's previous attempts at suicide, and a doctor considered that on the day in question, in view of her general state, it was likely that she may have attempted suicide again. On appeal Martin succeeded in demonstrating this claim and his appeal was allowed and the conviction quashed.

SIMON BROWN J

The appellant's case on the facts was that he genuinely, and he would suggest reasonably, believed that his wife would carry out the threat unless he did as she demanded. Despite his disqualification he therefore drove the boy.

Sceptically though one may regard that defence on the facts the sole question before this court is whether those facts, had the jury accepted they were or might be true, amounted in law to a defence. . . .

. . . First, English law does, in extreme circumstances, recognise a defence of necessity. Most commonly this defence arises as duress. Equally, however, it can arise from other objective dangers threatening the accused or others. Arising thus it is conveniently called 'duress of circumstances'.

Secondly, the defence is available only if, from an objective standpoint, the accused can be said to be acting reasonably and proportionately in order to avoid a threat of death or serious injury.

Thirdly the issue should be left to the jury, who should be directed to determine these two questions: first was the accused, or may he have been, impelled to act as he did because as a result of what he reasonably believed to be the situation he had good cause to fear that otherwise death or serious physical injury would result? Second, if so, would a sober person of reasonable firmness, sharing the characteristics of the accused, have responded to that situation by acting as the accused acted? If the answer to both those questions was Yes, then the jury would acquit; the defence of necessity would have been established.

Questions

Read the two extracts above and answer the questions.

1. In *Howe* what do you think Lord Hailsham means by 'a concession to human frailty'?
2. What are the limitations to a successful plea of defence, according to Lord Hailsham in that case?
3. What important aspect of the defence, is identified in Lord Griffiths' judgment?
4. Looking at the case of *Martin*, what connections can be seen with the defence of duress?
5. When will a defence of 'duress of circumstances' be successful?

SECTION 14: PARTICIPATION

There are principals who carry out crimes but there can also be secondary parties such as those who give support or assistance. The question is what degree of involvement will lead to actually participating and therefore possible conviction as a criminal. A further problem concerns joint enterprise. What happens when two people set out to carry out one crime but another, possibly more serious, is committed by one party and the other knew that this was a possible outcome?

EXTRACT FROM S8 ACCESSORIES AND ABETTORS ACT 1861

8. Abettors in misdemeanours

Whosoever shall aid, abet, counsel or procure the commission of [any indictable offence], whether the same be at common law or by virtue of any Act passed or to be passed, shall be liable to be tried, indicted, and punished as a principal offender.

EXTRACT ADAPTED FROM THE JUDGMENT IN *ATTORNEY-GENERAL'S REFERENCE (NO 1 OF 1975)* [1975] 2 ALL ER 684, CA

The accused laced his friend's drink with double measures of spirits, knowing that his friend had to drive home. The friend then drove and was convicted of a drink driving offence. The question for the court was whether an accused should succeed on a claim of there being no case to answer, there being no positive encouragement by the accused to the driver to drive the vehicle with excess alcohol in his blood.

LORD WIDGERY CJ

The language in the section which determines whether a 'secondary party', as he is sometimes called, is guilty of a criminal offence committed by another embraces the four words 'aid, abet, counsel or procure'.

... it is the fact that in the great majority of instances where a secondary party is sought to be convicted of an offence there has been a contact between the principal offender and the secondary party. Aiding and abetting almost inevitably involves a situation in which the secondary party and the main offender are together at some stage discussing the plans which they may be making in respect of the alleged offence, and are in contact so that each knows what is in the mind of the other.

In the same way ... a person who counsels the commission of a crime of another, almost inevitably comes to a moment when he is in contact with that other, when he is discussing the offence with that other and when, to use the words of the statute, he counsels the other to commit the offence.

The fact that so often the relationship between the secondary party and the principal will be such that there is a meeting of minds between them caused the trial judge in the case to think that this was really an essential feature of proving or establishing the guilt of the secondary party and, he took the view that in the absence of some sort of meeting of minds, there could be no aiding, abetting or counselling of the offence within the meaning of the section.

So far as aiding, abetting and counselling is concerned we would go a long way with that conclusion. But we do not see why a similar principle should apply to procuring. We approach the section on the basis that if four words are employed here, the probability is that there is a difference between each of those four words and the other three, because, if there were no such difference, then Parliament would be wasting time in using four words where two or three would do.

To procure means to produce by endeavour. You procure a thing by setting out to see that it happens and taking appropriate steps to produce this happening ... there are plenty of instances in which a person may be said to procure the commission of a crime by another even though there is no sort of conspiracy between the two, even though there is no attempt at agreement or agreement as to the form which the offence should take. In our judgment the offence described ... is such a case.

If one looks at the facts ... the accused surreptitiously laced his friend's drink. This is an important element ... the conception of another procuring the commission of the offence by the driver is very much stronger where the driver is innocent of all knowledge of what is happening, as in the present case where the lacing of the drink was surreptitious.

The second thing which is important in the facts ... is that following and in consequence of the introduction of the extra alcohol, the friend drove with an excess quantity of alcohol in his blood. Causation here is important. You cannot procure an offence unless there is a causal link between what you do and the commission of the offence, and here we are told that in consequence of the addition of this alcohol the driver, when he drove home, drove with an excess quantity of alcohol in his body.

Giving the words their ordinary meaning in English, and asking oneself whether in those circumstances the offence has been procured, we are in no doubt that it has.

Questions

1. What are the different ways of acting as an accomplice?
2. According to Lord Widgery in the Attorney-General's Reference, in what way do they differ from one another?
3. What feature is usually common to both aiding and abetting?
4. Why is it not necessary for a procurer to communicate directly with the principal?
5. What feature does Lord Widgery suggest is the most vital element of procuring?

EXTRACT ADAPTED FROM THE JUDGMENT IN *R V POWELL AND ANOTHER; R V ENGLISH* 4 ALL ER 545, HL

The case involved joint appeals on joint enterprise.

Powell and Daniels and one other went to purchase drugs from a drug dealer, which was their joint enterprise. The dealer was shot dead and the Crown was unable to prove which of the men had fired the shot. The Crown's case was that the other two were guilty of murder in any case because they knew that the third man was armed and realised that he might use the gun and kill or seriously injure the drug dealer. They were convicted and their appeal to the Court of Appeal failed.

The joint enterprise between English and Weddle was to attack a police officer with wooden posts. During the attack Weddle killed the policeman with a knife. It was possible that English had no knowledge of the knife but the trial judge directed that he could be convicted of murder if he knew that there was a substantial risk that death or serious injury might be caused with the wooden post. English was convicted and his appeal rejected by the Court of Appeal.

Powell's and Daniels' appeals were rejected on the basis that they knew that the primary party might kill or cause serious injury to the drug dealer. English's appeal was granted on the basis that the lethal act by Weddle was fundamentally different from the act that he foresaw.

LORD HUTTON

The first issue is whether there is a principle established in the authorities that where there is a joint enterprise to commit a crime, foresight or contemplation ... by one party to the enterprise that another party to the enterprise may in the course of it commit another crime, is sufficient to impose criminal liability for that crime if committed by the other party even if the first party did not intend that criminal act to be carried out.

I consider that there is a strong line of authority that where two parties embark on a joint enterprise to commit a crime, and one party foresees that in the course of the enterprise the other party may carry out, with the requisite *mens rea*, an act constituting another crime, the former is liable for that crime if committed by the latter in the course of the enterprise.

... in *R v Smith* the Court of Appeal recognised that the secondary party will be guilty of unlawful killing committed by the primary party with a knife if he contemplates that the primary party may use such a weapon.

As a matter of strict analysis there is ... a distinction between a party to a common enterprise contemplating that in the course of the enterprise another party may use a gun or a knife and a party tacitly agreeing that in the course of the enterprise another party may use such a weapon. However, it is clear from a number of decisions that ... when two parties embark on a joint criminal enterprise one party will be liable for an act which he contemplates may be carried out by the other party in the course of the enterprise even if he has not tacitly agreed to the act.

The second issue which arises on these appeals is whether the line of authority exemplified by *R v Smith* is good law in the light of the decisions of this House in *R v Moloney* and *R v Hancock*. In reliance upon [those cases] the appellants submitted that as a matter of principle there is an anomaly in requiring proof against a secondary party of a lesser *mens rea* than needs to be proved against the principal who commits the *actus reus* of murder. If foreseeability of risk is insufficient to found the *mens rea* of murder for a principal then the same test of liability should apply in the case of a secondary party to the joint enterprise.

I recognise that as a matter of logic there is force in the argument ... and that on one view it is anomalous that if foreseeability of death or really serious harm is not sufficient to constitute *mens rea* for murder in the party who actually carries out the killing, it is sufficient to constitute *mens rea* in a secondary party. But the rules of the common law are not based solely on logic but relate to practical concerns . . .

There is, in my opinion, an argument of considerable force that the secondary party who takes part in a criminal enterprise with foresight that a deadly weapon may be used, should not escape liability for murder because he, unlike the principal party, is not suddenly confronted by the security officer so that he has to decide whether to use the gun or knife . . .

Therefore for the reasons which I have given . . . it is sufficient to found a conviction for murder for a secondary party to have realised that in the course of the joint enterprise the primary party might kill with intent to do so or with intent to cause grievous bodily harm. Accordingly I would dismiss the appeals.

The second certified question in the appeal of English arises because of the trial judge's summing up.

The appellant advanced the submission that in a case such as the present one where the primary party kills with a deadly weapon which the secondary party did not know that he had and therefore did not foresee his use of it, the secondary party should not be guilty of murder.

I consider that this submission is correct.

Accordingly, in the appeal of English, I consider that the direction of the learned trial judge was defective because he did not qualify his direction on foresight of really serious injury by stating that if the jury considered that the use of the knife by Weddle was the use of a weapon and an action which English did not foresee as a possibility then English should not be convicted of murder.

On the evidence the jury could have found that English did not know that Weddle had a knife. Therefore the judge's direction made the conviction unsafe and the appeal should be allowed.

Questions

1. What were the joint enterprises in the cases of *Powell and Daniels* and of *English*?
2. Why were none of these parties principal offenders in the killings that occurred?
3. What does Lord Hutton say is 'sufficient to found a conviction for murder' in the case of a secondary participant?
4. Why were the appeals of *Powell and Daniels* decided differently to the appeal of *English*?

SECTION 15: INCHOATE OFFENCES

These are incomplete crimes. There are three: incitement, conspiracy and attempt, but only the latter is considered here. Natural problems of attempt are what the defendant has to do to have done something 'more than merely preparatory' and what happens when the defendant attempts the impossible.

EXTRACT FROM S1 CRIMINAL ATTEMPTS ACT 1981

1. Attempting to commit an offence

(1) If, with intent to commit an offence to which this section applies, a person does an act which is more than merely preparatory to the commission of the offence, he is guilty of attempting to commit the offence.

(2) A person may be guilty of attempting to commit an offence to which this section applies even though the facts are such that the commission of the offence is impossible.

EXTRACT ADAPTED FROM THE JUDGMENT IN *R V CAMPBELL* [1991] 93 CR APP R 350, CA

Police who had been tipped off that he was going to rob it arrested Campbell outside a post office.

Campbell had in his possession an imitation gun and a threatening note which he had planned to pass to the assistant. He was convicted of attempted robbery and appealed successfully on the ground that he had not done sufficient to amount to an attempt.

WATKINS LJ

... it was beyond dispute that the appellant, at the material time, was carrying an imitation firearm which he made no attempt to remove from his clothing.

In order to effect the robbery it is equally beyond dispute it would have been quite impossible unless obviously he had entered the post office, gone to the counter and made some kind of hostile act—directed, of course, at whoever was behind the counter and in a position to hand him some money. A number of acts remained undone and the series of acts which he had already performed—were clearly acts which were, in the judgment of this court, indicative of mere preparation.

If a person, in circumstances such as this, has not even gained the place where he could be in a position to carry out the offence, it is extremely unlikely that it could ever be said that he had performed an act which could properly be said to be an attempt.

EXTRACT ADAPTED FROM THE JUDGMENT IN *R V SHIVPURI* [1987] AC 1, HL

When arrested Shivpuri believed that he was actually carrying large quantities of prohibited drugs. In fact the substance that he was carrying was described later as 'harmless vegetable matter' and not drugs at all. He was convicted of attempting to be knowingly concerned in dealing with and harbouring Class A and Class B drugs. He appealed on the basis of the earlier decisions in *Haughton v Smith* and *Anderton v Ryan* that he could not be convicted of attempting a crime that it was factually impossible for him to commit. His appeal in the House of Lords failed.

LORD BRIDGE

The first question ... is whether the appellant intended to commit the offences ... did the appellant intend to receive and store (harbour) and in due course pass on to third parties (deal with) packages of heroin or cannabis which he knew had been smuggled into England from India? The answer is plainly yes ... Next, did he in relation to each offence, do an act which was more than merely preparatory to the commission of the offence? The act relied on in relation to harbouring was the receipt and retention of the packages found in the lining of the suitcase. The act relied on in relation to dealing was the meeting at Southall station with the intended recipient of one of the packages. In each case the act was clearly more than merely preparatory to the commission of the *intended* offence; it was not and could not be more than merely preparatory to the commission of the *actual* offence, because the facts were such that the commission of the actual offence was impossible. Here then is the nub of the matter. Does the 'act which is more than merely preparatory to the commission of the offence' in section 1(1) of the Act ... (the *actus reus* of the statutory offence of attempt) require any more than an act which is more than merely preparatory to the commission of the offence which the defendant intended to commit? Section 1(2) must surely indicate a negative answer; if it were otherwise, whenever the facts were such that the commission of the actual offence was impossible, it would be impossible to prove an act more than merely preparatory to the commission of that offence and subsections (1) and (2) would contradict each other.

Questions

Read the three extracts above and answer the questions.

1. According to s1(1) of the Act and the case of *Campbell* how far towards the actual commission of the offence does an accused have to go in order to be guilty of attempting to commit the full offence?
2. Why precisely was *Campbell* not guilty of attempt?
3. What particular act on the part of the police might have made a difference?
4. What, according to the sources, is the necessary *mens rea* for attempt?
5. Why could *Shivpuri* not be guilty of dealing in or harbouring the prohibited drugs?
6. Why does Lord Bridge suggest that he can still be guilty of attempt?

Activity

Consider whether I could be guilty of attempted burglary in the following example:

An accomplice has given me a set of keys to an off licence in High Street, Low Town. Intending to steal large quantities of alcohol, I set off and arrive by mistake at the off licence in Low Street, High Town. Police arrest me as I am puzzling over why the keys look far too big for the lock.

CHAPTER 2

CONTRACT LAW

SECTION 1: OFFER AND ACCEPTANCE

A contract is formed only once an agreement has been reached between two parties. An agreement is a valid offer followed by a valid acceptance. Offers must be distinguished from other things like mere statements of price and an invitation to treat, which is an invitation to the other party to make an offer to buy. Problems also occur when a unilateral offer is made. An acceptance must be a 'mirror image' of the offer, with no variation of the terms of the offer. Other problems concern communication. Offers, revocations of offers and acceptance must all be communicated. In the case of acceptance where the postal rule applies the acceptance takes place when the letter is posted rather than when it is received.

EXTRACT ADAPTED FROM THE JUDGMENT IN *PHARMACEUTICAL SOCIETY OF GREAT BRITAIN V BOOTS CASH CHEMISTS (SOUTHERN) LTD* [1953] 1 QB 401, CA

The Pharmacy and Poisons Act 1933 provided that it was unlawful to sell drugs and medicines specified by the Act other than under the supervision of a qualified pharmacist. Boots the Chemists had opened a 'self service' shop, something of a novelty at the time. Customers would select articles they wished to purchase and take them to the assistant at the cash desk. If the items fell under the control of the Act the pharmacist would be there to supervise, or to refuse the sale if necessary. The question for the court was at what point the contract was formed: when the customer selected the goods, or not until the sale had been approved at the counter.

SOMERVELL LJ

[The plaintiffs] said that the purchase is complete if and when a customer going round the shelves takes an article and puts it in the receptacle which he or she is carrying, and that ... if that is right, when the customer comes to the pay desk, the registered pharmacist ... has no power to say: 'This drug ought not to be sold to this customer.'

Whether the view ... is a right view depends on what are the legal implications of this layout—the invitation to the customer. Is a contract to be regarded as being completed when the article is put into the receptacle, or is this to be regarded as a more organised way of doing what is already done in many other shops namely, enabling customers to have free access to what is in the shop, to look at the different articles, and then, ultimately, having got the ones which they wish to buy, to come up to the assistant saying 'I want this'? In the case of an ordinary shop, although goods are displayed and it is intended that customers should go and choose what they want, the contract is not completed until, the customer having indicated the articles which he needs, the shopkeeper, or someone on his behalf, accepts that offer. Then the contract is completed. I can see no reason at all, that being clearly the normal position, for drawing any different implications as a result of this layout.

If the plaintiffs are right, once an article has been placed in the receptacle the customer himself is bound and would have no right, without paying for the first article, to substitute an article which he saw later . . . and which he perhaps preferred.

EXTRACT ADAPTED FROM THE JUDGMENT IN *CARLILL V CARBOLIC SMOKE BALL CO* [1893] 1 QB 256, CA

The defendants produced and sold a patent medicine called the 'Carbolic Smoke Ball'. In their advertisement for the product they stated that anybody who used it for a prescribed period in the prescribed manner and still caught flu would receive £100. Furthermore they showed their *bona fides* on this matter by indicating that they had lodged £1,000 at a bank for such purposes. The claimant used the medicine in the prescribed manner and still caught flu, and so wished to claim the £100. The company claimed that the advertisement was a mere puff, and that in any case they had no contract with Mrs Carlill on the matter since they had made no offer directly to her which she could then accept. The Court of Appeal held that there was indeed a contract based on acceptance of a unilateral offer.

BOWEN LJ

The first observation which arises is that the document itself is not a contract at all, it is only an offer made to the public. The defendants contend next, that it is an offer the terms of which are too vague to be treated as a definite offer, inasmuch as there is no limit of time fixed for the catching of the influenza, and it cannot be supposed that the advertisers seriously promised to pay money to every person who catches the influenza at any time after the inhaling of the smoke ball. It was urged also, that if you look at this document you will find much vagueness as to the persons with whom the contract was intended to be made—that, in the first place, its terms are wide enough to include persons who may have used the smoke ball before the advertisement was issued; at all events, that is an offer to the world in general, and, also, that it was unreasonable to suppose it to be a definite offer, because nobody in their senses would contract themselves out of the opportunity of checking the experiment which was going to be made at their own expense. . . . in order to arrive at a right conclusion we must read this advertisement in its plain meaning . . . It was intended unquestionably to have some effect. And it seems . . . that the way in which the public would read would be . . . that if anybody, after the advertisement was published, used three times daily for two weeks the carbolic smoke ball, and then caught cold, he would be entitled to the reward.

It was also said that the contract is made with all the world—that is with everybody; and that you cannot contract with everybody . . . It is not a contract made with all the world. It is an offer made to all the world; and why should not an offer be made to all the world which is to ripen into a contract with anybody who comes forward and performs the condition? . . . although the offer is made to the world, the contract is made with that limited portion of the public who come forward and perform the condition on the faith of the advertisement. It is not like cases in which you offer to negotiate, or you issue advertisements that you have got a stock of books to sell, or houses to let, in which case there is no offer to be bound by any contract. If this is an offer to be bound, then it is a contract the moment the person fulfils the condition.

Then it was said that there was no notification of the acceptance of the contract. One cannot doubt that, as an ordinary rule of law, an acceptance of an offer made ought to be notified to the person who makes the offer, in order that the two minds may come together. Unless this is done . . . there is not that consensus which is necessary according to . . . English law to make a contract. But there is this clear gloss to be made upon that doctrine, that as notification of acceptance is required for the benefit of the person who makes the offer, the person who makes the offer may dispense with notice to himself if he thinks it desirable to do so, and . . . there can be no doubt that where a person in an offer made by him to another person, expressly or impliedly intimates in his offer that it will be sufficient to act on the proposal without communicating acceptance of it to himself, performance of the condition is a sufficient acceptance without notification.

Questions

Read the two extracts above and answer the questions.

1. According to the *Boots* case, when goods are displayed in a shop setting when is the offer actually made?
2. Looking at the reasoning in the same case, when is the acceptance made?
3. How does this differ from the formation of agreements generally in contract law?
4. According to the judgment in *Carlill v The Carbolic Smoke Ball Co*, to whom can an offer be made?
5. How is the acceptance made in relation to such offers?

EXTRACT ADAPTED FROM THE JUDGMENT IN *HYDE V WRENCH* [1840] 3 BEAV 334

These are simple enough. The defendant offered to sell his farm to the plaintiff for £1,000. The plaintiff, instead of agreeing, offered to pay £950 which the defendant then rejected. The plaintiff at a later stage then claimed to accept the original offer and brought an action for specific performance. The court rejected the claim that there was a contract since the original offer had been rejected and was no longer open to acceptance.

LORD LANGDALE MR

Under the circumstances stated in this bill, I think there exists no valid binding contract between the parties for the purchase of the property. The defendant offered to sell it for £1,000, and if that had been at once unconditionally accepted, there would undoubtedly have been a perfect binding contract; instead of that, the plaintiff made an offer of his own, to purchase the property for £950, and he thereby rejected the offer previously made by the defendant. I think that it was not afterwards competent for him to revive the proposal of the defendant, by tendering an acceptance of it; and that, therefore, there exists no obligation of any sort between the parties; the demurrer must be allowed.

EXTRACT ADAPTED FROM THE JUDGMENT IN *FELTHOUSE V BINDLEY* [1862] 11 CB (NS) 869; 142 ER 1037

The claimant had been discussing the purchase of his nephew's horse. The nephew was auctioning off various farming stock of which the horse was a part. At one point the claimant wrote to his nephew and said: 'If I hear no more about him, I consider the horse is mine at £30 15s'. No reply was made to this letter. The nephew did instruct the auctioneer to reserve the horse. However, the auctioneer put the horse into the sale by mistake and sold it. The claimant, to bring an action for conversion against the auctioneer, needed to prove that there was a contract between himself and his nephew for the purchase of the horse. He failed because there had been nothing to bind the horse to him.

WILLES J

It is clear that there was no complete bargain on January 2: and . . . that the uncle had no right to impose upon the nephew the sale of his horse for £30 15s unless he chose to comply with the condition of writing to repudiate the offer. The nephew might, no doubt, have bound his uncle to the bargain by writing to him: the uncle might also have retracted his offer at any time before acceptance. It stood an open offer; and so things remained until February 25, when the nephew was about to sell his farming stock by auction. The horse in question being catalogued with the rest of the stock, the auctioneer (the defendant) was told that it was already sold. It is clear, therefore, that the nephew in his own mind intended his uncle to have the horse at the price which he (the uncle) had named, £30 15s: but he had not communicated such ... intention to his uncle, or done anything to bind himself. Nothing, therefore, had been done to vest the property in the horse in the plaintiff down to February 25, when the horse was sold by the defendant. It appears ... there had been no bargain to pass the property in the horse to the plaintiff, and therefore that he had no right to complain of the sale.

EXTRACT ADAPTED FROM THE JUDGMENT IN *HOUSEHOLD FIRE INSURANCE CO V GRANT* [1879] 4 EX D 216

Grant agreed with an agent to buy 100 shares in a company, paying a £5 deposit and agreeing to pay the balance of £95 within 12 months of the date of allotment. The agent forwarded his application. Grant's name was entered on the register of shareholders. A letter of allotment was then posted to Grant, but it never arrived. When the company went into liquidation the liquidator sued Grant for the balance of money owing on the shares. His argument that there was no contract failed. The contract was formed when the letter was posted. It was irrelevant that he had never received the letter, and the fact his name was on the register was proof that he was indeed a shareholder.

THESIGER LJ

Now whatever in abstract discussion may be said as to the legal notion of its being necessary, in order to the effecting of a valid and binding contract, that the minds of the parties should be brought together at one and the same moment, that notion is practically the foundation of English law upon the subject of the formation of contracts ... on the other hand it is a principle of law, as well established as the legal notion to which I have referred, that the minds of the two parties must be brought together by mutual communication. An acceptance, which only remains in the breast of the acceptor without being actually and by legal implication communicated to the offeror, is no binding acceptance. How then are these elements of law to be harmonised in the case of contracts formed through correspondence through the post? I see no better mode than ... treating the post office as the agent of both parties. If the post office be such common agent. ... it seems ... to follow that, as soon as the letter of acceptance is delivered to the post office, the contract is made as complete ... and absolutely binding as if the acceptor had put his letter into the hands of a messenger sent by the offeror himself as his agent to deliver the offer and receive the acceptance. The contract is actually made when the letter is posted. How then can a casualty in the post, whether resulting in delay, which in commercial transactions is often as bad as no delivery, or in non-delivery, unbind the parties or unmake the contract? To me it appears that in practice a contract complete upon the acceptance of an offer being posted, but liable to be put an end to by an accident in the post, would be more mischievous than a contract only binding upon the parties to it upon acceptance actually reaching the offeror, and I can see no principle of law from which such an anomalous contract can be deduced.

Questions

Read the three extracts above and answer the questions.

1. According to the reasoning in *Hyde v Wrench*, what happens when an offer is rejected?

2 What does *Felthouse v Bindley* tell us about the communication of an acceptance?

3 In *Household Fire Assurance Co v Grant* what does Thesiger LJ's judgment tell us about the state of mind of the two parties when a contract is made?

4 On that basis should it be possible for there to be a contract if a party enters an agreement involuntarily?

5 What does the *Grant* case tell us about the use of postal services for making contracts?

6 How would this differ from face-to-face dealing?

7 What apparent inconsistency does there appear to be between the communicating of an offer and the communicating of an acceptance?

SECTION 2: CONSIDERATION

Consideration is also vital to the formation of contracts. Because a contract is a bargain there must be a price paid in return for the promise given by the other party. This is the consideration. Both sides must give consideration. Problems concern past consideration (consideration given prior to any agreement), offering what is already required under an existing agreement in return for a new promise, and the effect of agreements to accept part payment of debts as consideration for the whole debt.

EXTRACT ADAPTED FROM THE JUDGMENT IN *THOMAS V THOMAS* [1842] 2 QB 851

On his deathbed a man stated that he wished his wife to have his house and all that it contained, although he had not previously made any such provision. His executors decided to honour his wishes, and drew up a document giving the wife the property for life, but also charging her a nominal ground rent of £1 per year. An executor later tried to remove her and she successfully argued that she had a contract based on the payment of the ground rent. The defendant unsuccessfully tried to argue that there was no consideration because this figure was not adequate.

PATTESON J

Consideration means something which is of some value in the eye of the law, moving from the plaintiff: it may be some benefit to the plaintiff, or some detriment to the defendant; but at all events it must be moving from the plaintiff.

EXTRACT ADAPTED FROM THE JUDGMENT IN *CHAPPELL & CO LTD V NESTLE CO LTD* [1960] AC 87

The chocolate company offered, as a promotional campaign, a free gramophone record 'Rockin' Shoes' in return for 1s 6d (7½p now) to cover post and packing, together with three chocolate bar wrappers from their 6d chocolate which would only be thrown away. Nestle were then sued for breach of copyright that they could avoid if they paid a royalty of 6¼%. The issue was whether the royalty should be based only on the 1s 6d, and thus whether the wrappers were part of the consideration in return for the record.

LORD SOMERVELL

I think that they are part of the consideration. They are so described in the offer. 'They', the wrappers, 'will help you to get smash hit recordings'. It is said that, when received, the wrappers are of no value to the respondents, the Nestle Co Ltd. This I would have though to be irrelevant. A contracting party can stipulate for what consideration he chooses. A peppercorn does not cease to be good consideration if it is established that the promisee does not like pepper and will throw away the corn.

Questions

Read the two extracts above and answer the questions.

1. According to Patteson J in *Thomas v Thomas*, what is consideration?
2. What does this tell us about adequacy of consideration?
3. What is Lord Somervell's justification for finding that there is consideration in *Chappel v Nestle*?
4. What does this tell us about sufficiency of consideration?

Activity

Consider which of the following, if any, could be classed as consideration:

1. I am hungry and I offer you my house in return for a sandwich.
2. I will give you my car if you like my book.
3. I will give you a free copy of my book if your school or college buys ten copies.
4. I will like you enormously if you buy my book.

EXTRACT ADAPTED FROM THE JUDGMENT IN *ROSCORLA V THOMAS* [1842] 3 QB 234

Two parties contracted for the sale and purchase of a horse for £30. After the deal was concluded and the bargain struck, the defendant, in answer to the claimant's enquiry, promised that the horse was 'sound and free from vice'. In fact the horse turned out to be vicious and difficult to control. The claimant sued and failed. The promise was not incorporated in the contract since it came before the agreement. Any consideration was in the past.

DENMAN CJ

It may be taken as a general rule . . . that the promise must be co-extensive with the consideration. In the present case, the only promise that would result from the consideration, as stated, and be co-extensive with it, would be to deliver the horse upon request. The precedent sale, without a warranty, though at the request of the defendant, imposes no other duty or obligation upon him. It is clear, therefore, that the consideration stated would not raise an implied promise by the defendant that the horse was sound or free from vice.

Questions

1. The above case refers to the 'past consideration' rule. Why is there no contract in the above case, and what does past consideration mean?
2. What sorts of problems would we have if we allowed contracts to be made where the consideration has been supplied before any agreement has been reached?
3. The rule in *Lampleigh v Braithwaite* says that if a service has been requested with no mention of payment made at that time, a later promise to pay made after the service has been rendered will be enforced. Why is this exception to the past consideration rule necessary?

EXTRACT ADAPTED FROM THE JUDGMENT IN *STILK V MYRICK* [1809] 2 CAMP 317

Two sailors deserted and the master of the ship, not being able to replace them, then offered to share the wages of the two men among the remaining crew for their extra part in the return voyage. One sailor then sued when the extra sum remained unpaid. He was unsuccessful because there was no consideration to support the fresh promise made by the master of the ship.

LORD ELLENBOROUGH

There was no consideration for the ulterior pay promised to the mariners who remained with the ship. Before they sailed from London they had undertaken to do all that they could under all the emergencies of the voyage. They had sold all their services till the voyage should be completed. If they had been at liberty to quit the vessel at Cronstadt, the case would have been quite different; or if the captain had capriciously discharged the two men who were wanting, the others might not have been compellable to take the whole duty upon themselves, and their agreeing to do so might have been a sufficient consideration for the promise of an advance of wages. But the desertion of a part of the crew is to be considered an emergency of the voyage as much as their death; and those who remain are bound by the terms of their original contract to exert themselves to the utmost to bring the ship in safety to their destined port.

EXTRACT ADAPTED FROM THE JUDGMENT IN *WILLIAMS V ROFFEY BROS & NICHOLLS (CONTRACTORS) LTD* [1990] 1 ALL ER 512, CA

The defendants were building contractors who had agreed to refurbish 27 flats for a housing association under a contract containing a 'penalty clause' for late completion. The defendants employed the claimant, as a subcontractor, to do the carpentry for £20,000. The contract did not stipulate the manner of payment, but the claimant was paid as the work progressed. By April 1986 he had been paid £16,000 and had done some work on all the flats, but he had completed only nine and was in financial difficulties. This was partly because he failed to supervise his workmen properly but largely because, as the defendants agreed, the original price for the work was too low. The defendants therefore promised to pay him an extra amount of £10,300, at the rate of £575 per completed flat. The claimant completed work on eight further flats but the defendants paid only £1,500 more and the claimant stopped work and brought this action for payment.

PURCHAS LJ

What consideration has moved from the plaintiff to support the promise to pay the extra £10,300 added to the lump sum provision? In the particular circumstances ... there was clearly a commercial advantage to both sides from a pragmatic point of view in reaching the agreement of 9 April. The defendants were on risk that as a result of the bargain that they had struck the plaintiff would not or indeed possibly could not comply with his existing obligations without further finance. As a result of the agreement the defendants secured their position commercially. There was, however, no obligation added to the contractual duties imposed upon the plaintiff under the original contract. Prima facie this would appear to be a classic *Stilk v Myrick* case. It was, however, open to the plaintiff to be in deliberate breach of the contract in order to 'cut his losses' commercially. In normal circumstances the suggestion that a contracting party can rely upon his own breach to establish consideration is distinctly unattractive. In many cases it obviously would be and if there was any element of duress brought upon the other contracting party under the modern development of this branch of the law the proposed breaker of the contract would not benefit ... I consider that the modern approach to the question of consideration would be that where there were benefits derived by each party to a contract of variation even though one party did not suffer a detriment this would not be fatal to establishing sufficient consideration to support the agreement. If both parties benefit from an agreement it is not necessary that each also suffers a detriment. ... on the facts ... the judge ... was entitled to reach the conclusion that consideration existed ... I would not disturb that finding.

Questions

Read the two extracts above and answer the questions.

1. Why does Lord Ellenborough suggest that there is no consideration for the promise to share the wages of the two deserters between the rest of the crew in *Stilk v Myrick*?
2. What exactly was the consideration for the agreement by Roffey's to pay an extra £10,300 to Williams in *Williams v Roffey Bros & Nicholls*?
3. What would have happened if instead Williams had threatened Roffey's that he would do no more work without extra payment?
4. In your own words explain how Purchas LJ sees the principle in *Williams v Roffey Bros & Nicholls* conforming to the basic principle in *Stilk v Myrick*.

SECTION 3: INTENTION TO CREATE LEGAL RELATIONS

All contracts are formed only if the parties intend to be legally bound by their promises. Generally, intention operates on the basis of two rebuttable presumptions, that in social or domestic agreements there is no such intention, and in a business or commercial arrangement there will be an intention to be legally bound.

EXTRACT ADAPTED FROM THE JUDGMENT IN *BALFOUR V BALFOUR* [1919] ALL E R 860

A man had a government posting in Ceylon while his wife stayed in England because of her health. The couple later decided to part. The wife claimed that shortly before the husband left he had promised to pay her a regular income of £30 per month that he had never paid. She won at first instance but lost on her husband's appeal.

ATKIN LJ

The defence to this action . . . is that the husband says he entered into no contract with his wife, and for the determination of that it is necessary to remember that there are agreements between parties which do not result in contracts within the meaning of that term in our law. The ordinary example is where two parties agree to take a walk together, or where there is an offer and acceptance of hospitality. Nobody would suggest in ordinary circumstances that those agreements result in what we know as a contract, and one of the most usual forms of agreement which does not constitute a contract appears . . . to be the arrangements . . . made between husband and wife. . . . it is the natural and inevitable result of the relationship between husband and wife, that the two spouses should make agreements between themselves such as are in dispute in this action, agreements for allowances by which the husband agrees to pay to his wife a certain sum of money . . . to cover either her own expenses or the necessary expenses of the household . . . those agreements, or many of them, do not result in contracts at all . . . even though there may be what as between other parties would constitute consideration for the agreement. Nevertheless they are not contracts . . . because the parties did not intend that they should be attended by legal consequences. . . . The small courts of this country would have to be multiplied one hundredfold if these arrangements did result in fact in legal obligations. They are not sued upon . . . because the parties in the inception of the arrangement never intended that they should be . . .

EXTRACT ADAPTED FROM THE JUDGMENT IN *MERRITT V MERRITT* [1970] 1 WLR 1211

A husband left his wife and children to live with another woman. The matrimonial home was jointly owned. The husband later agreed to pay the wife an allowance of £40 per month out of which she would pay the mortgage. He also signed an agreement that once the mortgage payments were complete he would transfer sole ownership into her name. When the wife paid off the mortgage he nevertheless refused to transfer the house into her name. She sued and succeeded on appeal.

LORD DENNING MR

The first point taken on his behalf by counsel for the husband was that the arrangement was not intended to create legal relations. It was, he says, a family arrangement such as was considered by the court in *Balfour v Balfour* and *Jones v Padavatton.* So the wife could not sue on it. I do not think that those cases have any application here. The parties there were living together in amity. In such cases their domestic arrangements are ordinarily not intended to create legal relations. It is altogether different when the parties are not living together in amity but are separated, or about to separate. They then bargain keenly. It may be safely presumed that they intend to create legal relations.

Questions

Read the two extracts above and answer the questions.

1. What evidence does Lord Atkin suggest for the proposition that husbands and wives do not intend to create legal relations?
2. What other reasons does he give for not being prepared to enforce agreements between spouses?
3. How does Lord Denning distinguish *Balfour v Balfour* in *Merritt v Merritt*?

EXTRACT ADAPTED FROM THE JUDGMENT IN *ESSO PETROLEUM LTD V COMMISSIONERS OF CUSTOMS AND EXCISE* [1976] 1 WLR 1

Esso gave free 'World Cup coins' with every four gallons of petrol bought as a promotional campaign. The Commissioners argued that the coins should be subject to purchase tax on which basis they needed to show that the transaction was a contractual one. The House of Lords actually rejected the argument that the coins were part of a contract of sale, but some of them felt that there was definitely an intention to create legal relations.

LORD SIMON OF GLAISDALE

I am ... not prepared to accept that the promotion material put out by Esso was not envisaged by them as creating legal relations between the garage proprietors who adopted it and motorists who yielded to its blandishments. In the first place, Esso and the garage proprietors put the material out for their commercial advantage, and designed it to attract the custom of motorists. The whole transaction took place in a setting of business relations. In the second place, it seems ... undesirable to allow a commercial promoter to claim that what he has done is a mere puff, not intended to create legal relations. The coins may have been themselves of little intrinsic value; but all the evidence suggests that Esso contemplated that they would be attractive to motorists and that there would be a large commercial advantage to themselves from the scheme, an advantage in which the garage proprietors would also share. Thirdly, I think that authority supports the view that legal relations were envisaged.

EXTRACT ADAPTED FROM THE JUDGMENT IN *ROSE & FRANK CO V J R CROMPTON BROS* [1923] 2 KB 261

Under an agreement manufacturers of tissue gave a New York firm sales and distribution rights for the United States and Canada for a three-year period with an option to extend the time. The agreement contained an 'honour pledge' clause, specifically stating that the agreement should 'not be subject to legal jurisdiction in the law courts' of either country, but binding in honour only. The agreement was subsequently extended, but the manufacturers then terminated it too early and refused to process orders made before the termination. The distributors sued for breach of the original agreement and also for the failure to deliver the goods ordered. They failed on the first because there was no intention to create legal relations, though they succeeded in respect of the orders since this was accepted as being a separate contract inferred from the conduct of the parties and enforceable without any reference to the original agreement.

SCRUTTON LJ (IN THE COURT OF APPEAL)

It is quite possible for parties to come to an agreement by accepting a proposal with the result that the agreement does not give rise to legal relations. The reason of this is that the parties do not intend that their agreement shall give rise to legal relations. This intention may be implied from the subject-matter of the agreement, but it may also be expressed by the parties. In social and family relations such an intention is readily implied, while in business matters the opposite result would ordinarily follow. But I can see no reason why, even in business matters, the parties should not intend to rely on each other's good faith and honour, and to exclude all idea of settling disputes by any outside intervention, with the accompanying necessity of expressing themselves so precisely that outsiders may have no difficulty in understanding what they mean. If they clearly express such an intention I can see no reason in public policy why effect should not be given to their intention.

Questions

Read the two extracts above and answer the questions.

1. What reasons does Lord Simon give for thinking that there is intention to create legal relations in the *Esso* case?
2. What reasons does Scrutton LJ give for thinking that there is no intention to create legal relations in the *Rose & Frank* case?
3. What do the two cases suggest about the basic presumption of intention in business and commercial dealings?

Activity

Consider whether or not there is intention to create legal relations in the following arrangements:

1. Jaz arranges to meet his girlfriend at 6.30 p.m. to take her to the cinema.
2. Simon says that he will pay his secretary a bonus at Christmas for the hard work she has done over the year.
3. Terry borrows 50p from his friend with which to buy a raffle ticket and promises to share the prize if he wins.
4. Trevor gives Abdul a written agreement that he will not sell his photographic business to anybody else until he has heard back from Abdul. The written agreement finishes 'This agreement is binding in honour only'.

SECTION 4: PRIVITY OF CONTRACT

Historically only those who were parties to a contract could sue or be sued under it. This seemed generally unfair on named third parties who were granted rights under the contract which were not then enforceable by them. A variety of methods were devised to get round the hardship of this rule. Now Parliament has intervened with a Bill to make third party rights enforceable in certain circumstances.

EXTRACT ADAPTED FROM THE JUDGMENT IN *DUNLOP PNEUMATIC TYRE CO LTD V SELFRIDGE & CO LTD* [1915] AC 847, HL

Under a price maintenance agreement (which would now in any case be governed by statutory and European law controls) Dunlop sold tyres to a wholesaler, Dew and Co, who, by the agreement, were bound to sell on at specific prices and to include in their contracts with retailers a clause to the same effect. Selfridge bought Dunlop's tyres from Dew under an agreement containing the required clause but then sold on to customers at reduced prices. Dunlop sued on the basis of the price fixing clause but could not succeed because they were not a party to the contract between Dew and Selfridge, and therefore had no stake in it.

VISCOUNT HALDANE LC

... in the law of England certain principles are fundamental. One is that only a person who is a party to a contract can sue on it. Our law knows nothing of a *jus quaesitum tertio* arising by way of contract. Such a right may be conferred by way of property, as, for example, under a trust, but it cannot be conferred on a stranger to a contract as a right to enforce the contract *in personam*. A second principle is that if a person with whom a contract not under seal has been made is to be able to enforce it consideration must have been given by him to the promisor or to some other person at the promisor's request. A third proposition is that a principal not named in the contract may sue upon it if the promisee really contracted as his agent. But again in order to entitle him to sue, he must have given consideration either personally or through the promisee, acting as his agent in giving it.

EXTRACT ADAPTED FROM 'ABOLITION OF PRIVITY', RICHARD HUDSON, *NEW LAW JOURNAL*, 22 JANUARY 1999

Sixty two years after the Law Revision Committee ... first recommended that where a contract, by its express implication seeks to confer a benefit on a third party, that third party should be entitled to enforce the provision in his own name, the so-called doctrine of privity, a Bill to implement the Law Commission proposals contained in their 1996 report *Privity of Contract: Contracts for the Benefit of Third Parties* (Law Commission No 242) has been introduced by the Government.

According to the Law Commission, the non-recognition of third party rights has been the rule which senior judges have criticised more than any other rule of English contract law, ... yet the simple logic of the rule has been widely regarded as a fundamental principle ... although ... dating only from the mid nineteenth century.

The Bill provides that a third party will have the right to enforce a term of the contract both when the contract expressly provides that he should have that right and also where there is no such provision but there is a contractual term which purports to confer a benefit on him. Once the third party has a right to enforce the term, there will be limitations on the extent to which the contracting parties may modify their contract without the third party's consent. The contracting parties will not be obliged to give enforceable rights to the third party on whom the benefit is to be conferred. If it is apparent from the contract that they did not intend to do so, the third party will be unable to enforce the term as under the previous law.

There are a number of changes from the draft Bill annexed to the Law Commission report. One important new exception will prevent a third party from suing an employee for breach of his contract of employment.

Some unresolved problems remain. Principal amongst them is the one which vexed the Law Commission, namely the extent to which the Unfair Terms Act 1977 should protect a third party acquiring rights by virtue of abolition of the rule. Clause 7 of the Bill preserves any rights or remedies which may be available to a party at common law or by statute apart from the Bill, for example by rendering ineffective a contractual provision seeking to exclude liability for personal injury or death, but ensures that a third party cannot invoke the reasonableness test under s2(2) of the 1977 Act to contest the validity of a term excluding or limiting liability for negligently caused loss or damage. This is consistent with the underlying policy of the Bill, which is to enable contracting parties to confer rights on third parties but to allow them to retain control over the nature and extent of those newly conferred rights. The opposing view holds that the policy of the law should be against unreasonable contract terms whoever relies on them and in whatever circumstances.

Questions

Read the two extracts above and answer the questions.

1. In the *Dunlop v Selfridge* case in what situations does Viscount Haldane suggest that a person who is not actually a party to the contract might still have rights under it?
2. What is the significance of consideration in the doctrine of privity?
3. From Viscount Haldane's judgment what do you understand *jus quaesitum tertio* to mean?
4. In Richard Hudson's article why were the Law Commission in their Report No 242 concerned to see changes to the doctrine of privity?
5. In what circumstances does the Bill propose that third parties to contracts should be able to enforce rights identified in the contracts as affecting them?
6. Why do you think that the Bill contains the exception preventing a third party from suing an employee who is in breach of his contract of employment?
7. What problems that may arise in relation to exclusion clauses are identified in the source?

SECTION 5: CAPACITY AND MINORS' CONTRACTS

Sometimes a person or body lacks the capacity to contract fully. This generally means that contracts made by such parties are not fully enforceable against them. The group includes minors (those under the age of 18), drunkards, those with a mental incapacity, and corporations. Minors' contracts are enforceable when they are for necessaries or for training, education, or employment. Minors can avoid some contracts of continuous obligation, and certain agreements such as for loans are not enforceable against them. Legislation seeks to prevent a minor's unjust enrichment.

EXTRACT ADAPTED FROM THE JUDGMENT IN *CHAPPLE V COOPER* [1844] M & W 13 QB 252

A young woman who was also a minor became widowed by her husband's death. When the funeral expenses remained unpaid the undertaker sued her successfully for the cost of the funeral. It was held to be a necessary for which she was liable.

ALDERSON B

Things necessary are those without which an individual cannot reasonably exist. In the first place, food, raiment, lodging and the like. About these there is no doubt. Again, as the proper cultivation of the mind is as expedient as the support of the body, instruction in art or trade, or intellectual, moral and religious information may be a necessary also. Again, as man lives in society, the assistance and attendance of others may be a necessary to his well-being. . . . Then the classes being established, the subject matter and extent of the contract may vary according to the state of the infant himself. His clothes may be fine or coarse according to his rank; his education may vary according to the station he is to fill; and the medicines will depend on the illness with which he is afflicted, and the extent of his probable means when of full age. So again, the nature and extent of the attendance will depend on his position in society. But in all these cases it must first be made out that the class itself is one in which the things furnished are essential to the existence and reasonable advantage and comfort of the infant contractor. Thus articles of *mere* luxury are always excluded, though luxurious articles of utility are in some cases allowed.

Extract adapted from s3 Sale of Goods Act 1979

3.

Where necessaries are sold and delivered to an infant or minor, or to a person who by reason of mental incapacity or drunkenness is incompetent to contract, he must pay a reasonable price therefor.

Questions

Read the two extracts above and answer the questions.

1. In *Chapple v Cooper* what things does Baron Alderson suggest are obviously necessaries?
2. What tests does the case establish for determining whether in fact a given item is a necessary to a particular minor?
3. What reasoning is given for the funeral charges being a necessary to the minor in the case itself?
4. What important point is made in s3 of the Sale of Goods Act 1979 in respect of necessaries?

Extract adapted from the judgment in *North Western Railway Co v M'Michael* [1851] 5 Exch 114

A minor had bought railway shares without completing payment on them. In such circumstances the company would be entitled to make a 'call' for payment. The railway company did make a call on the minor who then pleaded that he had never in fact ratified the purchase of the shares and had received no benefit from them. The court, in its judgment, identified what the position would have been if the contract had been repudiated successfully instead.

PARKE B

Our opinion is that an infant is not absolutely bound, but is in the same situation as an infant acquiring real estate or any other permanent interest: he is not deprived of the right which the law gives every infant of waiving and disagreeing to a purchase which he has made; and if he waives it the estate acquired by the purchaser is at an end and with it his liability to pay calls, *though the avoidance may not have taken place till the call was due.*

Questions

1. What point is Baron Parke making about the enforceability of the share contract in the above case?
2. To which other type of contracts does this point apply, and what common feature do they share?

EXTRACT ADAPTED FROM THE JUDGMENT IN *R LESLIE LTD V SHEILL* [1914] 3 KB 607, CA

The defendant while still a minor borrowed £400 from the claimants who were moneylenders by misrepresenting his age as being over the age of contractual capacity. The claimants brought an action to recover the sum lent and the interest appropriate to the loan. They failed in their action because for them to succeed would have in effect meant enforcing the contract, rather than amounting to restitution, and would have been contrary to the Infants Relief Act 1874 in force at that time. Lord Sumner identified that there was a distinction between restitution and mere repayment and that the latter excluded the doctrine of restitution.

LORD SUMNER

I think that the whole current of decisions down to 1913, apart from dicta which are inconclusive, went to shew that, when an infant obtained an advantage by falsely stating himself to be of full age, ... equity required him to restore his ill-gotten gains, or to release the party deceived from obligations or acts in law induced by the fraud, but scrupulously stopped short of enforcing against him a contractual obligation, entered into while he was an infant, even by means of fraud. Restitution stopped where repayment began.

EXTRACT FROM S3 MINORS' CONTRACTS ACT 1987

3. Restitution

(1) Where—

(a) a person ('the plaintiff') has after the commencement of this Act entered into a contract with another ('the defendant'), and

(b) the contract is unenforceable against the defendant (or he repudiates it) because he was a minor when the contract was made,

the court may, if it is just and equitable to do so, require the defendant to transfer to the plaintiff any property acquired by the defendant under the contract, or any property representing it.

Questions

Read the two extracts above and answer the questions.

1. What does Lord Sumner say is the consequence of a minor gaining property by a fraudulent misrepresentation as to his age?
2. Why could the loan not be recovered in the case?
3. According to the Minors' Contracts Act 1987, when will restitution apply?

SECTION 6: TERMS

The terms of a contract are the obligations. They must first be incorporated to be terms. Terms can be expressed by the parties or implied. Terms are usually classified as 'conditions', which are important terms going to the root of the contract and with a broad range of remedies if they are breached; or warranties, ordinary terms. Sometimes judges call terms 'innominate' and determine what remedy is available from the consequences of the breach.

EXTRACT ADAPTED FROM THE JUDGMENT IN *OSCAR CHESS V WILLIAMS* [1957] 1 WLR 370, CA

The defendant purchased a new car from the claimant car dealers, who took his old car in part exchange. Relying on information in the registration documents, he described his old car as a 1948 model. The dealers in consequence gave him £290 off the price of the new car. Unknown to either party, the registration documents were wrong and the car was actually a 1939 model for which the dealers would have allowed only £175. When the truth was discovered they sued for the balance. They succeeded in County Court where the judge held that that the statement as to the age was a condition of the contract. The defendant, however, successfully appealed on the ground that any representation as to the age was a mere opinion and not, therefore, incorporated in the contract.

DENNING LJ

I entirely agree that both parties assumed that the Morris was a 1948 model and that this assumption was fundamental to the contract. But this does not prove that the representation was a term of the contract. ...

If the buyer had come promptly, he might have succeeded in getting the whole transaction set aside in equity on the ground of this mistake; but he did not do so. His only remedy is in damages and, to recover these, he must prove a warranty.

I use the word 'warranty' in its ordinary English meaning to denote a binding promise. During the last fifty years, however, some lawyers have come to use the word 'warranty' in another sense. They use it to denote a subsidiary term in contract, as distinct from a vital term, which they call a 'condition'. These different uses of the word seem to have been the source of confusion in the present case. The judge did not ask himself, 'Was the representation ... intended to be a warranty?' He asked himself 'Was it fundamental to the contract?' He answered it by saying ... it was fundamental; and therefore ... was a condition and not a warranty. By concentrating on whether it was fundamental, he ... missed the crucial point in the case, which is whether it was a term of the contract at all. The crucial question is: was it a binding promise or only an innocent misrepresentation? The technical distinction between a 'condition' and a 'warranty' is quite immaterial in this case. ...

The question whether a warranty was intended depends on the conduct of the parties ... If an intelligent bystander would reasonably infer that a warranty was intended, that will suffice ...

It is instructive to take some recent instances to show how the courts have approached this question. When the seller states a fact which is or should be within his own knowledge and of which the buyer is ignorant, intending that the buyer should act on it and he does so, it is easy to infer a warranty: see *Couchman v Hill*, where the farmer stated that the heifer was unserved. So also, if he makes a promise about something which is or should be within his own control: see *Birch v Paramount Estates*, where the seller stated that the house would be as good as the show house. But if the seller ... makes it clear that he has no knowledge of his own, but has got his information elsewhere and is merely passing it on, it is not easy to imply a warranty.

Turning now to the present case; much depends on the precise words that were used. If the seller says 'I believe it is a 1948 Morris, here is the registration book to prove it', there is clearly no warranty. It is a statement of belief, not a contractual promise. But if the seller says 'I guarantee that it is a 1948 Morris. This is borne out by the registration book, but you need not rely solely on that. I give you my own guarantee that it is', there is clearly a warranty. ...

It must have been obvious to both that the seller had himself no personal knowledge of the year when the car was made ... He must have been relying on the registration book. It is unlikely that such a person would warrant the year of manufacture. ... the intelligent bystander would, I suggest, say that the seller did not intend to bind himself ...

EXTRACT ADAPTED FROM THE JUDGMENT IN *SCHAWEL V READE* [1913] 2 IR REP 81, HL

The claimant wished to buy a stallion for stud purposes. He was stopped while examining a horse at the defendant's farm and the defendant stated: 'You need not look for anything, the horse is perfectly sound. If there was anything the matter with the horse I would tell you.' The claimant bought the horse but it proved incapable for stud purposes. In the claimant's action it was held that the defendant's statement amounted to a warranty as to the horse's fitness for the use required by the claimant.

LORD MOULTON

It would be impossible, in my mind, to have a clearer example of an express warranty where the word 'warranty' was not used. The essence of such warranty is that it becomes plain by the words and action of the parties that it is intended that in the purchase the responsibility of the soundness shall rest upon the vendor; and how in the world could a vendor more clearly indicate that he is prepared and intends to take upon himself the responsibility of the soundness than by saying: 'You need not look at that horse, because it is perfectly sound,' and sees that the purchaser thereupon desists from his immediate impending examination?

Questions

Read the two extracts above and answer the questions.

1. In what sense does Lord Denning use the word 'warranty' in Oscar Chess, and how does this meaning differ from that normally adopted by lawyers?
2. Why was Lord Denning not prepared to accept that a binding contract existed between the parties?
3. Why, on the contrary, does Lord Moulton suggest that there is a warranty in *Schawel v Reade*?

EXTRACT ADAPTED FROM THE JUDGMENT IN *POUSSARD V SPIERS AND POND* [1876] 1 QBD 410

The claimant, an opera singer, was contracted to take the lead role in an opera at the Criterion Theatre. During the rehearsals she became ill and as a result was unable to attend the remaining rehearsals or to appear in the opening performance. She was replaced with an understudy who was then given the part for the remaining performances. When the claimant returned her husband, as her agent, then brought an action for breach of contract.

BLACKBURN J

... from the nature of the engagement to take a leading, and indeed, the principal female part ... in a new opera which (as appears from the terms of the engagement) it was known might run for a longer or shorter time, and so be a profitable or a losing concern to the defendants, we can ... see that it must have been of great importance to the defendants that the piece should start well, and consequently that the failure of the plaintiff's wife to be able to perform on the opening and early performances was a very serious detriment to them.

This inability having been occasioned by sickness was not any breach of contract by the plaintiff, and no action can lie against him. But the damage to the defendants and the consequent failure of consideration is just as great as if it had been occasioned by the plaintiff's fault, instead of by his wife's misfortune.

... we must consider what were the courses open to the defendants under the circumstances. They might, it was said on the argument before us (though not on the trial), have postponed the bringing out of the piece till the recovery of Madame Poussard, and if her illness had been a temporary hoarseness incapacitating her from singing on the Saturday, but sure to be removed by the Monday, that might have been a proper course to pursue. But the illness here was a serious one, of uncertain duration, and if the plaintiff had at the trial suggested that this was the proper course, it would no doubt have been shewn that it would have been a ruinous course; and that it would have been much better to have abandoned the piece altogether than to have postponed it from day to day for an uncertain time, during which the theatre would have been a heavy loss.

The remaining alternatives were to employ a temporary substitute until such time as the plaintiff's wife should recover; and if a temporary substitute capable of performing the part adequately could have been obtained upon such a precarious engagement on any reasonable terms, that would have been a right course to pursue; but if no substitute capable of performing the part adequately could be obtained, except on the terms that she should be permanently engaged at higher pay than the plaintiff's wife, in our opinion it follows, as a matter of law, that the failure on the plaintiff's part went to the root of the matter and discharged the defendants.

Questions

1. According to Blackburn J, what were the choices open to the defendants when Madame Poussard fell ill and could not attend performances?
2. On what basis does the judge suggest that the choice made by the defendants was the only possible one to take?
3. What principal of law discharges the defendants from their obligation to continue to employ the claimant?
4. Using the case in support, what do you understand a 'condition' of a contract to be?

EXTRACT ADAPTED FROM THE JUDGMENT IN *REARDON SMITH LINE V HANSEN-TANGEN* [1976] 1 WLR 989, HL

A steamship company contracted for the purchase of a ship with the Osaka Shipbuilding Co. The contract named the vessel as Hull No 354. Osaka were then unable to complete the work so it was sub-contracted to another shipyard in which the company owned a 50 per cent shareholding, and for which it provided much of the workforce. The job was then renamed Oshima 004. The vessel, when completed was identical to how it would have been if built in the other yard. Nevertheless the buyers rejected it claiming a breach of a condition of the contract by Osaka. The House of Lords held that this was merely a technical breach and, applying the principles of innominate terms, did not justify repudiation of the contract.

LORD WILBERFORCE

... I am not prepared to accept that authorities as to 'description' in sale of goods cases are to be extended, or applied, to such a contract as we have here. Even if a strict and technical view must be taken as regards the description of unascertained future goods as to which each detail of the description must be assumed to be vital, it may be, and in my opinion is, right to treat other contracts of sale of goods in a similar manner to other contracts generally, so as to ask whether a particular item in a description constitutes a substantial ingredient of the 'identity' of the thing sold, and only if it does to treat it as a condition. It is one thing to say of given words that their purpose is to state an essential part of the description of the goods. It is another to say that they provide one party with a specific indication of the goods so that he can find them and if he wishes dispose of them. If the words are read in their first sense, then, unless I am right in the legal argument above, each element in them has to be given contractual force. The vessel must, as a matter of contract, and as an essential term, be built by Osaka, and must bear their yard number 354; if not, the description is not complied with and the vessel tendered is not that contracted for. If in the second sense, the only question is whether the words provide a means of identifying the vessel. If they fairly do this, they have fulfilled their function.

So the question becomes simply whether, as a mater of fact, it can be fairly said that—as a means of identification—the vessel was ... 'built by Osaka Shipping Co. Ltd and known as Hull No. 354, until named'. I have no doubt that an affirmative answer must be given. The act is that the vessel always was Osaka Hull No. 354—though also Oshima No. 004—and equally it can fairly be said to have been 'built' by Osaka as the company which planned, organised and directed the building and contractually engaged to build it, though also it can be said to have been built by Oshima.

Questions

1. Why do you think that Lord Wilberforce was 'not prepared to accept that authorities as to "description" in sale of goods cases are to be extended, or applied, to such a contract'?
2. What is the consequence of treating a term as a 'condition'?
3. The court applies the principle of 'innominate terms' to the case. How does the principle operate in general, and what is its effect in this case?

EXTRACT FROM THE LAW COMMISSION REPORT NO 160, *SALE AND SUPPLY OF GOODS* (CM 137 (1987)), PARAGRAPHS 3.5, 3.11 AND 3.12

2. Should the implied term as to quality be altered at all?

3.5 In the Consultative Document we suggested that the present implied term is not satisfactory. The reasons ... :

(i) The word 'merchantable' refers to transactions between merchants and is not suitable for consumer transactions, even in its dictionary meaning ... It is also a word of uncertain meaning ...

(ii) The present definition relies on the fitness of goods for their purpose and not on their other characteristics. ... the exact extent to which minor defects and defects of appearance and finish fall within the definition remains unclear.

(iii) The present definition does not expressly say that the goods must be reasonably durable. ...

3.11 The decision to recommend a single implied term as to the quality of goods to be supplied under all types of contract brings with it certain consequences. There is no one word which we have found or which has been suggested to us by which the appropriate standard can be defined. The term must be sufficiently flexible to be able to apply to all the many types of sale which can take place. Above all, there is no 'magic' formula which will provide an instant answer in every case to the question whether goods meet the standard of quality which they should have. ...

3.12 In the Consultative Document we suggested that the new definition of quality should consist of two elements:

(i) a basic principle formulated in language sufficiently general to apply to all kinds of goods and all kinds of transactions; this principle would also refer, as at present, to the description of the goods, their price, and any other relevant circumstances, which are factors which would be taken into account in determining how stringent the quality requirement should be ...; and

(ii) a list of aspects of quality, any of which could be important in a particular case; the list would, however, not be exhaustive.

Questions

1. In the 1994 Sale and Supply of Goods Act, which followed from the Law Commission Report, what word replaced the word 'merchantable' when considering quality?
2. In your own words explain why the word 'merchantable' was inadequate to protect consumers against sale of defective goods.
3. To what extent does the new s14(2) meet the shortcomings identified in paragraph 3.5 (ii) and (iii) of the Law Commission Report?
4. In what way did the 1994 Act meet the Law Commission's requirement in paragraph 3.12 (ii) of the Report?

SECTION 7: EXCLUSION CLAUSES

Exclusion clauses are terms inserted into a contract by one party to exclude liability for their breaches of the contract. They can be very damaging to the other party so the courts have regulated them. They will be invalid unless they are properly drawn to the attention of the other party at the time the contract was made. Where businesses contract on equal terms the courts are more prepared to allow such clauses to stand provided they are clearly expressed. Control of such clauses in contracts has also come as consumer protection from Parliament in the Unfair Contract Terms Act and Europe has also intervened.

EXTRACT ADAPTED FROM THE JUDGMENT IN *OLLEY V MARLBOROUGH COURT HOTEL LTD* [1949] 1 KB 532, CA

Mrs Olley booked in at reception in the hotel, at which point a contract was made. During her stay at the hotel clothing was stolen from her room. The hotel sought to rely on an exclusion clause exempting it from liability for valuables not left in the safekeeping of the management. The clause in question was to be found on a notice on the inside of the doors of guests' rooms. The hotel was unable to rely on the clause because it had not been incorporated into the contract.

DENNING LJ

The only point in the case is whether the hotel company are protected by the notice which they put in the bedrooms. 'The proprietors will not hold themselves responsible for articles lost or stolen, unless handed to the manageress for safe custody.' The first question is whether that notice formed part of the contract. Now people who rely on a contract to exempt themselves from their common law liability, must prove that contract strictly. Not only must the terms of the contract be clearly proved, but also the intention to create legal relations ... must also be clearly proved. The best way of proving it is by a written document, signed by the party to be bound.

Another way is by handing them, before or at the time of the contract, a written notice specifying its terms and making it clear ... that the contract is on those terms. A prominent public notice which is plain ... to see when he makes the contract, or an express oral stipulation would, no doubt, have the same effect. But nothing short of one of these three ways will suffice. It has been held that mere notices put on receipts for money do not make a contract. (See *Chapelton v Barry Urban District Council*). So also, in my opinion, notices put up in bedrooms do not of themselves make a contract. As a rule, the guest does not see them until after he has been accepted as a guest. The hotel company no doubt hopes that the guest will be bound by them, but the hope is vain unless they clearly show that he agreed to be bound by them, which is rarely the case.

EXTRACT ADAPTED FROM THE JUDGMENT IN *MCCUTCHEON V DAVID MACBRAYNE LTD* [1964] 1 WLR 125, HL

McSporran took his brother-in-law, McCutcheon's, car to load on to MacBrayne's ferry to the mainland. Although it was usual practice to get people to sign a risk note, on this occasion McSporran had not been asked to do so. The ferry sank. McCutcheon sued and claimed damages for negligence and the ferry company sought to rely on an exclusion clause exhibited in their office on their invoices and also in the risk notice. MacBrayne claimed that, since McCutcheon had dealt with them before he had implied knowledge of the exclusion clause. It was held that since there was an inconsistent course of dealing, sometimes McCutcheon had been required to sign the risk note and on other occasions he had not, the exclusion clause was not incorporated into the current contract.

LORD REID

The respondents contend that, by reason of the knowledge ... gained by the appellant and his agent in ... previous transactions, the appellant is bound by their conditions. But this case differs essentially from the ticket cases. There the carrier hands over a document containing or referring to conditions which he intends to be part of the contract. So if the consignor or passenger knows that this is the carrier's intention, he can hardly deny that the conditions are part of the contract. If it could be said that when making the contract [McSporran] knew ... the respondents always required the risk note to be signed and ... that the purser was simply forgetting, then it might be said ... neither he nor his principal could take advantage of the error ... of which he was aware. But counsel frankly admitted that he could not put his case as high as that. The only other ground on which it would seem possible to impute these conditions is that based on a course of dealing. But again the facts here will not support that ground. According to [McSporran] there had been no consistent course of dealing: sometimes he was asked to sign and sometimes not. And moreover he did not know what the conditions were. This time he was offered an oral contract without any reference to conditions and he accepted the offer in good faith.

EXTRACT ADAPTED FROM THE JUDGMENT IN *L'ESTRANGE V GRAUCOB (F) LTD* [1934] 2 KB 394, CA

The claimant bought a vending machine from the defendant, signing a written 'Sale Agreement'. When the machine turned out to be faulty and the claimant sued, the defendant sought to rely on an exclusion clause in the signed agreement. The court held that, because she had signed the agreement, the claimant was bound by its terms even though she had not read it.

SCRUTTON LJ

In this case the plaintiff has signed a document headed 'Sales Agreement' which she admits had to do with an intended purchase and which contained a clause excluding all conditions and warranties. That being so, the plaintiff, having put her signature to the document, and not having been induced to do so by any fraud or misrepresentation, cannot be heard to say that she is not bound by the terms of the document because she did not read them.

EXTRACT ADAPTED FROM THE JUDGMENT IN *PHOTO PRODUCTIONS LTD V SECURICOR TRANSPORT LTD* [1980] 2 WLR 283, HL

Securicor provided a security guard for night patrol at the claimant's factory. The guard lit a fire that got out of hand and burned down the factory and its contents, amounting to £615,000 worth of loss. Securicor sought to rely on a clause in the contract exempting them from liability and succeeded because the parties were of equal bargaining strength and the clause was clear and unambiguous.

LORD WILBERFORCE

... Securicor undertook to provide ... periodical visits for a very modest charge, which works out at 26p per visit. It did not agree to provide equipment. It would have no knowledge of the value of Photo Productions' factory; that and the efficacy of their fire precautions would be known to Photo Productions. In these circumstances nobody could consider it unreasonable that as between these two equal parties, the risk assumed by Securicor should be a modest one and that Photo Productions should carry the substantial risk of damage or destruction.

The duty of Securicor was, as stated, to provide a service. There must be implied an obligation to use care in selecting their patrolmen, to take care of the keys, and ... to operate the service with due and proper regard to the safety and security of the premises. The breach of duty ... lay in a failure to discharge this latter obligation. Alternatively, it could be put on a vicarious responsibility for the wrongful act of Musgrove, viz starting a fire on the premises; Securicor would be responsible for this. This being the breach, does condition 1 apply? It is drafted in strong terms: 'Under no circumstances, any injurious act or default by any employee'. These words have to be approached with the aid of the cardinal rules of construction that they must be read contra preferentum and that in order to escape from the consequences of one's own wrongdoing, or that of one's servants, clear words are necessary. I think that these words are clear. Photo Productions in fact relied on them for an argument, that since they exempted from negligence, they must be taken as not exempting from the consequence of deliberate acts. But this is a perversion of the rule that if a clause can cover something other than negligence, it will not be applied to negligence. Whether, in addition to negligence, it covers other, e.g. deliberate acts, remains a matter of construction, requiring ... clear words. I am of the opinion that it does and, being free to construe and apply the clause, I must hold that liability is excluded.

Questions

Read the four extracts above and answer the questions.

1. In *Olley v Marlborough Court Hotel* what three methods does Lord Denning state can be used to show that an exclusion clause is a term of a contract?
2. In the case why were the hotel unable to show that the exclusion clause was part of the contract made with Mrs Olley?
3. In *McCutcheon v MacBrayne* how were the defendants trying to claim that the exclusion clause had been incorporated into the contract?
4. Why did their argument fail?
5. How does the case of *L'Estrange v Graucob* bear out what Lord Denning said in his judgment in *Olley v Marlborough Court Hotel*?
6. How does the judgment in *Photo Productions v Securicor* differ significantly from the other cases?
7. Why do you think that is?

EXTRACT FROM THE UNFAIR CONTRACT TERMS ACT 1977

11. The 'reasonableness' test

(1) In relation to a contract term, the requirement of reasonableness ... is that the term shall have been a fair and reasonable one to be

included having regard to the circumstances which were, or ought reasonably to have been, known to or in the contemplation of the parties when the contract was made.

(2) In determining for the purposes of section 6 and 7 above whether a contract term satisfies the requirements of reasonableness, regard shall be had in particular to the matters specified in Schedule 2 to this Act; but this subsection does not prevent the court or arbitrator from holding, in accordance with any rule of law, that a term which purports to exclude or restrict any relevant liability is not a term of the contract.

Schedule 2
'Guidelines' for Application of Reasonableness Test

The matters to which regard is to be had in particular for the purposes of sections 6(3), 7(3) and (4), 20 and 21 are any of the following which appear to be relevant—

(a) the strength of the bargaining positions of the parties relative to each other, taking into account (among other things) alternative means by which the customer's requirements could have been met;

(b) whether the customer received an inducement to agree to the term, or in accepting it had an opportunity of entering into a similar contract with other persons, but without having to accept a similar term;

(c) whether the customer knew or ought reasonably to have known of the existence and extent of the term (having regard, among other things, to any custom of the trade and any previous course of dealings between the parties);

(d) where the term excludes or restricts any relevant liability if some condition is not complied with, whether it was reasonable at the time of the contract to expect that compliance with that condition would be practicable;

(e) whether the goods were manufactured, processed or adapted to the special order of the customer.

EXTRACT ADAPTED FROM 'LIMITATION CLAUSES IN STANDARD TERM CONTRACTS—ARE THEY EVER ENFORCEABLE?' SYLVIA ELWES, *THE LEGAL EXECUTIVE JOURNAL*, SEPTEMBER 1995

The principle of freedom of contract would dictate that the terms of a contract should stand in their entirety. These are the conditions of trading, whether in standard form contract or otherwise, upon which the seller is willing to supply the goods at the contract price.

The consequences of breach of contract may be enormous and it is obvious that a supplier may only provide the goods if his liability can be excluded or limited by the terms of the agreement.

On the other hand, there may be no real equality of bargaining power. The buyer may not agree to the terms at all but have them imposed upon him. It is the question of which party should bear the risk in the event of a breach of contract and in many cases it is the supplier, who should be adequately covered by insurance.

Current law under the Unfair Contract Terms Act 1977 does not differentiate between contracts in standard terms and those individually negotiated, so far as consumers are concerned.

SI 1994/3159 was made in December 1994 and brought into effect the Unfair Terms in Consumer Contracts Regulations 1994.

Under the Regulations 'unfair' terms in standard term contracts between a seller or supplier, and a consumer are not binding on the consumer.

The Regulations define standard terms as those which have not been individually negotiated. They are not so negotiated where they have been drafted in advance and the consumer has been unable to influence the substance of the term.

An unfair term is a term which, contrary to the requirement of good faith, causes a significant imbalance in the parties' rights and obligations under the contract to the detriment of the consumer.

Certainly a term excluding or limiting liability would be such an unfair term, but unfair terms are not limited to these terms. Schedule 3 contains a non-exhaustive list of terms that may be regarded as unfair.

For example a term that irrevocably binds the consumer to terms which he had no opportunity of becoming acquainted before the conclusion of the contract may be unfair.

Unfair terms are not automatically unenforceable against the consumer .... They must be 'contrary to the requirement of good faith' ... the court must consider:

- the strength of the bargaining position of the parties;
- whether the consumer had an inducement to agree to the terms;
- whether the goods were sold to the special order of the consumer;
- the extent to which the seller had dealt fairly and equitably with the consumer.

The first three are the same factors laid down under Schedule 2 of the UCTA 1977. However, the fourth factor is a different factor.

In addition, the regulations provide that, if there is ... doubt about the meaning of a term in a written contract, the interpretation most favourable to the consumer will prevail. This is a statutory reinforcement of the common law 'Contra preferentum' rule.

Further, although a term in a standard term agreement may be unfair, the contract may still be enforceable if it can be carried out without the term.

These Regulations are far reaching and erode significantly the principle of freedom of contract in consumer sales.

Whereas at present, an exclusion or limitation clause must be reasonable in any type of contract, standard term or otherwise, with a consumer the new law will mean that additionally it must be entered into in good faith. If not it will not be binding on the consumer.

It is becoming increasingly difficult to have valid limitation clauses in standard term contracts. New regulations will afford additional protection to consumers against these and other unfair terms.

Questions

Read the two extracts above and answer the questions.

1. Under the Unfair Contract Terms Act 1977 what must be 'reasonable' to satisfy the test of reasonableness?
2. Against whose standards is reasonableness measured?
3. In Sylvia Elwes' article why do you think she is suggesting that sellers may wish to exclude liability for breaches of contract?
4. What are 'standard terms' and why according to the article do they need regulation?
5. What is an 'unfair term' according to the 1994 Regulations?
6. How according to the author do the Regulations 'erode significantly the principle of freedom of contract'?

SECTION 8: MISREPRESENTATION

A misrepresentation is a form of vitiating factor rendering a contract voidable by the other party. It is a false statement of fact, made at the time the contract was formed, intended to induce the other party to enter the contract but not intended to be a term. Misrepresentations can be fraudulently, negligently or innocently made. The available remedy may depend on the type. Misrepresentation is most commonly controlled now by statute.

EXTRACT ADAPTED FROM THE JUDGMENT IN *BISSET V WILKINSON* [1927] AC 177, PC

The claimant had bought land in New Zealand from the defendant. He claimed that he had only done so because he relied on a representation made to him by the defendant that the land would carry 2,000 sheep. In fact the land did not have this capacity at all. The claimant sought rescission of the contract for misrepresentation. His action failed, as did his appeal.

LORD MERRIVALE

In an action for rescission, as in an action for specific performance of an executory contract, when misrepresentation is the alleged ground of relief of the party who repudiates the contract, it is, of course, essential to ascertain whether that which is relied on is a representation of a specific fact, or a statement of opinion, since an erroneous opinion stated by the party affirming the contract, though it may have been relied on and have induced the contract on the part of the party who seeks rescission, gives no title to relief unless fraud is established.

In the present case the material facts of the transaction, the knowledge of the parties respectively, the words of representation used, and the actual condition of the subject matter spoken of, are relevant.

As was said by Sim J: 'In ordinary circumstances, any statement made by an owner who has been occupying his own farm as to its carrying capacity would be regarded as a statement of fact. This, however, is not such a case. The purchasers knew all about Hogan's Block and knew also what sheep it was carrying when they inspected it. In these circumstances the purchasers were not justified in regarding anything said by the vendor as to the carrying capacity as being anything more than an expression of his opinion on the subject.'

In this view of the matter their Lordships concur.

Questions

1. What question does Lord Merrivale feel is critical to the resolution of the case?
2. What would be the consequences if the statement were one of fact rather than opinion?

EXTRACT ADAPTED FROM THE JUDGMENT IN *HEDLEY BYRNE & CO LTD V HELLER & PARTNERS LTD* [1964] AC 465, HL

Hedley Byrne were advertisers approached by a small company Easipower to prepare an advertising campaign. Sensibly, since they had not previously dealt with the company, they approached their bank for a credit reference. The reference given was that Easipower were 'good for normal business'. In fact Easipower went into liquidation and Hedley Byrne lost money as a result. They sued the bank that had failed to check Easipower's current financial status properly. They failed because a disclaimer of liability included in the reference was accepted as valid. The House of Lords, however, accepted in principle that there could be an action, in tort, for a negligent misrepresentation causing financial loss.

LORD REID

... there is good sense behind our present law that in general an innocent but negligent misrepresentation gives no cause of action. There must be something more than the mere misstatement. ... The most natural requirement would be that expressly or by implication from the circumstances the speaker or writer has undertaken some responsibility, and that appears to me not to conflict with any authority that is binding on this House. Where there is a contract there is no difficulty as regards the contracting parties: the question is whether there is a warranty. Then there are cases where a person does not merely make a statement but performs a gratuitous service ... the cases ... show that in some cases that person owes a duty of care apart from any contract, and to that extent they pave the way to holding that in some cases that person owes a duty of care in making a statement of fact or opinion which is independent of contract ...

I can see no logical stopping place short of all those relationships where it is plain that the party seeking information or advice was trusting the other to exercise such a degree of care as the circumstances required, where it was reasonable for him to do that, and where the other gave the information or advice when he knew or ought to have known that the inquirer was relying on him.

A reasonable man, knowing that he was being trusted or that his skill and judgment were being relied on, would, I think, have three courses open to him. He could keep silent or decline to give the information or advice sought: or he could give an answer with a clear qualification that he accepted no responsibility for it or that it was given without that reflection or inquiry which a careful answer would require: or he could simply answer without any such qualification. If he chooses to adopt the last course he must, I think, be held to have accepted some responsibility for his answer being given carefully, or to have accepted a relationship with the inquirer which requires him to exercise such care as the circumstances require.

Questions

1. In what way does Lord Reid suggest that the law prior to the case was sensible?
2. What extra requirement, other than the negligent misstatement itself, does Lord Reid say is necessary to bring an action?
3. What are the important characteristics of the relationship that lead to liability for negligent misstatement being possible?
4. What does Lord Reid say are the choices available to a person asked to give advice on which the person asking will rely?
5. What is it in the course of action of the person giving the advice that leads on to liability if their advice is negligently given?

EXTRACT FROM S2 MISREPRESENTATION ACT 1967

2. Damages for misrepresentation

(1) Where a person has entered into a contract after a misrepresentation has been made to him by another party thereto and as a result thereof he has suffered loss, then, if the person making the misrepresentation would be liable to damages in respect thereof had the misrepresentation been made fraudulently, that person shall be so liable notwithstanding that the misrepresentation was not made fraudulently, unless he proves that he had reasonable ground to believe and did believe up to the time the contract was made that the facts represented were true.

(2) Where a person has entered into a contract after a misrepresentation has been made to him otherwise than fraudulently, and he would be entitled, by reason of the misrepresentation, to rescind the contract, then, if it is claimed, in any proceedings arising out of the contract, that the contract ought to be or has been rescinded the court or arbitrator may declare the contract

subsisting and award damages in lieu of rescission, if of opinion that it would be equitable to do so, having regard to the nature of the misrepresentation and the loss that would be caused by it if the contract were upheld, as well as to the loss that rescission would cause to the other party.

EXTRACT ADAPTED FROM THE JUDGMENT IN *HOWARD MARINE & DREDGING CO LTD V A OGDEN & SONS (EXCAVATIONS) LTD* [1978] 2 WLR 515, CA

Contractors who were to excavate the site of a new sewage were obliged to dump the waste material at sea. Since they knew nothing about earth carrying barges, they sought the advice of Howards from whom they were hiring the barges as to the weight they could carry and they based their estimate for the work on the answer that they were given. They were mistakenly told that the barges' payload was 1,600 tonnes since Howards' marine manager relied on a mistaken entry in Lloyds register. When the true payload of 1,055 became apparent, Ogden refused to pay more towards the cost of hire of the barges, Howard withdrew the barges, and sued for the balance of the price, and Ogden successfully countered with misrepresentation under s2(1).

BRIDGE LJ

The first question is whether Howards would be liable in damages in respect of Mr O'Loughlin's misrepresentation if it had been made fraudulently, that is to say, if he had known that it was untrue. An affirmative answer to that question is inescapable. It follows then that, on the plain language of the 1967 Act that, although there was no allegation of fraud, Howards must be liable unless they proved that Mr O'Loughlin had reasonable ground to believe what he said about the barges' capacity.

SHAW LJ

... the chartering of barges for the purpose of carrying clay out to sea and there dumping it is a business transaction whose nature makes clear the importance and influence of an answer to the question: what is their carrying capacity? The information sought would govern the performance by Ogdens of their contract with the Tyneside authority and this must have been apparent to any man of business. ... The information which had been asked for more than once cannot be regarded as other than important whatever the circumstances in which it was sought and given. Moreover it was not expert advice that was sought which might honestly and reasonably have assumed different forms according to the source of it. What was asked for was a specific fact. Ogdens had not ... any direct means of ascertaining what the fact was. Certainly they had no such ready and facile means as were available to Mr O'Loughlin [of Howards]. These factors in association with the relationship of the parties did in my judgment give rise to a duty on the owners to exercise reasonable care to be accurate in giving information of a material character which was peculiarly within their knowledge. All Mr O'Loughlin had to do was to look at the documents in Howards' possession and to read them accurately. Had he done so there would have been no room for error of fact or for misconceived opinion or wrong advice.

Questions

Read the two extracts above and answer the questions.

1. What advantages does s2(1) of the Misrepresentation Act 1967 have over the previous law?
2. In what circumstances is a person likely to use s2(2) of the Act?

3 What class of misrepresentation was apparent in *Howard Marine & Dredging*?

4 How according to the source could Howard have avoided the misrepresentation?

5 Would Ogden have been able to sue under the previous law?

6 Why were they able to succeed in the case?

EXTRACT ADAPTED FROM THE JUDGMENT IN *WITH V O'FLANAGAN* [1936] CH 575, CA

The defendant doctor was selling his medical practice. He truthfully told the claimant it had cost him £2,000 and had a panel of 1,480 people. During the next four months, while negotiations were taking place, the defendant was ill, his takings dwindled to virtually nothing, and the panel of patients fell considerably, to 1,260. He failed to tell the claimant of these facts. When the claimant discovered the current state of the practice on completion he sought rescission for the defendant's misrepresentation, and succeeded.

ROMER LJ

The only principle invoked by the plaintiff in this case is as follows. If A, with a view to inducing B to enter into a contract makes a representation as to a material fact, then if at a later date and before the contract is actually entered into, owing to a change of circumstances, the representation then made would to the knowledge of A be untrue and B subsequently enters into the contract in ignorance of that change of circumstances and relying upon that representation, A cannot hold B to the bargain. There is ample authority for that statement and ... I doubt myself whether any authority is necessary, it being ... so obviously consistent with the plainest principles of equity.

Questions

1 How are the facts in *With v O'Flanagan* connected with misrepresentation?

2 In what other situations do you think that a failure to disclose certain information can amount to a misrepresentation?

SECTION 9: MISTAKE

A mistake, if operative (that is if the contract has been made because of the mistake) will render the contract void. If the mistake is not operative then it can still be set aside because of equity. A mistake can be common to both parties, or both parties can be at cross purposes, or only one of the parties may be mistaken usually with the other knowing of the mistake. A common problem concerns mistaken identity when the parties contract face to face.

EXTRACT ADAPTED FROM THE JUDGMENT IN *COUTURIER V HASTIE* [1856] 9 EX 102, COURT OF EXCHEQUER CHAMBER

A contract was made for the sale and purchase of a cargo of grain in transit. Unknown to either buyer or seller, at the time they made the contract, the cargo had been sold when it had begun to ferment. The contract was void for mistake and the seller could legitimately repudiate his obligations without a breach of contract.

COLERIDGE J

For the plaintiffs it was contended that the parties plainly contracted for the sale and purchase of goods ... that a vendor of goods undertakes that they exist and that they are capable of being transferred ... and that as the goods in question had been sold and delivered to other parties before the contract in question was made, there was nothing on which it could operate.

On the other hand, it was argued that this was not a mere contract for the sale of an ascertained cargo, but that the purchaser bought the adventure and took upon himself all risks from the shipment of the cargo ... it appears to us that the contract in question was for the sale of a cargo supposed to exist and to be capable of transfer and that inasmuch as it had been sold and delivered to others by the captain before the contract in question was made, the plaintiffs cannot recover in this action.

EXTRACT ADAPTED FROM THE JUDGMENT IN *BELL V LEVER BROTHERS* [1932] AC 161, HL

Levers owned 99.5 per cent of the shares of Niger Co Ltd. The company was making heavy losses. Levers approached Bell and gave him a five-year fixed-term contract with a view to improving the fortunes of the small subsidiary. He did that in well under the time expected. The company's assets were then transferred into another company, and his services to Niger Co were no longer required. As a result an agreement was reached to pay Bell £30,000 as compensation for his fixed-term contract being terminated years earlier than expected, and in acknowledgment of his exceptional service. The company later discovered Bell had been dealing on his own account contrary to the terms of a 'directors clause' in his contract, though there was no question of fraud. Levers then tried to claim that Bell's private dealings amounted to misconduct that would have justified his dismissal. They sought to recover the money paid over on the basis that the agreement to pay resulted from a common mistake, since both parties thought Bell was entitled to the payment. They failed as the mistake was not operative and so did not void the agreement to recompense Bell for early termination of his contract and the agreement was valid.

LORD WARRINGTON

The learned judge thus describes the mistake involved in this case as sufficient to justify a court in saying that there was no true consent—namely: 'Some mistake or misapprehension as to some facts which, by the common intention of the parties, whether expressed or more generally implied, constitute the underlying assumption, without which the parties would not have made the contract they did.'

That a mistake of this nature, common to both parties, is, if proved, sufficient to render a contract void is ... established law. This principle, however, is confined to cases in which 'the mistake is as to the substance of the whole consideration, going, as it were, to the root of the matter'. In the present case it is ... clear that each party believed that the remunerative offices, compensation for the loss of which was the subject of the negotiations, were offices which could not be determined except by the consent of the holder thereof and further believed that the other party was under the same belief and was treating on that footing. The real question, therefore, is whether the erroneous assumption on ... both parties to the agreements that the service contracts were indeterminable except by agreement, was of such a fundamental character as to constitute an underlying assumption without which the parties would not have made the contract they in fact made, or whether it was only a common error as to a material element, but not one going to the root of the matter and not affecting the substance of the consideration.

LORD ATKIN

Mistake as to quality of the thing contracted for raises more difficult questions. In such a case, a mistake will not affect assent unless it is the mistake of both parties and is as to the existence of some quality which makes the thing without the quality essentially different from the thing as it was believed to be.

EXTRACT ADAPTED FROM THE JUDGMENT IN *SMITH V HUGHES* [1871] LR 6 QB 597

A racehorse trainer contracted to buy oats for feeding the horses from the defendant. He believed he was purchasing 'old oats', oats from the previous season, but in fact when delivered they were 'green oats', oats from the current season. He refused to pay and won at the County Court. On appeal it was held that there should be a new hearing.

BLACKBURN LJ

On the sale of a specific article, unless there be a warranty making it part of the bargain that it possesses some particular quality, the purchaser must take the article he has bought, though it does not possess that quality. ... even if the vendor was aware that the purchaser thought ... the article possessed that quality, and would not have entered ... the contract unless he had so thought, still the purchaser is bound, unless the vendor was guilty of some fraud or deceit .... A mere abstinence from disabusing the purchaser of that impression is not fraud or deceit, for, whatever may be the case in a court of morals, there is no legal obligation on the vendor to inform the purchaser that he is under a mistake which has not been induced by the act of the vendor.

Questions

Read the three extracts above and answer the questions.

1. What was the mistake that made the contract void in *Couturier v Hastie*?
2. Why is it described as a common mistake?
3. According to Lord Warrington in *Bell v Lever Brothers* when will a mistake common to both parties be sufficient to invalidate the contract?
4. Why, according to both Lord Warrington and Lord Atkin, was the contract not void in the case?
5. What effect does a mistake about the quality of a contract have on the contract?
6. How do the facts in *Smith v Hughes* differ from those in the previous two cases?
7. According to Blackburn LJ in *Smith v Hughes*, what obligation does the party who is not mistaken have to correct the mistake being made by the other party?

EXTRACT ADAPTED FROM THE JUDGMENT IN *CUNDY V LINDSAY* [1878] 3 APP CAS 459, HL

A rogue called Blenkarn hired a room in a house on the corner of Wood Street where there was also situated a respectable firm called Blenkiron & Co. He then ordered goods from Lindsay in the name of Blenkiron. They had heard of this firm and thought that they were dealing with the genuine firm. Blenkarn then sold the goods on to an innocent third party, Cundy. When Lindsay discovered the mistake they sued Cundy successfully for conversion of their goods.

LORD PENZANCE

I am not aware ... that there is any decided case in which a sale and delivery intended to be made to one man, has been held to be a sale and delivery so as to pass the property to another, against the intent and will of the vendor. In the present case Blenkarn pretended ... he was Blenkiron & Co with whom, alone, the vendors meant to deal. No contract was ever intended with him and the contract which was intended failed for want of another party to it ... the respondents were never brought personally into contact with Blenkarn; all their letters were addressed to Blenkiron & Co and finally the goods in dispute were sent to Blenkiron & Co, though at a wrong address.

EXTRACT ADAPTED FROM THE JUDGMENT IN *LEWIS V AVERAY* [1971] 3 ALL ER 907, CA

Lewis advertised his car for sale and a man, in fact a rogue, who introduced himself as Richard Green came to buy it. The buyer wrote out a cheque for the car and wanted to take it at once. Lewis was hesitant and the man produced a pass for Pinewood Studios with the man's picture on it. Richard Green was a famous actor at the time and Lewis was taken in. The cheque bounced. Lewis then discovered the car with Averay, who had bought it from the rogue in good faith and in all innocence. Lewis sued for conversion, winning the case but losing on appeal.

LORD DENNING MR

It has been suggested that a mistake as to the identity of a person is one thing; and a mistake as to his attributes is another. A mistake as to identity, it is said, avoids a contract; whereas a mistake as to attributes does not.

As I listened to the argument in this case, I felt it wrong that an innocent purchaser (who knew nothing of what passed between the seller and the rogue) should have his title depend on such refinements. After all, he has acted with complete circumspection and in entire good faith; whereas it was the seller who let the rogue have the goods and thus enabled him to commit the fraud.

...

When a dealing is had between a seller like Mr Lewis and a person who is actually there present before him, then the presumption in law is that there is a contract, even though there is a fraudulent impersonation by the buyer representing himself as a different man than he is. There is a contract made with the very person there, who is present in person. It is liable no doubt to be avoided for fraud but it is still a good contract under which title will pass unless and until it is avoided.

Questions

Read the two extracts above and answer the questions.

1. To what type of mistake do the two above cases refer?
2. Why were the claimants able to succeed in the case of *Cundy v Lindsay*?
3. What is the significantly different feature of the relationship between the contracting parties in the two cases?
4. According to Lord Denning in *Lewis v Averay* what effect does a mistake of identity normally have on a contract?
5. Why does the claimant fail in that case?

SECTION 10: DURESS AND UNDUE INFLUENCE

Duress and undue influence cover those areas where a party is coerced and therefore does not enter the contract voluntarily. Duress was traditionally associated with violence or the threats of violence. A recent development is 'economic duress' that is coercion in a commercial context. Undue influence was traditionally of two types: one where because of the closeness of the relationship the influence could be presumed, and one where actual proof of the undue influence was required. A common modern problem is the situation where a wife is persuaded to let her husband remortgage their property as surety for a loan. The question then is what the lender has to do to escape the consequences of the undue influence when the husband defaults on the loan.

EXTRACT ADAPTED FROM THE JUDGMENT IN *NORTH OCEAN SHIPPING CO V HYUNDAI CONSTRUCTION CO (THE ATLANTIC BARON)* [1978] 3 ALL ER 1170

Shipbuilders agreed to build a tanker, the price to be paid in five instalments. The buyers then asked the shipbuilders to open a 'reverse letter of credit' so that they could be assured of repayment in the event of the shipbuilders' default. After the first instalment was paid the shipbuilders put the price up by 10 per cent without any justification. The buyers, frightened that they might lose a lucrative contract they had secured with Shell if the tanker was not built on time, agreed reluctantly to the shipbuilders' demand. The letter of credit was also increased proportionately. The ship was delivered, the buyers paid the final instalment, and then, after eight months, they tried to claim back the extra 10 per cent. The buyers were able to show that they had been the victims of economic duress but their claim failed. They had delayed in making any complaint and the increase in the letter of credit amounted to good consideration for the new agreement to increase the price.

MOCATTA J

... the facts ... in this case do establish that the agreement to increase the price by ten per cent was caused by what may be called 'economic duress'. The yard were adamant in insisting on the increased price without having any legal justification for so doing and the owners realised that the yard would not accept anything other than an unqualified agreement to the increase. The owners might have claimed damages in arbitration against the yard with all the inherent unavoidable uncertainties of litigation, but in the view of the position of the owners vis-à-vis their relations with Shell it would be unreasonable to hold ... that this is the course they should have taken. The owners made a very reasonable offer of arbitration coupled with security for any award in the yard's favour ... but this was refused. They then made their agreement, which can truly ... be said to have been made under compulsion.

...

On the other hand the findings of fact present difficulties. There was a delay between the 27th November 1974 when the Atlantic Baron was delivered and 30th July 1975 before the owners put forward their claim.

The owners were, therefore, free from duress on 27th November 1974 and took no action by way of protest.

... the important points here are that (i) since there was no danger at this time in registering a protest, (ii) the final payments were made without any qualification, and (iii) were followed by a delay before the owners put forward their claim, the correct inference to draw, taking an objective view of the facts, is that the action and inaction of the owners can only be regarded as an affirmation of the variation of the terms of the original contract by the agreement to pay the additional ten per cent.

Questions

1. Looking at both the facts of the case and the judgment of Mocatta J, how would you describe 'economic duress'?
2. What was the economic duress in this case?
3. Why does the claimants' claim fail?

EXTRACT ADAPTED FROM 'THE CREDITOR, THE HOUSE, THE MISLED AND HER LOVER', SIMON BROOMAN, *THE LEGAL EXECUTIVE JOURNAL*, OCTOBER 1995

As the old saying goes 'an Englishman's home is his castle'. What this phrase misses is the obvious possibility that it might be his wife's castle too.

The recent case history of the area of undue influence has confirmed that the courts are not only willing to find that undue influence may occur between heterosexual and homosexual couples, but also that this may lead to a creditor (usually a bank) being unable to enforce a charge on the 'matrimonial' property unless they have taken care in obtaining the signature of the party who loses out.

The doctrine of undue influence is basically split up into two areas.

In the case of *actual* undue influence, the plaintiff must prove that a person gained a dominating influence over him/her and then used this influence to pressure the plaintiff into a transaction which they would not otherwise have entered.

The second, and more common area, is where no *actual* undue influence needs to be proved but, because of the trust and confidence placed by the plaintiff in the defendant, a *presumption* of undue influence arises.

This allows the doctrine to be used where the influence falls short of domination but still represents an abuse of a position of trust held by the defendant.

The related question, discussed recently by the courts is whether a creditor lending money to one partner in a relationship, secured on the 'matrimonial' property, can be affected by the undue influence of that partner on the other in obtaining a signature.

Past decisions have recognised that a creditor owes an obligation to take steps to ensure that the cohabitee knows what he/she is signing.

. . .

TSB plc v Camfield [1995] has confirmed that the creditor loses the charge in . . . entirety and that it cannot be partially set aside on the grounds that it was a valid security for the specified amount for which the cohabitee *thought* they were at risk. It is an all or nothing situation.

What steps should creditors take? Do they need to *ensure* that the cohabitee takes independent advice or merely to suggest that they should?

The leading decision . . . is the judgment of Lord Browne-Wilkinson in ***Barclays Bank plc v O'Brien [1993]***. He outlined that in such cases . . . there is a two stage analysis of the facts. The first stage is to consider whether the creditor has been 'put on enquiry'. This occurs when the transaction is on its face not to the financial advantage of the wife and there is a substantial risk that the husband has committed a legal or equitable wrong in persuading her to put her interest behind that of the creditor.

This acts as a trigger to set off alarm bells with the creditor to encourage them to take steps to avoid the possibility that undue influence may be taking place.

The second stage is to assess whether the creditor has taken *reasonable* steps to ensure that the wife's agreement to the charge was properly obtained.

It was this point that was considered in ***Massey v Midland Bank plc [1995]***.

Miss Massey was persuaded by her lover to charge her house to the bank as security for an overdraft used by the lover's business. The bank was put on enquiry because of the nature of the transaction and the potential risks to Miss Massey. The bank then indicated that they would require her to be independently advised by a solicitor before they would proceed.

The lover arranged for his own solicitor to advise her which was done with him present. When the business failed the bank sought possession. Miss Massey claimed she had been induced to sign the charge by the lover's undue influence.

Following this she claimed that the bank's right to claim was affected due to them being put on enquiry and not taking enough care to ensure that she had been properly and independently advised.

The Court of Appeal unanimously held that the bank was entitled to believe that Miss Massey had received independent advice from a reputable firm of solicitors. There was no duty to enquire how the interview had been conducted and who by.

This judgment fails to protect adequately the vulnerable position of people like Miss Massey. It leaves open the possibility of poor advice being given in the presence of the influencing party.

Banks and other creditors could easily tighten up the procedure by asking the giver of advice to confirm that they do not act for the 'partner' or the business concerned and that the interview was conducted without the 'partner' being present.

It would be unfair and unworkable to *require* that independent advice *is* taken as that would be too great a burden on creditors. But when advice is taken it adds credibility, gives assurance to the person concerned and legitimises the transaction ... removing any responsibility on the part of the bank to check the circumstances of the advice will only serve to eventually undermine confidence in the system.

The same type of problem came up for consideration in ***Banco Exterior International v Mann [1995]***. A loan to a company was partially secured by a second charge on the matrimonial home owned by the husband and occupied by him and his wife.

The loan was given conditionally on the understanding that the nature of the charge would be explained to her by her solicitor.

It was the husband and the company's solicitor who was involved on this occasion. It was also found that the husband was present for part at least of the time when matters were explained to the wife.

The ... judge found ... the bank had not done all that it was reasonable to expect because they '*said nothing about the need for that solicitor to be acting only for the wife*'.

In the Court of Appeal, the question was whether the bank should be affected by their constructive notice of it due to not taking sufficient precautions.

The Court of Appeal decided that the bank had done all that could be required of it.

In spite of this there is a strong argument that not only should banks be compelled to recommend that independent advice be taken but that there should be back-up procedure to ensure that the advice was given truly independently.

Questions

1. What, according to Simon Brooman's article, must be shown if 'actual undue influence' is claimed?
2. When will there be a possibility of 'presumed undue influence'?
3. What will be the effect on a creditor when a loan is secured on the basis of undue influence by the debtor on their partner or cohabitee?
4. How can the creditor avoid this and what is the test in *Barclays Bank v O'Brien*?
5. What significant point about this test is made in *Massey v Midland Bank*?
6. Why was the bank able to succeed in *Banco Exterior International v Mann*?
7. What do you think of the argument referred to in the last paragraph?

SECTION 11: ILLEGALITY

Certain contracts are illegal, usually because of policy reasons. Contracts declared illegal are void. Both statute and the common law have declared types of contract illegal. The most common form of illegality to be considered in depth in contract courses is restraint of trade clauses. These are *prima facie* void, but can be validated if they are reasonable in all the circumstances, a series of tests having been developed to determine this. Sometimes it is possible to sever an illegal restraint clause from a contract and leave the rest of the contract intact.

EXTRACT ADAPTED FROM THE JUDGMENT IN *RE MAHMOUD AND ISPAHANI* [1921] 2 KB 716, CA

An Act required that parties trading in linseed oil should be licenced. Mahmoud, who had a licence, contracted to sell 150 tons to Ispahani, who, unknown to Mahmoud, did not. Ispahani had told Mahmoud that he did indeed have a licence and it was found that Mahmoud was in no way negligent for failing to ask to see Ispahani's licence. When Ispahani failed to take the goods the court was required to consider whether he was bound by the contract with Mahmoud or whether it was illegal and unenforceable. The court held that the latter was the case.

SCRUTTON LJ

Two reasons are given why the court should enforce this contract. First ..., it is said ... the court will not listen to a person who says: 'Protect me from my own illegality'. In my view, the court is bound, once it knows that the contract is illegal, itself to take the objection and to refuse to enforce the contract, whether its knowledge comes from the statement of the party who was guilty of the illegality, or whether its knowledge comes from outside sources. The court does not sit to enforce illegal contracts ... it is for the protection of the public that the court refuses to enforce such a contract.

The other point is that where a contract can be performed either lawfully or unlawfully, and the defendant without the knowledge of the plaintiff elects to perform it unlawfully, he cannot plead its illegality. That ... does not apply to a case where the contract sought to be enforced is altogether prohibited, and in this case to contract with a person who had no licence was altogether prohibited. The contract was absolutely prohibited; and ... if an act is prohibited by statute for the public benefit, the court must enforce the prohibition, even though the person breaking the law relies upon his own illegality.

EXTRACT ADAPTED FROM THE JUDGMENT IN *FITCH V DEWES* [1921] AC 158, HL

The defendant was employed as a managing clerk by the claimants, solicitors. In his contract was a clause that he would not 'directly or indirectly become engaged or manage or be concerned in the office, profession or business of a solicitor within a radius of seven miles of the town hall of Tamworth' after expiry of his contract. When he proposed to do so the claimants successfully sought to enforce the provision.

LORD BIRKENHEAD

The controversy is the old one between freedom of contract and certain considerations of public policy, which have received much attention at the hands of the courts in the last few years. The appellant was a young man alert and very competent both to understand and to safeguard his own interests. The agreement then into which he entered, and in respect of which he has accepted for a lengthy period the consideration which was to move from the covenantee towards himself, will naturally stand unless he satisfies your Lordships that it is bad as being in restraint of trade.

What then is said by the appellant under that head? He does not complain of the restriction of space, and indeed it would have been very difficult for him to do so. The clause only restricts him from being directly or indirectly engaged in the office profession or business of a solicitor within a radius of seven miles of the Town Hall of Tamworth. We need not therefore trouble ourselves with any question of the restriction in respect of space but may confine ourselves to the complaint which is made that the agreement cannot stand, because the restriction in respect of time is unlimited and is against the public interest. But it is to be noticed here that guidance may be derived in dealing with a restriction in relation to time from an examination of the restriction which is made in respect of space. And the converse remark is of course equally true. For instance, if the restriction in respect of space is extremely limited, it is evident that a considerable restriction in respect of time may be more acceptable than would otherwise have been the case.

The courts have been generous in elucidating these matters and I am extremely anxious not to carry this process further today; I hope simply that such an agreement as this, if it is to be impeached, is to be measured by reference to two considerations: first, is it against the public interest? And, second, does that which has been stipulated for exceed what is required for the protection of the covenantee?

EXTRACT ADAPTED FROM THE JUDGMENT IN *GOLDSOLL V GOLDMAN* [1915] 1 CH 292, CA

Dealers in imitation jewellery in the UK covenanted with a competitor not to engage in dealing with real or imitation jewellery in the UK or USA, France, Germany, Russia, Poland, Spain and Austria for a period of two years from the agreement, on their own or as agents to any other business. They did in fact go on to assist another business in the same street as the claimant's business was situated. The covenant was 'severed' by the court in order to give effect to the reasonable parts.

LORD COZENS-HARDY MR

On the question of the space covered by the covenant, Neville J, has held, and I entirely agree with him, that it is unreasonably large, in so far as it is intended to cover not merely the United Kingdom and the Isle of Man, but also the foreign countries mentioned in the covenant. He has also held—and his decision is consistent with a long series of authorities—that the covenant can be severed as regards the space covered by it. It is clear that part of the covenant dealing with the area is reasonable, and the learned judge in the court below has limited the injunction which he has granted to 'London, England, Scotland, Ireland and Wales, or any part of the United Kingdom of Great Britain and Ireland and the Isle of Man'. That such a covenant is severable in this respect has been decided by authorities nearly two hundred years old.

No objection is taken, or could be taken, with regard to the limit of time. But the further difficulty has been raised that while the business of the plaintiffs was, as I have said, a business in imitation jewellery, the covenant is against carrying on or being engaged, concerned, or interested in 'the business of a vendor of or dealer in real or imitation jewellery'. It is admitted that the business of a dealer in real jewellery is not the same as that of a dealer in imitation jewellery. That being so it is difficult to support the whole of this provision, for the covenant must be limited to what is reasonably necessary for the protection of the covenantee's business.

Then comes the question whether the doctrine of severability is applicable to this part of the covenant. In my opinion it is, and the covenant is good in so far as it purports to restrain the covenantor from carrying on business in imitation jewellery.

Questions

Read the extracts above and answer the questions.

1. For what reason was the contract in *Re Mahmoud and Ispahani* unenforceable?

2 What restrictions on the legitimacy of restraint of trade clauses are identified in the case of *Fitch v Dewes*?

3 By what criteria does Lord Birkenhead measure whether the clause is reasonable in the case?

4 How does the court deal with the clauses in *Goldsoll v Goldman*?

SECTION 12: DISCHARGE BY PERFORMANCE

A contract is said to be discharged when all of the obligations have ceased. The simplest way to complete a contract is to perform the obligations. Sometimes one party carries out less than what they are supposed to do under the contract. In this situation the question arises whether they can receive payment for what has already been done under the contract. Another question is whether an acceptance of that part performance by the other party ends the contract.

EXTRACT ADAPTED FROM THE JUDGMENT IN *SUMPTER V HEDGES* [1898] 1 QB 673, CA

A builder contracted to build buildings for the defendant for £565. He did part of the work and received payment of part of the price, but he then said that he was unable to continue work because he had insufficient funds. The defendant then had the buildings completed by someone else, but using some of the materials that the builder had left on site. The builder sued for the cost of the materials and also for the balance of his pay. His action failed and his appeal was rejected.

COLLINS LJ

... the case is really concluded by the finding of the learned judge to the effect that the plaintiff had abandoned the contract. If the plaintiff had merely broken his contract in some way so as not to give the defendant the right to treat him as having abandoned the contract, and the defendant had then proceeded to finish the work himself, the plaintiff might perhaps have been entitled to sue on a *quantum meruit* on the ground that the defendant had taken the benefit of the work done. But that is not the present case. There are cases in which, though the plaintiff has abandoned the performance of a contract, it is possible ... to raise the inference of a new contract to pay for the work done on a *quantum meruit* from the defendant's having taken the benefit of that work but, in order that that may be done, the circumstances must be such as to give the option to the defendant to take or not to take the benefit of the work done. It is only where the circumstances are such as to give that option that there is any evidence on which to ground the inference of a new contract. Where, as in the case of work done on land, the circumstances are such as to give the defendant no option whether he will take the benefit of the work or not, then one must look to other facts than the mere taking the benefit of the work in order to ground the inference of a new contract. In this case I can see no other facts on which such an inference can be founded. The mere fact that a defendant is in possession of what he cannot help keeping, or even has done work upon it, affords no ground for such an inference. He is not bound to keep unfinished a building which in an incomplete state would be a nuisance on his land. I am therefore of the opinion that the plaintiff was not entitled to recover for the work which he has done.

EXTRACT ADAPTED FROM THE JUDGMENT IN *HOENIG V ISAACS* [1952] 2 ALL ER 176

The defendant employed the claimant to decorate and furnish his flat at a price of £750. The defendant paid £400 by instalments and the balance was due on completion of the work. He then refused to pay the balance because of defects in the workmanship. The claimant decorator sued for the balance of the price due to him and succeeded less the price relevant to putting the defects right.

DENNING LJ

In determining this issue the first question is whether, on true construction of the contract, entire performance was a condition precedent to payment. It was a lump sum contract, but that does not mean that entire performance was a condition precedent to payment. When a contract provides for a specific sum to be paid on completion of specified work, the courts lean against a construction of the contract which would deprive the contractor of any payment simply because there are some defects or omissions. The promise to complete the work is, therefore, construed as a term of the contract, but not as a condition. It is not every breach of that term which absolves the employer from his promise to pay the price, but only a breach which goes to the root of the contract, such as an abandonment of the work when it is only half done. Unless the breach does go to the root of the matter, the employer cannot resist payment of the price. He must pay it and bring a cross-claim for the defects and omissions, or, alternatively, set them up in diminution of the price. The measure is the amount which the work is worth less by reason of the defects and omissions, and is usually calculated by the cost of making them good.

Questions

Read the two extracts above and answer the questions.

1. Why was the contract discharged in *Sumpter v Hedges*?
2. Why was the builder unable to claim a *quantum meruit*?
3. Why was the contract not an 'entire contract' in *Hoenig v Isaacs*?
4. Why was the purchaser bound to pay in this case?
5. How do the two cases differ on the issue of performance?

SECTION 13: DISCHARGE BY AGREEMENT

A contract is made by an agreement between two parties, so it is said that it can also be unmade by an agreement. Problems arise when only one party is trying to back out of the agreement. A common way of ending a contract by agreement is the 'waiving' of the rights under it.

EXTRACT ADAPTED FROM THE JUDGMENT IN *BRIKOM INVESTMENTS LTD V CARR & OTHERS* [1979] QB 467, CA

A landlord of flats offered to sell 99-year leases to the sitting tenants. The flats all needed repairs and the landlord made an oral promise that he would carry out all necessary repairs. The leases were then all created and signed, and these stipulated that tenants would contribute to maintenance and expenditure incurred by the landlord. The landlord carried out the necessary repairs and then tried to claim contributions from the tenants. The Court of Appeal refused to allow the landlord's claim. Lord Justice Roskill held that the doctrine of waiver prevented the landlord from going back on his assurance that he would stand the cost of the repairs.

ROSKILL LJ

It is necessary to do no more than to apply what was said by the House of Lords and especially Lord Cairns LC in *Hughes v Metropolitan Railway*

Co . . . : '. . . it is the first principle upon which all Courts of Equity proceed, that if parties who have entered into definite and distinct terms involving certain legal results—certain penalties or legal forfeiture—afterwards by their own act or with their own consent enter upon a course of negotiation which has the effect of leading one of the parties to suppose that the strict rights arising under the contract will not be enforced, or will be kept in suspense, or held in abeyance, the person who otherwise might have enforced those rights will not be allowed to enforce them where it would be inequitable, having regard to the dealings which have thus taken place between the parties.'

For my own part, I would respectfully prefer to regard that as an illustration of contractual variation of strict contractual rights. But it could equally well be put as an illustration of equity relieving from the consequences of strict adherence to the letter of the lease.

But, whichever is the right way of putting it, ever since *Hughes v Metropolitan Railway Co* one finds that where parties have made a contract which provides one thing and where, by a subsequent course of dealing, the parties have worked that contract out in such a way that one party leads the other to believe that the strict rights under that contract will not be adhered to, the courts will not allow that party who has led the other to think the strict rights will not be adhered to, suddenly to seek to enforce those rights against him. That seems to be precisely what the landlords are trying to do here. I do not think that the common law or equity will allow them to take that step.

Questions

1. What, according to Lord Cairns in *Hughes v Metropolitan Railway Co*, is the basic rule when parties bound by legal arrangements decide not to be bound by them?
2. On whom does the principle have the major effect and in what way?
3. Why does Lord Justice Roskill think that this principle should apply in *Brikom Investments v Carr*?

SECTION 14: DISCHARGE BY FRUSTRATION

Frustration occurs when through no fault of either party to the contract an intervening event occurs which makes it impossible to continue with the contract. The contractual obligations are discharged at the point of the frustration. It will not be frustration where one party is responsible for the frustrating event. Problems in frustration concern what happens when one party has handed over money in advance of a contract which is not then performed, and when one party has carried out work under the contract for which (s)he then can claim no payment. Parliament has intervened in this area.

EXTRACT ADAPTED FROM THE JUDGMENT IN *TAYLOR V CALDWELL* [1863] 3 B & S 826

The plaintiffs contracted to hire the Surrey Gardens and Music Hall from the defendants for four days during which they intended to stage a series of concerts. After the contract was formed but before the due time of the concerts the Music Hall burned down through no fault of either party, but making the staging of the concerts impossible. The plaintiffs had incurred considerable costs in preparing for the concerts and sued to recover their losses. They failed because the court held that the contract was frustrated, all obligations ceasing at the point of the frustrating event, the fire in the Music Hall.

BLACKBURN J

The principle seems to us to be that, in contracts in which the performance depends on the continued existence of a given person or thing, a condition is implied that the impossibility of performance arising from the perishing of the person or thing shall excuse the performance.

In none of these cases is the promise in words other than positive, nor is there any express stipulation that the destruction of the person or thing shall excuse the performance; but that excuse is by law implied, because from the nature of the contract it is apparent that the parties contracted on the basis of the continued existence of the particular person or chattel. In the present case, looking at the whole contract, we find that the parties contracted on the basis of the continued existence of the Music Hall at the time when the concerts were to be given; that being essential to their performance.

We think, therefore, that the Music Hall having ceased to exist, without fault of either party, both parties are excused . . .

EXTRACT ADAPTED FROM THE JUDGMENT IN *KRELL V HENRY* [1903] 2 KB 740, CA

The defendant hired a room in Pall Mall from which to watch the procession during the coronation of the King. The King was taken ill, the coronation postponed, and the defendant had no purpose for renting the flat. The claimant sued for the agreed price but failed. The contract was frustrated because its commercial purpose was destroyed.

VAUGHAN WILLIAMS LJ

It is plain that English law applies the principles not only to cases where the performance of the contract becomes impossible by the cessation of existence of the thing which is the subject matter of the contract, but also to cases where the event which renders the contract incapable of performance is the cessation or non-existence of an express condition or state of things, going to the root of the contract and essential to its performance . . .

In each case one must ask oneself, first, what, having regard to all the circumstances, was the foundation of the contract? Secondly: was the performance of the contract prevented? And thirdly: was the event which prevented the performance of the contract of such a character that it cannot reasonably be said to have been in the contemplation of the parties at the date of the contract? If all these questions are answered in the affirmative (as I think they should be in this case) I think both parties are discharged from further performance of the contract.

EXTRACT ADAPTED FROM THE JUDGMENT IN *FIBROSA SPOLKA AKCYJNA V FAIRBAIRN LAWSON COMBE BARBOUR LTD* [1943] AC 32, HL (THE FIBROSA CASE)

A company in Leeds contracted to supply a Polish company with machinery. The Polish company paid £1,000 advance payment, but before delivery could take place Poland was invaded by the German army and the contract was frustrated. The Polish company then sued successfully for the return of the advance.

LORD MACMILLAN

The plaintiffs made a payment to the defendants on account of the price of certain plant which the defendants were to manufacture and deliver to them. Owing to circumstances arising out of present hostilities the contract has become impossible of fulfilment according to its terms. Neither party is to blame. In return for their money the plaintiffs have received nothing whatever from the defendants by way of fulfilment of any part of the contract. It is thus a typical case of a total failure of consideration. The money paid must be repaid.

EXTRACT ADAPTED FROM THE JUDGMENT IN *MARITIME NATIONAL FISH LTD V OCEAN TRAWLERS LTD* [1935] AC 524, PC

Owners of trawlers also chartered a trawler for a coming season. A government licence was required for each trawler used. In the event the government did not grant the company sufficient licences to operate all of the trawlers and the company used the licences for its own trawlers and claimed that the charter was frustrated. Their claim failed as the frustration was self-induced. They could have applied the licence to the trawler that they chartered, but chose not to.

LORD WRIGHT

The essence of frustration is that it should not be due to an act or election of the party ... Lord Sumner in *Bank Line Ltd v Arthur Capel and Co* ... says ...: ... 'I think it is now well settled that the principle of frustration of an adventure assumes that the frustration arises without blame or fault on either side. Reliance cannot be placed on a self-induced frustration ...'

EXTRACT FROM THE LAW REFORM (FRUSTRATED CONTRACTS) ACT 1943

1. Adjustment of rights and liabilities of parties to frustrated contracts

(2) All sums paid or payable to any party in pursuance of the contract before the time when the parties were so discharged (in this Act referred to as 'the time of discharge') shall, in the case of sums so paid, be recoverable from him as money received by him for the use of the party by whom the sums were paid, and, in the case of sums so payable, cease to be so payable.

Provided that, if the party to whom the sums were so paid or payable incurred expenses before the time of discharge in, or for the purpose of, the performance of the contract, the court may, if it considers it just to do so having regard to all the circumstances of the case, allow him to retain or, as the case may be, recover the whole or any part of the sums so paid or payable, not being an amount in excess of the expenses so incurred.

Questions

Read the five extracts above and answer the questions.

1. Why were the parties excused from further performance of the contract in *Taylor v Caldwell*?
2. How is this principle extended in the case of *Krell v Henry*?
3. According to Vaughan Williams LJ in that case, what three requirements are needed to demonstrate frustration?
4. What point does the *Fibrosa* case demonstrate about the rights of a party who has suffered a frustrated contract?
5. What limitation on the doctrine of frustration is demonstrated in the case of *Maritime National Fish v Ocean Trawlers*?
6. What adjustments does s1(2) of the Law Reform (Frustrated Contracts) Act make to the basic common law principles contained in the cases?

SECTION 15: DISCHARGE BY BREACH OF CONTRACT

The effects of a breach of contract may depend on the type of term that is breached and/or the consequences of the breach. A breach of contract can be 'anticipatory' where one party signals his/her intention before performance is due not to carry out the contract. In this instance the other party has the choice whether to sue at that point or to wait until the contract is actually breached.

EXTRACT ADAPTED FROM THE JUDGMENT IN *SCHULER (L) AG v WICKMAN MACHINE TOOL SALES LTD* [1973] 2 WLR 683, HL

Under an agency agreement Wickman were exclusive selling agents of Schuler's presses. Clause 7 provided: 'It shall be a condition of this agreement that [Wickman] shall send its representative to visit [the six large UK motor manufacturers] at least once in every week for the purpose of soliciting orders.' By clause 11 either side might terminate the agreement in writing if 'the other shall have committed a material breach of its obligations'. Wickman never maintained a weekly schedule of visits, causing no apparent concern. Two years into the contract after a breach of the term Schuler terminated the agreement, claiming they were entitled to because it was a condition of the contract. They succeeded in arbitration but this was reversed by the Court of Appeal and its reasoning was accepted by the House of Lords.

LORD REID

Schuler maintain that the word 'condition' has now acquired a precise legal meaning, its recognised meaning in English law is a term of a contract any breach of which by one party gives to the other party an immediate right to rescind the whole contract. Undoubtedly the word is frequently used in that sense. But it is frequently used with less stringent meaning. One is familiar with printed 'conditions of sale' incorporated into a contract, and with the words 'for conditions see back' printed on a ticket. This simply means that the 'conditions' are terms of the contract.

...

In the present case it is not contended that Wickman's failure to make visits amounted, in themselves, to fundamental breaches. What is contended is that the terms of clause 7 'sufficiently express an intention' to make any breach, however small, to entitle Schuler to rescind the whole contract if they so desire.

Schuler maintain that the use of the word 'condition' is, in itself, sufficient to establish this intention. ... Use of the word 'condition' is an indication—even a strong indication—of such an intention, but it is not conclusive. The fact that a particular construction leads to a very unreasonable result must be a relevant consideration. ... the parties must have realised the probability that in a few cases a visit would be impossible. But if Schuler's contention is right, failure to make even one visit entitles them to terminate the contract, however blameless Wickman might be. This is so unreasonable that it must make me search for some other meaning ...

If clause 7 must be read with clause 11 the difficulty disappears. The word 'conditions' would make any breach of clause 7(b), however excusable, a material breach. That would entitle Schuler to give notice under clause 11, requiring the breach to be remedied. There would be no point in giving such a notice if Wickman were clearly not in fault, but if it were given, Wickman would have no difficulty in showing that the breach had been remedied. If Wickman were at fault, then on receiving such a notice, they would have to amend their system so that they could show that the breach had been remedied. If they did not do that within the period of the notice, then Schuler would be entitled to rescind.

EXTRACT ADAPTED FROM THE JUDGMENT IN *WHITE AND CARTER (COUNCILS) LTD v MCGREGOR* [1962] 2 WLR 17, HL

The claimants produced litter bins with plates carrying advertisements from which they gained their revenue. The defendant had agreed to pay for advertising on the litter bins for three years, but later cancelled the contract. The claimants continued to produce the bins with advertisements for the defendants and then sued for the price agreed. The action was originally dismissed, and failed on appeal to the Scottish Court of Session, but the claimants succeeded on appeal to the House of Lords.

LORD REID

The general rule cannot be in doubt. ... If one party to a contract repudiates ... in the sense of making it clear to the other party that he refuses or will refuse to carry out his part of the contract, the other party, the innocent party, has an option. He may accept that repudiation and sue for damages for breach of contract, whether or not the time for performance has come or he may; if he chooses, disregard or refuse to accept it and then the contract remains in full effect.

I need not refer to the numerous authorities. They are not disputed by the respondent, but he points out that in all of them, the party who refused to accept repudiation had no active duties under the contract. The innocent party's option is generally said to be to *wait* until the date of performance and then to claim damages estimated as at that date. There is no case in which it is said that he may, in the face of the repudiation, go on and incur useless expenses in performing the contract and then claim the contract price.

... the respondent points out that in most cases the innocent party cannot complete the contract without the other party doing, allowing or accepting something. ... In most cases, by refusing co-operation, the party in breach can compel the innocent party to restrict his claim to damages. Then it was said that even where the innocent party can complete the contract without such co-operation, it is against the public interest that he be allowed to do so.

The other ground would be that there is some general equitable principle or element of public policy which requires this limitation of the contractual rights of the innocent party. If a party has no interest to enforce a stipulation, he cannot in general enforce it: so it might be said that if a party has no interest to insist on a particular remedy, he ought not to be allowed to insist upon it. And just as a party is not allowed to enforce a penalty, so he ought not to be allowed to penalise the other party by taking one course when another is equally advantageous to him.

Here, the respondent did not set out to prove that the appellants had no legitimate interests in completing the contract and claiming the contract price rather than claiming damages; there is nothing in the findings of fact to support such a case and it seems improbable that any such case could have been proved. It is, in my judgment, impossible to say that the appellants should be deprived of their right to claim the contract price merely because the benefit to them, as against claiming damages and re-letting their advertising space, might be small in comparison to the loss to the respondent.

Questions

Read the two extracts above and answer the questions.

1. According to the judgment in *Schuler v Wickman*, what is a 'condition' and what are the consequences of breach of a condition?
2. Why were Schuler unable to repudiate legally in the case?
3. Why were the claimants in *White & Carter v McGregor* able to continue with the contract and sue despite the fact that the defendants had signalled their intentions not to continue with the contract?

SECTION 16: DAMAGES

A sum of money compensation in the form of damages is the most usual remedy for contractual breaches. The victim of the breach can only claim for damage that is a foreseeable consequence of the breach. It is also possible to recover consequential losses. In some rare circumstances a party can recover for mental distress caused by the breach of contract, but only where the contract is to do with creating peace of mind.

EXTRACT ADAPTED FROM THE JUDGMENT IN *VICTORIA LAUNDRY (WINDSOR) LTD V NEWMAN INDUSTRIES LTD* [1949] 2 KB 528

A firm of launderers and dyers ordered a new boiler from the defendants in order to expand their business. Under the contract the boiler was due for delivery on 5th June but it was not actually delivered until November. The laundry firm sued claiming damages for their loss of regular profit and also for loss of a dyeing contract that they had procured with a government department. It was held that they could recover for the loss of profits, which was a natural consequence of the supplier's breach of contract. They could not recover for the loss of the government contract as this was not within the contemplation of the suppliers at the time they entered the contract.

ASQUITH LJ

What propositions applicable to the present case emerge from the authorities as a whole? We think they include the following:

1 It is well settled that the governing purpose of damages is to put the party whose rights have been violated in the same position, so far as money can do so, as if his rights had been observed. This purpose if pursued relentlessly would provide him with a complete indemnity for all loss, however unpredictable. This, in contract at least, is recognised as too harsh a rule. Hence:

2 In cases of breach of contract the aggrieved party is only entitled to recover such part of the loss actually resulting as was at the time of the contract reasonably foreseeable as liable to result from the breach.

3 What was at the time reasonably foreseeable depends on the knowledge then possessed by the parties, or . . . by the party who later commits the breach.

4 For this purpose, knowledge possessed is of two kinds, one imputed, the other actual. Everyone is taken to know the 'ordinary course of things' and consequently what loss is liable to result from a breach of contract in the ordinary course. But to this knowledge there may have to be added in a particular case knowledge which he actually possesses, of special circumstances outside the 'ordinary course of things', of such a kind that breach in those circumstances would be liable to cause more loss.

5 In order to make the contract-breaker liable under either rule it is not necessary that he should have asked himself what loss is liable to result from a breach. It suffices that, if he had considered the question, he would as a reasonable man have concluded that the loss in question was liable to result.

6 Nor . . ., to make a particular loss recoverable, need it be proved that upon a given state of knowledge the defendant could, as a reasonable man, foresee it was likely . . . to result. It is . . . enough if the loss is a 'serious possibility' or a 'real danger'.

EXTRACT ADAPTED FROM THE JUDGMENT IN *ANGLIA TELEVISION LTD V REED* [1972] 1 QB 60

Reed was hired to appear in a television play. The company incurred a number of expenses in planning for the production, including director's fees. The defendant then refused to carry out the contract. The company tried but was unable to find a suitable actor to replace him. They sued successfully for their losses, including the expenditure that, in reliance on the contract, had been wasted.

LORD DENNING MR

... a plaintiff in such a case as this has an option: he can either claim for loss of profits, or for his wasted expenditure. ... He cannot claim both. If he has not suffered any loss of profits—or if he cannot prove what his profits would have been—he can claim in the alternative the expenditure which has been ... wasted by reason of the breach.

If the plaintiff claims the wasted expenditure, he is not limited to the expenditure involved after the contract was concluded. He can claim also for the expenditure before the contract, provided that it was such as would reasonably be in the contemplation of the parties as likely to be wasted if the contract was broken. Applying this principle here, it is plain that, when Mr Reed entered into this contract, he must have known perfectly well that much expenditure had already been incurred on the director's fees and the like. He must have contemplated—or, at any rate, it is reasonable to be imputed to him—that if he broke his contract, all that expenditure would be wasted, whether or not it was incurred before or after the contract. He must pay damages for all expenditure so wasted and thrown away.

EXTRACT ADAPTED FROM THE JUDGMENT IN *JARVIS V SAWN TOURS LTD* [1973] QB 233 CA

The claimant bought a holiday in a Swiss hotel, described as a 'houseparty' and offering a variety of entertainments. In the first week there were only 13 people in the hotel and in the second week he was completely alone. There were few entertainments and those that were there did not match the description given to them. He was awarded half the value of the holiday when he sued, but on appeal he recovered also for the mental distress he suffered.

LORD DENNING MR

... It has often been said that on a breach of contract damages cannot be given for mental distress. I think that those limitations are out of date. In a proper case damages for mental distress can be recovered in contract, just as damages for shock can be recovered in tort. One such case is a contract for a holiday, or any other contract to provide entertainment and enjoyment. If the contracting party breaks his contract, damages can be given for the disappointment, the distress, the upset and frustration caused by the breach. I know that it is difficult to assess in terms of money, but it is no more difficult than the assessment which the courts have to make every day in personal injury cases for loss of amenities.

I think the judge was in error in taking the sum paid for the holiday £63.45 and halving it. The right measure of damages is to compensate him for the loss of entertainment and enjoyment which he was promised, and which he did not get.

Questions

Read the three extracts above and answer the questions.

1. What, according to the judgment of Lord Justice Asquith in *Victoria Laundry v Newman Industries*, is the purpose of awarding damages in a claim for a breach of contract?
2. What measure is applied to the damages that are recoverable?
3. In what ways is it possible to determine what is a foreseeable loss?
4. What is the difference between 'actual knowledge' and 'imputed knowledge'?

5 What choices of claim does Lord Denning say in *Anglia TV v Reed* are open to a claimant in a contract case, and what are the consequences of making one choice or the other?

6 For what were the claimants able to recover in that case?

7 In *Jarvis v Swan Tours* what does Lord Denning suggest is the normal rule in relation to mental distress in contract cases?

8 What are his justifications for allowing such a claim in the case?

SECTION 17: EQUITABLE REMEDIES

Equitable remedies are traditionally available where damages is an inadequate remedy. There are three main types: an injunction which will prevent the other party from breaching the contract in some way; specific performance of the contract, usually only available where the subject matter is land, or at least is unique in some way; and rescission, which is to put the parties back into their pre-contractual positions, if this is possible to achieve.

EXTRACT ADAPTED FROM THE JUDGMENT IN *PAGE ONE RECORDS LTD V BRITTON* [1968] 1 WLR 157

A sixties pop group, The Troggs, had entered into a contract with their manager that was more advantageous to him than to them and tied them to him absolutely. Once famous they lost confidence in him and wished to appoint another manager. The manager unsuccessfully sought an injunction to prevent them from doing so.

STAMP J

The present case is clearly distinguishable, in principle, from such cases as *Lumley v Wagner*, for there the only obligation on the part of the plaintiff seeking to enforce the negative stipulation was an obligation to pay remuneration and an obligation which could clearly be enforced by the defendants. Here, however, the obligations to the first plaintiff involving personal services were obligations of trust and confidence and were obligations which, plainly, could not be enforced at the suit of The Troggs. Here, indeed ... the totality of the obligations between the parties are more a joint venture almost approaching the relationship of partners than anything else, involving mutual confidence and reciprocal obligations on all sides ...

where a contract of personal services contains negative covenants, the enforcement of which will amount either to a decree of specific performance of the positive covenant ... or to giving a decree under which the defendant must either remain idle or perform those positive covenants, the court will not enforce those negative covenants.

EXTRACT ADAPTED FROM THE JUDGMENT IN *POSNER V SCOTT LEWIS* [1986] 3 ALL ER 513

Tenants leased flats in a block of flats from the defendant landlords. By the tenancy agreement the defendants were bound to provide a resident porter but in fact hired only a non-resident porter. The tenants succeeded in their action for specific performance of the provision of the tenancy agreement.

MERVYN DAVIES J

I was referred to *Ryan v Mutual Tontine [1893]* ... a case where the Court of Appeal considered a contract between a landlord and his tenant by which the landlord undertook to employ a porter to perform certain services for the benefit of the tenant. The contract was held not to be specifically enforceable. One ground ... was that the execution of the contract would require 'constant superintendence by the court'.

A close examination of the facts in *Ryan's* case shows that the situation in that case differs in some respects from the situation before me. For example in *Ryan's* case the porter was to 'be and act as the servant of the tenants'. Again the lease has, but the *Ryan* lease had not, covenants by the lessor whereby the porter's duties are seen as direct obligations of the lessor to the lessee.

... it is, I think open to me to consider the making of an order for specific performance in this case ... Damages here could hardly be regarded as an adequate remedy.

Whether or not an order for specific performance should be made seems to me to depend on the following considerations: (a) is there a sufficient definition of what has to be done in order to comply with the order of the court; (b) will enforcing the compliance involve superintendence by the court to an unacceptable degree; and (c) what are the respective prejudices or hardships that will be suffered by the parties if the order is made or not made?

EXTRACT ADAPTED FROM THE JUDGMENT IN *CLARKE V DICKSON* [1858] 120 ER 463

As a result of a misrepresentation the plaintiff was induced to buy shares in a partnership which later became a limited company. It was later wound up and it was only at this time that the plaintiff discovered the misrepresentation. He claimed rescission of the contract but failed.

CROMPTON J

When once it is settled that a contract induced by fraud is not void, but voidable at the option of the party defrauded, it seems to me to follow that, when that party exercises his option to rescind the contract, he must be in a state to rescind, that is, he must be in such a situation as to be able to put the parties into their original state before the contract. ... If he cannot return the article he must keep it, and sue for his real damage. Take the case I put in the argument, of a butcher buying live cattle, killing them, and even selling the meat to his customers. If the rule of law were as the plaintiff contends, that butcher might, upon discovering a fraud on the part of the grazier who sold him the cattle, rescind the contract and get back the whole price: but how could that be consistent with justice? The true doctrine is that a party can never repudiate a contract after, by his own act, it has become out of his power to restore the parties to the original condition.

However, so long as 'restitutio in integrum' is substantially possible, rescission may remain an available remedy.

Questions

Read the three extracts above and answer the questions.

1. Why was Stamp J not prepared to accept that an injunction should be awarded in *Page One Records v Britton*?
2. Why does Mervyn Davies J say that specific performance was refused in *Ryan v Mutual Tontine*?
3. On what basis did he then award the remedy in *Posner v Scott Lewis*?
4. With reference to the judgment in *Clarke v Dickson* explain the meaning of the term *restitutio in integrum* and the effect that this principle has on a claim for rescission?

Activity

Suggest what equitable remedy, if any, may be awarded in the following circumstances:

1. Jasvinder is contracted to buy Eric's factory but Eric has failed to hand over the title deeds on the due date.

2. Ali has discovered that the mileage on the car that he has just bought from Naomi is in fact 111,000 rather than the 11,000 that she told him.
3. Simon wishes to make his employee, Dan, come to work. Dan is currently on strike for more wages.
4. In 1990 Rachel bought a shop from Damon, who falsely misrepresented that the net profits were £45,000 per year. They were in fact only £30,000 when Rachel bought the shop. They are now only £20,000 and Rachel wants her money back from Damon.
5. Marcia contracted to buy Raj's Porsche car for £40,000. Raj is refusing to hand the car over now because he has a buyer who will pay him £45,000.

CHAPTER 3

THE LAW OF TORTS

SECTION 1: NEGLIGENCE: DUTY OF CARE

Negligence has developed from Lord Atkin's 'neighbour principle'. It depends first upon identifying the existence of a duty of care owed by the defendant to the claimant. At one stage Lord Wilberforce introduced a two-part test based only on proximity of the two parties and policy reasons for denying the existence of a duty. This test was always unpopular with judges and was eventually removed. It was replaced with the traditional incremental approach and is measured according to the proximity of the parties, the foreseeability of harm, and whether or not it is just and reasonable to impose a duty on the defendant.

EXTRACT ADAPTED FROM THE JUDGMENT IN *DONOGHUE V STEVENSON* [1932] AC 532

The claimant alleged that she had suffered injury as the result of drinking ginger beer from an opaque bottle bought for her by her friend that contained the remains of a decomposing snail. The House of Lords held that the manufacturer did owe her a duty of care and that in the instance there was an actionable claim.

LORD ATKIN

The liability for negligence ... is no doubt based upon a general public sentiment of moral wrongdoing for which the offender must pay. But acts or omissions which any moral code would censure cannot in a practical world be treated so as to give a right to every person injured by them to demand relief. In this way rules of law arise which limit the range of complaints and the extent of their remedy. The rule that you are to love your neighbour becomes in law, you must not injure your neighbour; and the lawyer's question, Who is my neighbour? receives a restricted reply. You must take reasonable care to avoid acts or omissions which you can reasonably foresee would be likely to injure your neighbour. Who, then, in law is my neighbour? The answer seems to be—persons who are so closely affected by my act that I ought reasonably to have them in my contemplation as being so affected when I am directing my mind to the acts or omissions which are called in question.

EXTRACT ADAPTED FROM THE JUDGMENT IN *ANNS V MERTON LONDON BOROUGH COUNCIL* [1978] AC 728, HL

A local authority failed to ensure that a building complied with plans in relation to the depth of its foundations with the result that a later tenant of the property suffered loss and sued successfully. The House of Lords modified the basic test from *Donoghue v Stevenson* for establishing when a duty of care exists.

LORD WILBERFORCE

... the position has now been reached that in order to establish that a duty of care arises in a particular situation, it is not necessary to bring the facts of that situation within those of previous situations in which a duty of care has been held to exist. Rather the question has to be approached in two stages. First one has to ask whether, as between the alleged wrongdoer and the person who has suffered damage there is a sufficient relationship of proximity or neighbourhood such that, in the reasonable contemplation of the former, carelessness on his part may be likely to cause damage to the latter—in which case a prima facie duty of care arises. Secondly, if the first question is answered affirmatively, it is necessary to consider whether there are any considerations which ought to negative, or to reduce or limit the scope of the duty or the class of person to whom it is owed or the damages to which a breach of it may give rise . . .

EXTRACT ADAPTED FROM THE JUDGMENT IN *CAPARO V DICKMAN* [1990] 2 AC 605

Shareholders in a company bought further shares in order to stage a take-over bid which proved successful. They claimed that, in doing this, they relied on the audited accounts of the company which showed a profit of £1.3 million when in fact the accurate figure was a loss of £465,000. The House of Lords held that the auditors owed no duty of care to the claimants in the case.

LORD BRIDGE

. . . since the *Anns* case a series of decisions of the Privy Council and of your Lordship's House have emphasised the inability of any single general principle to provide a practical test which can be applied to every situation to determine whether a duty of care is owed and, if so what is its scope. What emerges is that, in addition to the foreseeability of damage, necessary ingredients in any situation giving rise to a duty of care are that there should exist between the party owing the duty and the party to whom it is owed a relationship characterised by the law as one of 'proximity' or 'neighbourhood' and that the situation should be one in which the court considers it fair, just and reasonable that the law should impose a duty of a given scope upon the one party for the benefit of the other. . . . We must . . . recognise the wisdom of . . . Brennan J in *Sutherland Shire Council v Heyman* . . .: 'It is preferable . . . that the law should develop novel categories of negligence incrementally and by analogy with established categories, rather than by a massive extension of a prima facie duty of care restrained only by indefinable "considerations which ought to negative or to reduce or limit the scope of the duty or the class of the person to whom it is owed".'

Questions

Read the three extracts above and answer the questions.

1. In *Donoghue v Stevenson* why does Lord Atkin suggest there is a limit to the range of possible complaints?
2. How did Lord Wilberforce in *Anns* propose to alter the way in which the courts would establish the existence of a duty of care?
3. In what way would policy be a major factor in determining the existence of a duty of care as a result of the test in *Anns*?
4. Why would subsequent judges have been reluctant to follow Lord Wilberforce's two-part test?
5. In *Caparo v Dickman* what considerations does Lord Bridge think that the existence of a duty of care depends on, and what weight does he think should be attached to them?

SECTION 2: NEGLIGENCE: BREACH OF THE DUTY OF CARE

The second requirement is to show a breach of the duty. This is a falling below the standard appropriate to the particular duty. The standard of care owed is usually measured against the standards of the 'reasonable man'. A variety of factors can be taken into account in determining whether the standard of care has been breached, such as the foreseeability of damage occurring. The standard of care owed by professionals on the other hand is measured against the standards of reasonable members of the profession and this is not always felt to give satisfactory results.

EXTRACT ADAPTED FROM THE CASE OF *BLYTH V BIRMINGHAM WATERWORKS*, COURT OF EXCHEQUER [1856] 11 EX 781

The defendants laid a water main and inserted a 'fire plug'. This was a hole in the main blocked up with a wooden plug which could then be opened to release water up a pipe to the street. Following frost the pipe became blocked with ice, the plug became detached from the main, and water escaping up the pipe flooded the plaintiff's house. There was no negligence.

ALDERSON B

The case turns upon the question, whether the facts proved show that the defendants were guilty of negligence. Negligence is the omission to do something which a reasonable man guided upon those considerations which ordinarily regulate the conduct of human affairs, would do, or doing something which a prudent and reasonable man would not do. The defendants might have been liable for negligence, if, unintentionally, they omitted to do that which a reasonable person would have done, or did that which a person taking reasonable precautions would not have done. A reasonable man would act with reference to the average circumstances of the temperature in ordinary years. The defendants had provided against such frosts as experience would have led men, acting prudently, to provide against; and they are not guilty of negligence, because their precautions proved insufficient against the effects of the extreme ... frost of 1855 ... Such ... circumstances constitutes a contingency against which no reasonable man can provide.

EXTRACT ADAPTED FROM THE JUDGMENT IN *BOLTON V STONE* [1951] AC 850, HL

A cricket ball hit Miss Stone when she was outside a cricket ground in Manchester. A fence surrounded the ground 17 feet above the level of the pitch and 78 yards away from the cricket square. Miss Stone was in fact 100 yards away from the batsman when she was struck. Evidence showed that only six balls had been hit outside the ground in 28 years. Miss Stone's action for damages eventually failed in the club's appeal. There was no negligence by the cricket club that had done everything it could to avoid such accidents.

LORD RADCLIFFE

If the test whether there has been a breach of duty were to depend merely on the answer to the question whether this accident was a reasonably foreseeable risk, I think there would have been a breach of duty, for that such an accident might take place some time or other might very reasonably have been present in the minds of the appellants. It was quite foreseeable, and there would have been nothing unreasonable in allowing the imagination to dwell on the possibility of its occurring. But there was only a remote, perhaps I ought to say only a very remote, chance of the accident taking place at any particular time, for if it was to happen, not only was the ball to carry the fence around the ground but it had also to coincide in its arrival with the presence of some person on what does not look like a crowded thoroughfare and actually to strike that person in some way that would cause sensible injury.

Those being the facts, a breach of duty has taken place if they show the appellants guilty of a failure to take reasonable care to prevent the accident ... unless there has been something which a reasonable man would blame as falling beneath the standard of conduct that he would set for himself and require of his neighbour, there has been no breach of legal duty. ... here. I think, the respondent's case breaks down. It seems to me that a reasonable man, taking account of the chances against an accident happening, would not have felt ... called upon either to abandon the use of the ground for cricket or to increase the height of his surrounding fences. He would have done what the appellants did: in other words, he would have done nothing.

EXTRACT ADAPTED FROM THE JUDGMENT IN *NETTLESHIP V WESTON* [1971] 2 QB 691

Nettleship was teaching his friend to drive when she negligently hit a lamp post, injuring his knee. She was found liable on appeal. One issue on appeal was the appropriate standard of care owed by a learner driver.

LORD DENNING MR

Mrs Weston is clearly liable for the damage to the lamp post. In the civil law if a driver goes off the road on to the pavement and injures a pedestrian or damages property, he is prima facie liable. It is no answer ... to say: 'I was a learner driver under instructions. I was doing my best and could not help it.' The civil law permits no such excuse. It requires of him the same standard of care as of any other driver. The learner driver may be doing his best, but his incompetent best is not good enough. He must drive in as good a manner as a driver of skill, experience and care, who is sound in mind and limb, who makes no errors of judgment, has good eyesight and hearing, and is free from any infirmity ...

I take it to be clear that if a driver has a passenger in the car he owes a duty of care to him. But what is the standard of care ... ? Is it a lower standard than he or she owes towards a pedestrian on the pavement? ... The driver owes a duty of care to every passenger in the car, just as he does to every pedestrian on the road: and he must attain the same standard of care in respect of each.

EXTRACT ADAPTED FROM 'WHEN THE PITCH BECOMES A BATTLE GROUND ...', SARAH PHILBROOK, *THE LEGAL EXECUTIVE JOURNAL*, JUNE 1997

There are no hard and fast rules when it comes to tackling sporting injury in negligence cases. Every case is unique.

In general, every time an adult participates in a sporting activity, he/she automatically accepts a degree of personal risk.

However this implied consent is finite. Even in the case of high risk pursuits such as rugby and motor racing, there will be situations that fall outside what participants can be reasonably expected to accept on the basis of this unwritten agreement.

A classic case ... was *Smolden v Whitworth* ... which saw rugby player Smoldon sue referee Whitworth for not controlling the game in which he, Smoldon, sustained ... horrific spinal injuries.

At the heart of the plaintiff's case was the fact that the referee had repeatedly allowed the scrum to collapse without intervening.

Everyone knows that rugby is an aggressive contact sport, and that people frequently are hurt while playing ... players must accept that they may get injured in the 'rough and tumble'—possibly seriously ... indeed, had Smoldon sustained his injuries earlier in the match there would probably have been no case to answer.

However, in this case it was argued that by letting the scrum collapse as many times as he did, the referee had allowed the match to reach a point where it was reasonable to expect that someone would get hurt—and had therefore breached his duty of care to the players. The court agreed.

Questions

Read the four extracts above and answer the questions.

1. How does Baron Alderson define negligence in *Blyth v Birmingham Waterworks*?
2. Why do you think he uses a 'reasonable man' against which to measure the standards of the waterworks?
3. How does this principle of doing what the reasonable man would do apply in the case of *Bolton v Stone*?
4. Does the standard of care differ at all in the cases of *Bolton v Stone* and *Nettleship v Weston*? If not, why not?
5. According to *Nettleship v Weston* does the standard of care we owe depend on the level of experience and competence we have?
6. Why was the defendant in *Smolden v Whitworth* liable when the cricket club in *Bolton v Stone* was not?

EXTRACT ADAPTED FROM *'BOLAM AND BOLITHO: A NEW STANDARD OF CARE FOR DOCTORS?'*, DR WALTER SCOTT, *NEW LAW JOURNAL*, 16 JANUARY 1998, P 64

For 40 years doctors defending negligence actions have been able to rely on evidence of opinion from colleagues to justify their actions. In *Bolam v Friern HMC*, a psychiatrist and an anaesthetist were sued for negligence because they failed to use muscle relaxants when giving electroconvulsive therapy to a patient suffering from depressive illness. They produced expert evidence that this method amounted to an accepted practice by some of their colleagues. Put another way, there were some doctors who thought that muscle relaxants should be used and some who thought that they were unnecessary. This proved to be a successful defence and the relevant part of the judgment in *Bolam* was in terms that 'a doctor is not negligent if he is acting in accordance with such a practice merely because there is a body of opinion which takes a contrary view'.

. . .

Although doctors have been able to rely on the *Bolam* proposition in countless successful defences, the cynics have argued that it is wrong for doctors to be able to justify their actions merely by showing that a few of their colleagues would have done the same in the circumstances.

Patrick Bolitho was admitted to hospital with croup at the age of two. His respiratory efforts soon deteriorated further and the nursing sister called the resident doctors twice but there was a breakdown in communications and they failed to attend. Soon after the second call, Patrick collapsed and suffered very severe brain damage. Negligence was conceded by the defendants with regard to the failure to attend. The plaintiff's case was that, if they had attended they would have passed a tube into Patrick's throat to avert respiratory obstruction and that the brain damage would therefore not have occurred. . . . the defendants' case was that even if the doctors had responded in good time they would have refrained from the procedure because it was too risky. The trial judge found himself faced with . . . conflicting bodies of medical opinion and in accordance with *Bolam*, . . . felt compelled to accept both . . . Patrick lost . . .

The family then appealed . . . the Court of Appeal upheld the . . . judge's findings in favour of the . . . doctors. A further appeal led the House of Lords to consider the matter . . .

Lawyers for the plaintiff argued that the views of the defendants' experts should not be accepted because they were founded on an overestimate of the risks involved in intubation of such a young child. Lord Browne-Wilkinson ... was impressed with this argument but ... refused to accept it because ... 'it invited me to substitute my own views for those of the medical experts'. For the third and last time Patrick lost his case.

A very important point has emerged from the House of Lords decision ... Their Lordships focused on the words used in earlier medical negligence judgments and found the adjectives 'responsible', 'reasonable' and 'respectable' being used to describe a body of opinion which would act as a successful defence. They held that this 'showed that the court had to be satisfied that the exponents of the body of opinion relied upon could demonstrate that such opinion had a logical basis'. This means that it will become increasingly difficult for doctors to justify their actions on the basis of producing colleagues who will say that they would have done the same. To escape liability they will have to present a convincing and logical argument to a judge who has little or no medical knowledge.

EXTRACT ADAPTED FROM THE JUDGMENT IN *BOLAM V FRIERN HOSPITAL MANAGEMENT COMMITTEE* [1957] 1 WLR 582

The facts have already been outlined in the above article.

MCNAIR J

In the ordinary case which does not involve any special skill, negligence in law means a failure to do some act which a reasonable man would do, or doing some act which a reasonable man would not do ... How do you test whether this act or failure is negligent? In an ordinary case it is generally said you judge it by the action of the man in the street. In one case it has been said that you judge it by the conduct of the man on top of the Clapham omnibus. ... where you get a situation which involves the use of some special skill or competence, then the test as to whether there has been negligence or not is not the test of the man on top of the Clapham omnibus, because he has not got this special skill. The test is the standard of the ordinary skilled man exercising and professing to have this special skill. A man need not possess the highest expert skill; it is well established law that it is sufficient if he exercises the ordinary skill of an ordinary competent man exercising that particular art.

EXTRACT ADAPTED FROM THE JUDGMENT IN *BOLITHO V CITY AND HACKNEY HEALTH AUTHORITY* [1997] 4 ALL ER 771

The facts have already been outlined in the above article.

LORD BROWNE-WILKINSON

... the judge [at first instance] expressed these doubts:

'Mr Brennan also advanced a powerful argument—which I have to say, as a layman, appealed to me—to the effect that the views of the defendant's experts simply were not logical or sensible. Given the recent and the more remote history of Patrick's illness, culminating in these two episodes, surely it was unreasonable and illogical not to anticipate the recurrence of a life-threatening event and take the step which it was acknowledged would probably have saved Patrick from harm?'

Mr Brennan ... submitted that the judge had wrongly treated the *Bolam* test as requiring him to accept the views of one truthful body of expert professional advice even though he was unpersuaded by its logical force. He submitted that the judge was wrong in law in adopting that approach and that ultimately it was for the court, not for medical opinion, to decide what was the standard of care required of a professional ...

I agree ... that ... the court is not bound to hold that a defendant doctor escapes liability for negligent treatment or diagnosis just because he leads evidence from a number of medical experts who are genuinely of the opinion that the defendant's treatment accorded with sound medical practice. The use of the adjectives—responsible, reasonable, and respectable—all show that the court has to be satisfied that the exponents of the body of opinion relied upon can demonstrate that such opinion has a logical basis. In particular in cases involving, as they so often do, the weighing of risks against benefits, the judge before accepting a body of opinion as being responsible, reasonable or respectable, will need to be satisfied that ... the experts have directed their minds to the question of comparative risks and benefits and ... reached a defensible conclusion ...

in cases of diagnosis and treatment there are cases where, despite a body of professional opinion sanctioning the defendant's conduct, the defendant can properly be held liable for negligence. In my judgment that is because, in some cases, it cannot be demonstrated to the judge's satisfaction that the body of opinion relied upon is reasonable or responsible ... if, in a rare case, it can be demonstrated that the professional opinion is not capable of withstanding logical analysis, the judge is entitled to hold that the body of opinion is not reasonable or responsible.

Questions

Read the three extracts above and answer the questions.

1. According to McNair J in *Bolam*, why is the ordinary standard of care in negligence cases, the reasonable man's standard, not appropriate in determining whether or not a person exercising a skill has been negligent?
2. What standard of care is appropriate in assessing a skilled person's negligence?
3. According to Dr Walter Scott's article, how have doctors been able to take advantage of this principle in defences to medical negligence claims?
4. In *Bolitho* who did the claimants believe should be the judge of whether the standard of care exercised by the defendants was appropriate or not?
5. To what extent did Lord Browne-Wilkinson agree with this?
6. How does Dr Scott in his article suggest that the judgment in *Bolitho* will alter the basic principle in *Bolam*?
7. To what extent do you think that it is fair that people's actions in general are judged according to the standards of the 'reasonable man' while doctors and other professionals are judged according to their own standards?

SECTION 3: NEGLIGENCE: CAUSATION AND REMOTENESS OF DAMAGE

There will only be liability where a defendant's acts or omissions have actually caused the damage suffered by the claimant. This is measured by the 'but for test'. Problems arise where there are multiple causes of the same damage.

A claimant will only be able to recover in respect of damage that is a foreseeable consequence of his/her breach of the duty of care, and cannot recover for any damage that is too remote a consequence of the breach. Only the type of damage, not the specific damage itself, need be foreseen by the defendant.

EXTRACT ADAPTED FROM THE JUDGMENT IN *BARNETT V CHELSEA HOSPITAL MANAGEMENT BOARD* [1969] 1 QB 428

A night watchman went to the casualty department of the hospital complaining of being very ill and vomiting after drinking tea. The doctor, rather than attending to him, advised him to go home and see his own doctor in the morning. The man then died, and it was found that he had arsenic poisoning. The doctor had been negligent, however, it was shown that the man would have died even if the doctor had treated him, so there was no liability on the hospital.

NEILD J

Without doubt the casualty officer should have seen and examined the deceased. His failure to do either cannot be described as an excusable error ... It was negligence.

It remains to consider whether ... the deceased's death was caused by that negligence or whether, as the defendants have said, the deceased must have died in any event.

Without going in detail into the considerable volume of technical evidence ... it seems to me to be the case that when death results from arsenic poisoning it is bought about by two conditions; on the one hand dehydration and on the other disturbance of the enzyme process. If the principal condition is one of enzyme disturbance—as I am of the view it was here—then the only method of treatment ... likely to succeed is the use of the specific antidote ... commonly called B.A.L. Dr Goulding said ... in ... evidence:

'I see no reasonable prospect of B.A.L. being administered before the time at which he died.'

and at a later point ...

'I feel that even if fluid loss had been discovered death would have been caused by the enzyme disturbances. Death might have occurred later.'

So if damage would have occurred in any event without the breach of the duty of care on the part of the defendant, then the defendant will not be liable.

EXTRACT ADAPTED FROM THE JUDGMENT IN *BAKER V WILLOUGHBY* [1970] 2 WLR 50, HL

The claimant was knocked down and his leg injured through the negligence of the defendant. He was unable to carry on his present employment as a result of those injuries. At a later stage the claimant was shot in the leg during an armed robbery causing his leg to require amputation. The defendant's argument, that he should be liable only for the damages to the point where the leg was amputated, failed.

LORD REID

A man is not compensated for the physical injury; he is compensated for the loss ... he suffers as a result of that injury. His loss is not in having a stiff leg; it is in his inability to lead a full life, his inability to enjoy those amenities which depend on freedom of movement and his inability to earn as much as he used to earn or could have earned if there had been no accident. In this case the second injury did not diminish any of these. So why should it be regarded as having obliterated or superseded them?

EXTRACT ADAPTED FROM THE JUDGMENT IN *OVERSEAS TANKSHIP (UK) LTD V MORT'S DOCK AND ENGINEERING CO LTD (THE WAGON MOUND (NO 1))* [1961] AC 388

Fuel leaked into Sydney Harbour from a tanker. Contractors were welding on a ship in a wharf to which the oil drifted. Sparks from the welding ignited waste cotton wadding in the water that then set fire to the oil and the resulting fire caused much damage. The oil was thought at the time not to be likely to ignite because it had such a high flashpoint. The Privy Council decided that the previous test of remoteness of damage from *Re Polemis*, based on 'direct consequences', was no longer appropriate and that the appropriate test was that a claimant should recover for foreseeable damage.

VISCOUNT SIMONDS

... if it is asked why a man should be responsible for the natural or necessary or probable consequences of his act the answer is that it is not because they are natural or necessary or probable, but because, since they have this quality, it is judged by the standard of the reasonable man that he ought to have foreseen them.

... In the case of *Liesbosch* the appellants, whose vessel had been fouled by the respondents, claimed damages under various heads. The respondents were admittedly at fault; therefore, said the appellants, invoking the rule in *Polemis*, they were responsible for all damage whether foreseeable or not. Here was the opportunity to deny the rule or to place it secure upon its pedestal. But the House of Lords took neither course; ... it distinguished *Polemis* on the ground that in that case the injuries suffered were the 'immediate physical consequences' of the negligent act. It is not easy to understand why a distinction should be drawn between 'immediate physical' and other consequences, nor where the line should be drawn.

In the same connection may be mentioned the conclusion to which the Full Court finally came in the present case. Applying the rule in *Polemis* and holding therefore that the unforeseeability of the damage by fire afforded no defence, they then went on to consider the remaining question. Was it a 'direct' consequence? Upon this Manning J said: 'Notwithstanding that, if regard is had separately to each individual occurrence in the chain of events that led to this fire, each occurrence was improbable and, in one sense, improbability was heaped upon improbability, I cannot escape from the conclusion that if the ordinary man in the street had been asked, as a matter of common sense, without any detailed analysis of the circumstances, to state the cause of the fire at Mort's Dock, he would unhesitatingly have assigned such cause to the spillage of oil by the appellant's employees.' Perhaps he would, and probably he would have added: 'I never should have thought it possible.' But with great respect to the Full Court this is surely irrelevant, or if it is relevant, only serves to show that the Polemis rule works in a very strange way. After the event even a fool is wise. But it is not the hindsight of a fool; it is the foresight of the reasonable man which alone can determine responsibility. The Polemis rule by substituting 'direct' for 'reasonably foreseeable' consequences leads to a conclusion equally illogical and unjust.

EXTRACT ADAPTED FROM THE JUDGMENT IN *BRADFORD V ROBINSON RENTALS* [1967] 1 WLR 337

A TV engineer was required by his employers to travel a round journey of more than 450 miles in a van without a heater. He got frostbite in his hands and feet and suffered permanent damage as a result. The Court of Appeal held that there was a reasonably foreseeable risk of injury.

LORD GUEST

The question I have to consider is whether the plaintiff has proved that the injury to his health by 'frost-bite' which is admittedly unusual in this country, is nevertheless of the kind and type of injury which was reasonably foreseeable.

In order to establish a coherent chain of causation it is not necessary that the precise details leading up to the accident should have been reasonably foreseeable: it is sufficient if the accident which occurred is of a type which should have been foreseeable by a reasonably careful person ...

the defendants ... knew that the weather during January 9 and 10 was likely to be severe with temperatures at or about freezing point with ice and snow on the roads; that the road journey of about 450 to 500 miles in two days would be likely to involve the plaintiff in at least 20 hours of driving, when the old Austin van was unheated . . . From all these facts it is plain in my mind that the defendants knew that the plaintiff was being called upon to carry out an unusual task which would be likely to expose him for prolonged periods to extreme cold and considerable fatigue.

. . . the defendants did, by sending the plaintiff out on this journey, expose him to a reasonably foreseeable risk of injury arising from exposure to severe cold and fatigue. Even if there had been—and there is not—evidence that the plaintiff was extremely susceptible to 'frost-bite' as opposed to the more common sequels of prolonged exposure to severe cold and fatigue, he would be entitled to succeed on the footing that a tortfeaser must take his victim as he finds him.

Questions

Read the four extracts above and answer the questions.

1. Why was the doctor not liable in the *Barnett* case?
2. In *Baker v Willoughby* why was the original defendant still liable?
3. In *The Wagon Mound* what does Viscount Simonds suggest is the easier way of describing consequences that are 'natural or necessary or probable'?
4. What, according to Viscount Simonds, was the problem faced by the judge in the case at first instance in applying the rule in *Re Polemis*?
5. Why might the defendants have believed that they should not be liable in *Bradford v Robinson Rentals*?
6. What is Lord Guest's reasoning in saying that the defendant's were liable for the damage suffered by the claimant?
7. In what way does this develop the basic principle in *The Wagon Mound*?

SECTION 4: NEGLIGENCE: NOVEL DUTY SITUATIONS: NEGLIGENT MISSTATEMENT

One novel duty situation is where a claimant can recover for a financial loss caused by a negligently made misstatement by the other party. This is only possible where a special relationship exists between the two parties, where the party giving the advice does so in a capacity of professional expertise, and the other party relies on the advice for his future conduct.

EXTRACT ADAPTED FROM THE JUDGMENT IN *HEDLEY BYRNE & CO LTD V HELLER & PARTNERS LTD* [1964] AC 465, HL

Hedley Byrne were advertisers who were approached by a small company, Easipower, to prepare an advertising campaign. They approached that company's bank for a credit reference. The reference said that Easipower were 'good for normal business'. In fact Easipower went into liquidation and Hedley Byrne lost money as a result. They sued the bank for failing to check Easipower's current financial status properly. They failed because of a valid disclaimer of liability included in the reference. The House of Lords, however, accepted in principle that there could be an action.

LORD REID

A reasonable man, knowing that he was being trusted or that his skill and judgment were being relied on, would, I think, have three courses open to him. He could keep silent or decline to give the information or advice sought: or he could give an answer with a clear qualification that he accepted no responsibility for it or that it was given without that reflection or inquiry which a careful answer would require: or he could simply answer without any such qualification. If he chooses to adopt the last course he must, I think, be held to have accepted some responsibility for his answer being given carefully, or to have accepted a relationship with the inquirer which requires him to exercise such care as the circumstances require.

LORD PEARCE

Was there such a special relationship in the present case as to impose on the defendants a duty of care to the plaintiffs? The answer depends on the circumstances of the transaction. To import such a duty the representation must normally, I think, concern a business or professional transaction whose nature makes clear the gravity of the inquiry and the importance and influence attached to the answer. A most important circumstance is the form of the inquiry and of the answer. Both were here plainly stated to be without liability.

EXTRACT ADAPTED FROM THE JUDGMENT IN *SMITH V ERIC S BUSH* [1990] 1 AC 831, HL

Mrs Smith bought a house on a mortgage with the Abbey National Building Society. They ordered a valuation carried out by a surveyor hired by the society but paid for by Mrs Bush. The valuation was negligent in that, while the surveyor noticed that chimney breasts had been removed, he failed to check whether the walls above were properly supported. They were not, the chimney later fell into the main bedroom, and Mrs Smith claimed in negligent misstatement. The surveyor's argument that there was no duty owed to Mrs Smith failed on appeal since it was clear that she would rely on the survey although the contract for the valuation was between the surveyor and the building society.

LORD TEMPLEMAN

The common law imposes on a person who contracts to carry out an operation an obligation to exercise reasonable skill and care.

A valuer who values property as a security for a mortgage is liable either in contract or tort to the mortgagee for any failure on the part of the valuer to exercise reasonable skill and care in the valuation. The valuer is liable in contract if he receives instructions from and is paid by the mortgagee. The valuer is liable in tort if he receives instructions from and is paid by the mortgagee but knows that the valuation is for the purpose of a mortgage and will be relied upon by the mortgagee. The duty of professional men 'is not merely a duty to use care in their reports. They have also a duty to use care in their work which results in their reports'.

I agree that by obtaining and disclosing a valuation, a mortgagee does not assume responsibility to the purchaser for that valuation. But ... the valuer assumes responsibility to both mortgagee and purchaser by agreeing to carry out a valuation for mortgage purposes knowing that the valuation fee has been paid by the purchaser and ... that the valuation will probably be relied upon by the purchaser in order to decide whether or not to ... purchase the house.

The contractual duty of a valuer to value a house for the Abbey National did not prevent the valuer coming under a tortious duty to Mrs Smith who was furnished with a report of the valuer and relied upon the report.

In general I am of the opinion that in the absence of a disclaimer of liability the valuer who values houses for the purpose of a mortgage, knowing that the mortgagee will rely and the mortgagor will probably rely on the valuation, knowing that the purchaser mortgagor has in effect paid for the valuation, is under a duty to exercise reasonable skill and care and that duty is owed to both parties on the mortgage . . .

Questions

Read the two extracts above and answer the questions.

1. What choices does Lord Reid, in *Hedley Byrne*, think are open to a person who is called on to give advice to a party who will rely on it?
2. What relationships does Lord Pearce, in *Hedley Byrne*, see as the basis of establishing a duty situation for the tort?
3. What did Lord Templeman, in *Smith v Eric S Bush*, think that the full extent of the duty owed by the valuer was?
4. Why were the Smiths able to claim against the valuer in the case?
5. Having studied both judgments what are the three necessary requirements for a successful action to be bought under the *Hedley Byrne* principle?

SECTION 5: NEGLIGENCE: NOVEL DUTY SITUATIONS: PURE ECONOMIC LOSS

The traditional position was that the courts would not allow a claimant to recover for a pure economic loss, i.e. a loss of profit, because that was really more appropriate to contract law. The cases of *Anns* and *Junior Books* did seem to reverse this position for a while. However, the position now is that there can be no recovery for economic loss unless it is accompanied by physical damage or personal injury.

EXTRACT ADAPTED FROM THE JUDGMENT IN *SPARTAN STEEL ALLOYS V MARTIN & CO LTD* [1973] 1QB 27

The defendants negligently cut through an electricity cable while they were digging a road. This cut the electricity supply to the claimant's factory. The claimants lost the 'melt' that was already in their furnace. They also claimed for lost profit for their lost production while the supply was being reconnected. They succeeded in their claim for the physical damage but the lost profit, which was pure economic loss was not recoverable.

EXTRACT ADAPTED FROM THE JUDGMENT IN *MURPHY V BRENTWOOD DISTRICT COUNCIL* [1991] AC 398, HL

The claimant had bought a house built on a concrete raft that proved to be of inadequate construction leading to the house subsiding and cracks appearing in the walls. The claimant then was forced to sell the house for £35,000 less than it would have fetched without the defects. He then sued the local authority for negligently approving the construction of the concrete raft. In the House of Lords his claim was said to involve pure economic loss and the local authority's appeal succeeded.

LORD BRIDGE

If a manufacturer negligently puts into circulation a chattel containing a latent defect which renders it dangerous to persons or property, the manufacturer, on the well known principles established by *Donoghue v Stevenson*, will be liable in tort for injury to persons or damage to property which the chattel causes. But if a manufacturer produces and sells a chattel which is merely defective in quality, even to the extent that it is valueless for the purpose for which it is intended, the manufacturer's liability at common law arises only under and by reference to the terms of any contract to which he is a party in relation to the chattel; the common law does not impose on him any liability in tort to persons to whom he owes no duty in contract but who, having acquired the chattel, suffer economic loss because the chattel is defective in quality. If a dangerous defect in a chattel is discovered before it causes any personal injury or damage to property, because the danger is now known and the chattel cannot safely be used unless the defect is repaired, the defect becomes merely a defect in quality. The chattel is either capable of repair at economic cost or it is worthless and must be scrapped. In either case the loss sustained by the owner or hirer of the chattel is purely economic. It is recoverable against any party who owes the loser a relevant contractual duty. But it is not recoverable in tort . . .

Questions

1. What reasons does Lord Bridge give in *Murphy v Brentwood* why there should be no liability for 'pure economic loss'?
2. In what circumstances does he say that a claim is still possible?

SECTION 6: NEGLIGENCE: NOVEL DUTY SITUATIONS: NERVOUS SHOCK

It was originally impossible to recover for nervous shock while understanding of psychiatric disorders was still limited. A claimant will only be able to recover where the damage is a recognised psychiatric illness. The law distinguishes between primary victims, those present at the scene and injured or at risk of injury, and secondary victims, those who have some close tie of love and affection to an actual victim at the scene, and who are present at the scene or its immediate aftermath.

EXTRACT ADAPTED FROM 'DAMAGES FOR PSYCHIATRIC INJURIES', ANDREW RITCHIE, *NEW LAW JOURNAL*, 9 DECEMBER 1994

Nervous shock is a legal term covering a wide range of psychiatric injuries caused in a particular way for which the courts award damages. It encompasses various illnesses recognised by medical experts. For example: depression, post traumatic stress disorder, agoraphobia, paranoia, psychosis, personality change, phobia of driving, anxiety neurosis, etc.

In *Attia v British Gas* Bingham LJ said of nervous shock: 'Judges have in recent years become increasingly restive at the use of this misleading and inaccurate expression, and I shall use the general expression 'psychiatric damage' intending to comprehend within it all relevant forms of mental illness, neurosis and personality change.'

It is more than mere grief or distress, disgust or unhappiness, or fear either for one's own safety or that of others. In *McLoughlin v O'Brien* Lord Bridge stated that a plaintiff can recover: 'no damages for . . . emotional distress . . . when someone he loves is killed or injured. Anxiety and depression are normal human emotions. Yet an anxiety neurosis or a reactive depression may be recognisable psychiatric illness . . . so the first hurdle which a plaintiff must surmount is to establish that he is suffering not merely grief . . . but a positive psychiatric illness.'

Lawyers use the term nervous shock because, if the plaintiff is to recover damages for his psychiatric illness, he must prove that the cause of the condition was shock . . . seeing or experiencing an accident or disaster caused by the defendant's tortious act or omission.

A person suffering direct physical injury alongside nervous shock will recover for both. Where no direct physical injury was suffered then there are three elements which the plaintiff must prove to succeed in a nervous shock claim:

1 He suffered a psychiatric illness.
2 From a horrifying event.
3 He was close enough to the accident to be allowed to claim.

To recover the plaintiff must establish that a reasonably strong willed person would have suffered some psychiatric illness in the circumstances.

In most cases the evidence of a consultant psychiatrist who is experienced in the preparation of medico-legal reports is essential. ...

In some cases medical experts should be provided with a brief summary of the relevant law so that they understand that mere grief, stress or depression are not compensatable. It matters not that the plaintiff had a pre-disposition to psychiatric illness (an egg shell personality)—if it was foreseeable that he would suffer some psychiatric illness then damages will be awarded for the full extent of his suffering.

The plaintiff will also need to prove that he experienced a horrifying event. 'Shock ... involves the sudden appreciation by sight or sound of a horrifying event, which violently agitates the mind.' Per Lord Ackner in *Allcock v Chief Constable of South Yorkshire.*

The law does not yet award damages for psychiatric illness caused by the gradual accumulation of horror over a period of time. So caring for a dying person after an accident does not yet lead to damages even if the person caring, quite reasonably, suffered psychiatric illness as a result.

EXTRACT ADAPTED FROM THE JUDGMENT IN *ALCOCK V CHIEF CONSTABLE OF SOUTH YORKSHIRE. HOUSE OF LORDS* [1992] 3 WLR 1057

The case involved an FA Cup semi-final football match between Liverpool and Nottingham Forest at the Hillsborough Stadium in Sheffield. Shortly before kick-off the police opened the gates to allow a large crowd of supporters into a caged section of the ground that was already full. 95 people were killed in the crush that followed and over 400 were injured. Since the match was due to be televised the tragedy was shown on live TV. A number of relatives of the victims made claims against the police for psychiatric injuries. Their proximity to the events varied with some being present at the match, some hearing commentary of the disaster on radio and some seeing it on the television. The relationships with the victims also varied, with some being close relatives of the victims and some being friends. The House of Lords dismissed their appeals and held that the defendants did not owe a duty of care.

LORD ACKNER

It is now generally accepted that an analysis of the reported cases of nervous shock establishes that it is a type of claim in a category of its own. Shock is no longer a variant of physical injury but a separate kind of damage.

Because 'shock' in its nature is capable of affecting such a wide range of persons, Lord Wilberforce in *McLoughlin v O'Brian* [1983] concluded that there was a real need for the law to place some limitation upon the extent of admissible claims and ... he considered that there were three elements inherent in any claim.

...

(1) the class of persons whose claims should be recognised; (2) the proximity of such persons to the accident—in time and space; (3) the means by which the shock has been caused.

(1) The class of persons whose claims should be recognised

... Lord Wilberforce ... contrasted the closest of family ties—parent and child and husband and wife—with that of the ordinary bystander. As regards claims by those in the close family relationships. ... the justifications for admitting such claims is the presumption, ... I would accept as being rebuttable, that the love and affection normally associated with persons in those relationships is such that a defendant ought reasonably contemplate that they may be so closely and directly affected by his conduct as to suffer shock resulting in psychiatric illness. While as a generalisation more remote relatives and friends can reasonably be expected not to suffer illness from the shock, there can well be relatives and friends whose relationship is so close and intimate that their love and affection for the victim is comparable ...

(2) The proximity of the plaintiff to the accident

It is accepted that the proximity to the accident must be close both in time and space. Direct and immediate sight or hearing of the accident is not required. It is reasonably foreseeable that injury by shock can be caused to a plaintiff, not only through the sight or hearing of the event, but of its immediate aftermath.

Only two of the plaintiffs before us were at the ground. However, it is clear from *McLoughlin v O'Brian* ... that there may be liability where subsequent identification can be regarded as part of the 'immediate aftermath' of the accident. Mr Alcock identified his brother-in-law in a bad condition in the mortuary ... eight hours after the accident. This was the earliest of the identification cases. Even if this identification could be described as part of the 'aftermath', it could not in my judgment be described as part of the *immediate* aftermath.

(3) The means by which the shock is caused

Lord Wilberforce concluded that the shock must come through sight or hearing of the event or its immediate aftermath ... Of course it is common ground that it was clearly foreseeable by the defendant that the scenes at Hillsborough would be broadcast live and that amongst those who would be watching would be parents and spouses and other relatives and friends of those in the pens behind the Leppings Lane end. However he would also know of the code of ethics which the television authorities televising this event could be expected to follow, namely that they would not show pictures of suffering by recognisable individuals. Had they done so ... this would have been a 'novus actus' breaking the chain of causation between the defendants alleged breach of duty and the psychiatric illness ... there were no such pictures. Although the television pictures certainly gave rise to feelings of the deepest anxiety and distress, in the circumstances of this case the simultaneous television broadcasts of what occurred cannot be equated with the 'sight or hearing of the event or its immediate aftermath'. Accordingly shocks sustained by reason of these broadcasts cannot found a claim. I agree, however, with Nolan LJ that simultaneous broadcasts of a disaster cannot in all cases be ruled out as providing the equivalent of actual sight or hearing of the event or its immediate aftermath.

Questions

Read the two extracts above and answer the questions.

1. According to Andrew Ritchie's article, what sorts of illnesses or problems can be classed as 'nervous shock', and which ones cannot?
2. What does the article suggest is a better or more accurate term?
3. What does Andrew Ritchie conclude would be a more effective way of dealing with proving nervous shock? Is this a sensible suggestion?
4. In the *Allcock* case what does Lord Ackner say was Lord Wilberforce's reasoning in *McLoughlin v O'Brian* for wanting to limit the classes of people who can claim for nervous shock?

5 In *Allcock* how do the defence and the plaintiffs differ in the conclusions that they think should be drawn from the testing of the three elements?

6 How close must a relationship be with the victim of an accident in order to claim nervous shock?

7 Why was proximity in time and space such an important test to the plaintiffs in the *Allcock* case?

8 Who would be responsible if close up pictures of the suffering of recognisable individuals were shown on live television?

9 Is it fair that a bystander should be treated any differently than any other person present at the scene or immediate aftermath of an accident?

SECTION 7: NEGLIGENCE: NOVEL DUTY SITUATIONS: OMISSIONS

Generally, the law does not impose liability for what we do not do but rather for what we negligently have done. There are exceptions when because of specific types of relationship a duty to act is imposed. In the event of a failure to act in these circumstances a defendant can be liable for the consequences.

EXTRACT ADAPTED FROM THE JUDGMENT IN *SMITH V LITTLEWOODS ORGANISATION LTD* [1987] AC 1, HL

The organisation bought a cinema which they then left empty over several months. The building was regularly broken into and vandalised, which was known to contractors working for Littlewoods but not to Littlewoods themselves. At one stage a fire was started and this spread to nearby premises. A claim that Littlewoods were responsible for the damage caused because they failed to stop it was unsuccessful, since Littlewoods knew nothing about it and so did not owe a duty of care.

LORD GOFF

. . . a problem arises when the pursuer is seeking to hold the defender responsible for having failed to *prevent* a third party from causing damage to the pursuer or his property by the third party's own deliberate wrongdoing. In such a case, it is not possible to invoke a general duty of care: for it is well recognised that there is no *general* duty of care to prevent third parties from causing such damage.

That there are special circumstances in which a defender may be held responsible in law for injuries suffered by the pursuer through a third party's deliberate wrongdoing is not in doubt. For example a duty of care may arise from a relationship between the parties, which gives rise to an imposition or assumption of responsibility upon or by the defender, as in *Stansbie v Troman,* where such responsibility was said to arise from a contract. In that case a decorator, left alone on the premises by the householder's wife, was held liable when he went out leaving the door on the latch, and a thief entered the house and stole property.

But there is a more general circumstance in which a defender may be held liable in negligence to the pursuer although the immediate cause of the damage suffered by the pursuer is the deliberate wrongdoing of another. This may occur where the defender negligently causes or permits to be created a source of danger, and it is reasonably foreseeable that third parties may interfere with it and, sparking off the danger, thereby cause damage to persons in the position of the pursuer. The classic example of such a case is, perhaps, *Haynes v Harwood,* where the defendant's carter left a horse-drawn van unattended in a crowded street, and the horses bolted when a boy threw a stone at them. A police officer who suffered injury in stopping the horses ... was held to be entitled to recover damages from the defendant.

There is another basis upon which a defender may be held liable for damage to neighbouring property caused by a fire started on his (the defender's) property by the deliberate wrongdoing of a third party. This arises where he has knowledge or means of knowledge that a third party has created or is creating a risk of fire, or indeed has started a fire, on his premises, and then fails to take such steps as are reasonably open to him (in the limited sense explained by Lord Wilberforce in Goldman v Hargrave) to prevent any such fire from damaging neighbouring property. If, for example, an occupier of property has knowledge, or means of knowledge, that intruders are in the habit of trespassing upon his property and starting fires there, thereby creating a risk that fire may spread to and damage neighbouring property, a duty to take reasonable steps to prevent such damage may be held to fall upon him.

I wish to emphasise that I do not think that the problem in these cases can be solved simply through the mechanism of foreseeability. When a duty is cast upon a person to take precautions against the wrongdoing of third parties, the ordinary standard of foreseeability applies and so the possibility of such wrongdoing does not have to be very great before liability is imposed. So, for example, in Haynes v Harwood, liability was imposed although it cannot have been at all likely that a small boy would throw a stone at the horses left unattended; and in Stansbie v Troman, liability was imposed although it cannot have been at all likely that a thief would take advantage of the fact that the defendant left the door on the latch while he was out. Per contra, there is at present no general duty at common law to prevent persons from harming others by their deliberate wrongdoings, however foreseeable such harm may be if the defender does not take steps to prevent it.

Questions

1. What does Lord Goff say is the basic principle concerning liability for omissions or failures to act?
2. In what circumstances, according to Lord Goff, will a defendant be liable for the deliberate wrongdoings of a third party?
3. How does this amount to a failure to act by the defendant?

Activity

Consider whether there may be a duty to act in the following situations that could lead to an action in negligence for a failure to act:

1. Aaron sees Jane drowning in the pond in a park. He walks past and ignores her plight.
2. Simone gives her next door neighbour, Belinda, the key to her house while she is on holiday so that she can feed the fish. After one visit Belinda forgets to lock the door after leaving and burglars get in.
3. In a very cold winter Sid leaves his coal fire burning while he goes to the shops. While he is away burglars break in. Finding nothing to steal, they kick the burning coals around the room. This causes the house to catch fire and the fire spreads to next door, causing that house to burn to the ground.
4. Builders demolishing old properties regularly have large fires and leave them burning when they leave at night. On a number of occasions these fires have got out of control when, known to the builders, local children have kicked the burning material around. On this occasion the children set fire to occupied houses nearby.

SECTION 8: TRESPASS TO LAND

Trespass is one of the oldest torts. A trespass is a direct interference with someone's land. A person's rights in their land can extend even to the sub-soil below and the air space above, at least subject to certain statutory interventions.

EXTRACT ADAPTED FROM THE JUDGMENT IN *DELANEY V T P SMITH LTD* [1946] KB 393

Under an oral agreement the plaintiff was to become the tenant of the defendant's war damaged house once repairs were done to it. In fact the plaintiff entered the house secretly before the repairs were completed. The defendant then forcibly ejected him and the plaintiff brought an action for trespass. He succeeded in the county court because of the informal agreement.

TUCKER LJ

It is no doubt true that a plaintiff in an action for trespass to land need only in the first instance allege possession. This is sufficient to support his action against a wrongdoer, but it is not sufficient ... as against the lawful owner, and in an action against the freeholder the plaintiff must at some stage of the pleadings set up a title derived from the defendant.

EXTRACT ADAPTED FROM THE JUDGMENT IN *BERNSTEIN OF LEIGH (BARON) V SKYVIEWS AND GENERAL LTD* [1978] QB 479

The defendants were in the business of aerial photography. They took a photograph of the plaintiff's country house and then tried to sell it to him. He was annoyed and brought an action for trespass claiming that the defendants had unlawfully invaded his air space. His action failed.

GRIFFITHS J

The plaintiff claims that as owner of the land he is also owner of the air space above the land, or at least he has the right to exclude any entry into the air space above his land. He relies on the old Latin maxim, *cujus est solum ejus est usque ad coleum et ad inferos*... There are a number of cases in which the maxim has been used by English judges but an examination of those cases shows that they have all been concerned with structures attached to the adjoining land, such as overhanging buildings, signs or telegraph wires, and for their solution it has not been necessary for the judge to cast his eyes towards the heavens; he has been concerned with the rights of the owner in the air space immediately adjacent to the surface of the land.

That an owner has certain rights in the air space above his land is well established by authority. He has the right to lop the branches of trees that may overhang his boundary... In *Wandsworth Board of Works v United Telephone Co* [1884] the Court of Appeal did not doubt that the owner of land would have the right to cut a wire placed over his land.

In *Gifford v Dent* [1926] Romer J held that it was a trespass to erect a sign that projected four feet eight inches over the plaintiff's forecourt and ordered it to be removed. He invoked the old maxim in his judgment. That decision was followed by McNair J in *Kelsen v Imperial Tobacco Co Ltd* [1957] in which he granted a mandatory injunction ordering the defendant to remove a sign which projected only eight inches over the plaintiff's property.

I can find no support in authority for the view that a landowner's rights in the air space above his property extend to an unlimited height. In *Wandsworth Board of Works v United Telephone Co* Bowen LJ described the maxim, *usque ad coleum*, as a fanciful notion leading to the absurdity of a trespass at common law being committed by a satellite every time it passes over a suburban garden. The problem is to balance the rights of an owner to enjoy the use of his land against the rights of the general public to take advantage of all that science now offers in the use of air space. This balance is in my judgment best struck in our present society by restricting the rights of an owner in the air space above his land to such height as is necessary for the ordinary use and enjoyment of his land and the structures on it, and declaring that above that height he has no greater right in the air space than any other member of the public.

... The plaintiff's complaint is not that the aircraft interfered with the use of his land but that a photograph was taken from it. There is, however, no law against taking a photograph, and the mere taking of a photograph cannot turn an act which is not a trespass into the plaintiff's air space into one that is a trespass.

Questions

Read the three extracts above and answer the questions.

1. Why was the claimant unsuccessful in *Delaney v Smith*?
2. Why did Lord Bernstein fail in his action?
3. What do you understand by the maxim *cujus est solum ejus est usque ad coleum*?
4. How far do rights in the land extend in any direction?

SECTION 9: NUISANCE

Nuisance is generally an indirect interference with a person's enjoyment of their land. Because it involves competing claims by neighbours it is called the 'law of give and take' and subject to policy considerations. Generally interferences are only actionable if they are unreasonable. Factors such as the location of the property and the duration of the nuisance are important. A nuisance that causes damage is more likely to be actionable. The courts are reluctant to allow actions where the interference is only with a recreational use of land. Generally the action is available only to a person with a proprietary interest in the land.

EXTRACT ADAPTED FROM THE JUDGMENT IN *ST. HELEN'S SMELTING CO V TIPPING* [1865] 11 ER 1483, HL

Tipping bought an estate that was very valuable. Soon after he bought the estate a smelting works situated nearby, the use of which was uncertain when he bought the land, began extensive smelting operations. Tipping complained, not only of inconvenience in inhaling the vapours, but also that smuts from the process caused physical damage to shrubs and trees on his estate. Despite the locality and the prescriptive right claimed by the defendant, Tipping won the case and the appeals.

LORD WESTBURY LC

My Lords, in matters of this description it appears to me that it is a very desirable thing to mark the difference between an action brought for a nuisance upon the ground that the alleged nuisance produces material injury to the property, and an action brought for a nuisance on the ground that the thing alleged to be a nuisance is productive of sensible personal discomfort. With regard to the latter, namely, the personal inconvenience and interference with one's enjoyment, one's quiet, one's personal freedom, anything that discomposes or injuriously affects the senses or the nerves, whether that may or may not be denominated a nuisance, must undoubtedly depend greatly on the circumstances of the place where the thing complained of actually occurs. If a man lives in a town, it is necessary that he should subject himself to the consequences of those operations of trade which may be carried on in his immediate locality, which are actually necessary for trade and commerce, and also for the enjoyment of property, and for the benefit of the inhabitants of the town and of the public at large.

... But when an occupation is carried on by one person in the neighbourhood of another, and the result of that trade, ... occupation, or business, is material injury to property, ... there unquestionably arises a very different consideration.

Now, in the present case, it appears that the plaintiff purchased a very valuable estate, which lies within a mile and a half from certain large smelting works. Of the effect of the vapours exhaling from those works upon the plaintiff's property, and the injury done to his trees and shrubs, there is an abundance of evidence in the case.

The only ground upon which your Lordships are asked to set aside the verdict is that the whole neighbourhood where these copper smelting works were carried on, is ... more or less devoted to manufacturing purposes of a similar kind, and therefore it is said, that inasmuch as this copper smelting is carried on in what the appellant contends is a fit place, it may be carried on with impunity, although the result may be the destruction, or ... very considerable diminution of the value of the plaintiff's property. That is not the meaning of the word 'suitable', or ... of the word 'convenient', which has been used as applicable to the subject. The word 'suitable' unquestionably cannot carry with it this consequence, that a trade may be carried on ... the consequence of which ... may be injury and destruction to the neighbouring property.

EXTRACT ADAPTED FROM THE JUDGMENT IN *MILLER V JACKSON* [1977] QB 966, CA

New houses were built next to a cricket ground that had been in use for seventy years. The plaintiff bought one of these houses and became annoyed with cricket balls landing in his garden, the pitch being only 102 feet away. The club then erected a high wire fence to try to avoid cricket balls from going over. However, a few balls still came over despite batsmen being asked to avoid hitting in the direction of the plaintiff's garden as much as was possible. The plaintiff sought an injunction to prevent cricket from being played. The trial judge granted the injunction. The Court of Appeal held that there was an actionable nuisance. Lord Denning MR and Cumming-Bruce LJ, in the majority, however, granted the defendant's appeal and refused to grant the injunction on the grounds of public policy.

GEOFFREY LANE LJ

There is here in effect no dispute that there has been and is likely to be in the future an interference with the plaintiffs' enjoyment of no. 20 Brackenridge. The only question is whether it is unreasonable. It is a truism to say that this is a matter of degree. ... A balance has to be struck between on the one hand the rights of the individual to enjoy his house and garden without the threat of damage and on the other hand the rights of the public in general or a neighbour to engage in lawful pastimes. Difficult questions may sometimes arise when the defendants' activities are offensive to the sense, for example by way of noise. Where, as here, the damage or potential damage is physical the answer is more simple. There is ... no excuse I can see which exonerates the defendants from liability in nuisance for what they have done or for what they threaten to do.

There is, however, one obviously strong point in the defendants' favour. They or their predecessors have been playing cricket on this ground (and no doubt hitting sixes out of it) for 70 years or so. Precedent apart, justice would seem to demand that the plaintiffs should be left to make the most of the site they have elected to occupy with all its obvious advantages and all its equally obvious disadvantages. ... It does not seem just that a long-established activity, in itself innocuous, should be brought to an end because someone chooses to build a house nearby and so turn an innocent pastime into actionable nuisance. Unfortunately, however, the question is not open. In *Sturges v Bridgman* ... this very problem arose. It may be that this rule works injustice, ... we are bound by the decision.

LORD DENNING MR

This case is new. It should be approached on principles applicable to modern conditions. There is a contest here between the interest of the public at large and the interest of a private individual. The *public* interest lies in protecting the environment by preserving our playing fields in the face of mounting development, and by enabling our youth to enjoy all the benefits of outdoor games, such as cricket and football. The *private* interest lies in securing the privacy of his home and garden without intrusions or interference from anyone. In deciding between these two conflicting interests, it must be remembered that it is not a question of damages. If by a million-to-one chance a cricket ball does go out of the ground and cause damage the cricket club will pay. No, it is a question of an injunction. And in our law you will find it repeatedly affirmed that an injunction is a discretionary remedy. In a new situation like this, we have to think afresh as to how discretion should be exercised.

As between their conflicting interests, I am of the opinion that the public interest should prevail over the private interest. The cricket club should not be driven out. In my opinion the right exercise of discretion is to refuse an injunction . . .

EXTRACT ADAPTED FROM 'RIGHT, PRIVILEGE OR PASTIME?', BILL THOMAS, *THE LEGAL EXECUTIVE JOURNAL*, JULY 1997

Do you regard the opportunity to watch television as a right, a privilege or merely a pastime?

. . . the House of Lords had to consider that question in *Hunter v Canary Wharf Ltd.*

There were two issues before their Lordships: (a) whether putting up a large building which blocked television signals amounted to a nuisance; (b) who was had the right to sue for that tort.

The first point has far-reaching consequences. The construction of the Canary Wharf building—250 metres high and over 50 metres square—directly interfered with the reception of television signals by hundreds of people. The tower was between their homes and the transmitter.

We are all familiar with rights of air and light; the law recognises that such rights exist and will in appropriate cases protect them. Is there nowadays a right to be able to receive the necessary electronics so as to be able to watch the 'box'?

In 1965, there was a decision in which the judge held that the court would take judicial notice of the fact that the reception of television had become a 'very common feature of domestic life'; *Bridlington Relay v Yorkshire Electricity Board.*

There a relay television company sought an injunction against the electricity board to restrain them from electrifying a cable which might interfere with reception.

In the *Canary Wharf* case, the House of Lords decided that no action lay in private nuisance when the presence of a building interfered with television reception. They stated the well known principle that (subject to planning approval) a man was entitled to build what he liked on his own land . . . That the tower got in the way of the direct signal was not enough to found a claim.

The second issue was to decide who could sue in nuisance. The conclusion repeated the generally accepted legal proposition that only a person who is in possession of the adversely affected land could sue: . . . .

In *Hunter v Canary Wharf,* the Law Lords held that the only person who could sue (and there was a total of 690 plaintiffs) were those who owned or were tenants of properties. The parties had included wives, husbands, partners, children and other relatives but, however much their ability to watch television had been interfered with, they had no 'proprietary interest' and thus no right of action. . . .

In restating the law in this way the House of Lords overturned the Appeal Court decision in *Khorasandjian v Bush* where the lower court had held that a woman—who was a mere licensee—was entitled to use the law of private nuisance to apply for an injunction to restrain someone from telephoning her at her parents' house.

. . .

The upshot is that putting up a large building which shields adjoining property from a television signal is not nuisance .... The situation parallels that of 'view'. The rule that a person is not entitled to a view goes back to the 16th century.

It is interesting to note that planning considerations played a large part in the formulation of the rule that no one is entitled to a view—just as it does in 1997, although the 'view' now is that of a television screen.

Questions

Read the above three extracts and answer the questions.

1. What does the case of *St Helens Smelting v Tipping* tell us about the importance of locality in the tort of private nuisance?
2. Why was the company liable for nuisance even though it was in an industrial area?
3. What does Lord Denning's judgment in *Miller v Jackson* tell us about the importance of 'public policy' in nuisance?
4. Since damage was caused in *Miller v Jackson* how can this be consistent with the judgment in *Tipping*?
5. What does Bill Thomas's article tell us about who can sue in nuisance?
6. Why did interference with TV signals in *Hunter v Canary Wharf* not amount to a nuisance according to the article?

SECTION 10: RYLANDS V FLETCHER

This tort is generally considered to be a form of strict liability that deals specifically with escapes of dangerous things accumulated on land which are likely to 'cause peril' if they do escape. Liability is restricted because it is also only possible where the accumulation of the dangerous thing amounts to a 'non-natural' use of land. There also must be an escape from land controlled by the defendant to land over which he has no control. More recently the House of Lords has suggested that the tort is a form of nuisance with a requirement that the damage caused by the escaping danger is foreseeable, making it seem similar to negligence.

EXTRACT ADAPTED FROM THE JUDGMENT IN *RYLANDS V FLETCHER* [1868] LR 3 HL 330; [1866] LR 1 EX 265.

The defendant hired contractors to construct a reservoir on his land to use for his mill. The contractors came across old mine shafts during excavations, did not realise that they were connected to a nearby mine and failed to fill them adequately. As a result water from the reservoir flooded the neighbouring mine. The defendant was held liable and appealed unsuccessfully.

BLACKBURN J (IN THE COURT OF EXCHEQUER CHAMBER)

The question of law therefore arises, what is the obligation which the law casts on a person who, like the defendants, lawfully brings onto his land something which, though harmless whilst it remains there, will naturally do mischief if it escapes out of his land. It is agreed on all hands that he must take care to keep in that which he has bought onto the land and keeps there, in order that it may not escape and damage his neighbours, but the question arises whether the duty which the law casts upon him, under such circumstances, is an absolute duty to keep it in at his peril, or is ... merely a duty to take all reasonable and prudent precautions, in order to keep it in, but no more. If the first be the law, the person who has brought on his land and kept there something dangerous, and failed to keep it in, is responsible for all the natural consequences of its escape. If the second be the limit of his duty, he would not be answerable except on proof of negligence, and consequently would not be answerable for escape arising from any latent defect which ordinary prudence and skill could not detect.

We think that the true rule of law is, that the person who for his own purposes, brings on his land and collects and keeps there anything likely to do mischief if it escapes, must keep it in at his peril; and if he does not do so, is prima facie answerable for all the damage which is the natural consequence of its escape. The person whose grass or corn is eaten down by the escaping cattle of his neighbour, or whose mine is flooded by the water from his neighbour's reservoir, or whose cellar is invaded by the filth of his neighbour's privy, or whose habitation is made unhealthy by the fumes and noisome vapours of his neighbour's alkali works, is damnified without any fault of his own; and it seems but reasonable and just that the neighbour, who has brought something on his own property which was not naturally there, harmless to others so long as it is confined to his own property, but which he knows to be mischievous if it gets on his neighbour's, should be obliged to make good the damage which ensues ...

LORD CAIRNS (IN THE HOUSE OF LORDS)

... if the defendants not stopping at the natural use of their close, had desired to use it for any purpose which I may term a non-natural use, ... and if in consequence of their doing so, or in consequence of any imperfection in the mode of their doing so, the water came to escape and pass off into the close of the plaintiff, then ... that which the defendants were doing they were doing at their own peril; and, if in the course of their doing it, the evil arose to which I have referred ... then for the consequence of that ... the defendants would be liable.

Questions

1. What does Blackburn J say is the key question to be asked about the duty in relation to bringing things onto land that may cause peril if they escape?
2. How would we now refer to the principle of an 'absolute duty' to keep the thing in?
3. What did Blackburn suggest would have been the result for liability in such circumstances if the majority view of the Court of Exchequer were taken?
4. What does Blackburn J have to say about proving fault?
5. What extra element is Lord Cairns introducing in the House of Lords in order for there to be liability?

EXTRACT ADAPTED FROM THE JUDGMENT IN *READ V J LYONS & CO* [1947] AC 156, HL

The plaintiff was an inspector for the government at an ordnance factory where shells were made. She was injured when a shell exploded and some workers were injured and one man was killed. She did not claim in negligence and won the case under *Rylands v Fletcher* at first instance. The House of Lords dismissed her claim.

VISCOUNT SIMON

Now, the strict liability recognised ... to exist in *Rylands v Fletcher* is conditioned by two elements which I may call the condition of 'escape' from the land of something likely to do mischief if it escapes, and the condition of 'non-natural use' of the land.

'Escape' for the purposes of applying the proposition in *Rylands v Fletcher* means escape from a place where the defendant has occupation of or control over land to a place which is outside his occupation or control. Blackburn J several times refers to the defendant's duty as being the duty of 'keeping a thing in' at the defendant's peril, and by 'keeping in' he does not mean preventing an explosive substance from exploding but preventing a thing which may inflict mischief from escaping from the area which the defendant occupies or controls.

EXTRACT ADAPTED FROM THE JUDGMENT IN *CAMBRIDGE WATER CO V EASTERN COUNTIES LEATHER* [1994] 2 AC 264

Chemicals used in the defendant's tanning process splashed onto the floor and over a long period seeped through concrete, into the ground. It eventually seeped into the ground water that then contaminated a bore hole more than a mile away from the tannery as the result of which the claimants had to drill a new hole. It was generally unforeseeable at the time that such small seepages of the chemical could have contaminated the water supply in this way.

LORD GOFF

Blackburn J spoke of 'anything likely to do mischief if it escapes'; and later he spoke of something 'which he knows to be mischievous if it gets on his neighbour's [property],' and the liability to 'answer for the natural *and anticipated* consequences.' Furthermore, time and again he spoke of the strict liability imposed upon the defendant as being that he must keep the thing in at his peril; and, when referring to liability in actions for damage occasioned by animals, he referred to the established principle that 'it is quite immaterial whether the escape is by negligence or not'. The general tenor of his statement of principle is therefore that knowledge, or at least foreseeability of the risk, is a prerequisite of the recovery of damages under the principle; but that the principle is one of strict liability in the sense that the defendant may be liable notwithstanding that he has exercised all due care to prevent the escape from occurring ... the historical connection with the law of nuisance must now be regarded as pointing towards the conclusion that foreseeability of damage is a prerequisite of the recovery of damages under the rule.

... it can be argued that the rule in *Rylands v Fletcher* should not be regarded simply as an extension of the law of nuisance, but should rather be treated as a developing principle of strict liability from which can be developed a general rule of strict liability for damage caused by ultra-hazardous operations, on the basis of which persons conducting such operations may properly be held strictly liable for the extraordinary risk to others involved in such operations.

... I incline to the opinion that, as a general rule, it is more appropriate for strict liability in respect of operations of high risk to be imposed by Parliament, than by the courts. If such liability is imposed by statute, the relevant activities can be identified, and those concerned can know where they stand. Furthermore, statute can where appropriate lay down precise criteria establishing the incidence and scope of such liability.

It is of particular relevance that the present case is concerned with environmental pollution. The protection of the environment is now perceived as being of crucial importance to the future of mankind; and public bodies are taking significant steps towards the establishment of legislation which will promote the protection of the environment, and make the polluter pay for damage ... for which he is responsible ... But it does not follow from these developments that a common law principle, such as *Rylands v Fletcher*, should be developed or rendered more strict to provide for liability in respect of such pollution.

Questions

Read the two extracts above and answer the questions.

1. In the light of the judicial comments in the last two cases what do you understand 'strict liability' to mean?
2. Lord Goff in *Cambridge Water* speaks of a 'step to contain the scope of liability under the rule' taken in *Read v Lyons*. To which limitation to the rule is Lord Goff referring?
3. In what ways is it possible to disagree with Viscount Simon's interpretation of Blackburn J's judgment on this point?
4. How does Lord Goff justify his requirement for a test of foreseeability also to be a part of the rule?
5. In what ways does this affect the principle of strict liability?
6. What are Lord Goff's justifications for leaving environmental protection to Parliament rather than common law principles?
7. In what ways is it possible for the rule still to be used for the protection of the environment?

SECTION 11: OCCUPIERS' LIABILITY ACTS

Occupiers' liability is a statutory form of negligence. An occupier is whoever is in control of the land. The 1957 Act applies where the occupier owes a common duty of care to all legitimate visitors to the premises. An occupier must take particular care of children whom the law acknowledges are more at risk because they lack the caution of adults. The 1984 Act operates in respect of trespassers.

EXTRACT FROM THE OCCUPIERS' LIABILITY ACT 1957

2.—(1) An occupier of premises owes the same duty, the 'common duty of care', to all his visitors, except in so far as he is free to and does extend, restrict, modify or exclude his duty to any visitor or visitors by agreement or otherwise.

(2) The common duty of care is a duty to take such care as in all the circumstances of the case is reasonable to see that the visitor will be reasonably safe in using the premises for the purposes for which he is invited or permitted by the occupier to be there.

(3) . . .

(a) an occupier must be prepared for children to be less careful than adults; and

(b) an occupier may expect that a person, in the exercise of his calling, will appreciate and guard against any special risks ordinarily incident to it, so far as the occupier leaves him free to do so.

(4) In determining whether the occupier of premises has discharged the common duty of care to a visitor, regard is to be had to all the circumstances, so that (for example)—

(a) where damage is caused to a visitor by a danger of which he had been warned by the occupier, the warning is not to be treated without more as absolving the occupier from liability, unless in all the circumstances it was enough to enable the visitor to be reasonably safe; and

(b) where damage is caused to a visitor by a danger due to the faulty execution of any work of construction, maintenance or repair by an independent contractor employed by the occupier, the occupier is not to be treated without more as answerable for the danger if in all the circumstances he had acted reasonably in entrusting the work to an independent contractor and had taken such steps (if any) as he reasonably ought in order to satisfy himself that the contractor was competent and that the work had been properly done.

(5) The common duty of care does not impose on an occupier any obligation to a visitor in respect of risks willingly accepted as his by the visitor . . .

EXTRACT ADAPTED FROM THE JUDGMENT IN *WHEAT V E LACON & CO LTD* [1966] AC 552

Lacon employed a manager in a public house that they owned. They allowed the manager to have lodgers in his private quarters. The lodger was killed when he fell on stairs in the manager's quarters without a proper handrail. At the time there was no bulb in the light so it was dark, but the court accepted that this was because a stranger had removed it. As a result, while the Court of Appeal held that the brewers owed the lodger a duty they were not liable in the case.

LORD DENNING

I ask myself whether the brewery company had a sufficient degree of control over the premises to put them under a duty to a visitor. Obviously they had complete control over the ground floor and were 'occupiers' of it. . . . I think that they had also sufficient control over the private portion. They had not let it out to Mr Richardson by a demise. They had only granted him a licence to occupy it, having a right themselves to do repairs. That left them with a residuary degree of control . . . They were . . . 'an occupier' within the meaning of the Act of 1957. Mr Richardson, who had a licence to occupy, also had a considerable degree of control. So had Mrs Richardson, who catered for summer guests. All three . . . were . . . 'occupiers' of the private portion of the 'Golfer's Arms'. There is no difficulty in having more than one occupier at one and the same time, each of which is under a duty of care to visitors.

. . . Each was under a duty to take such care as 'in all the circumstances of the case' is reasonable to see that the visitor will be reasonably safe.

Questions

Read the two extracts above and answer the questions.

1. Explain whether, according to the Act, an occupier is obliged to keep his/her premises safe.
2. What common law defence in tort is s2(5) describing? In what situations will an occupier usually be able to claim this defence?
3. Try to give examples of when an occupier will and will not be liable for the torts of independent contractors as described in s2(4)(b).
4. According to the case of *Wheat v Lacon*, who exactly is an 'occupier' under the Act?
5. In what ways does the case suggest that is it possible for there be more than one occupier of land?

Activity

Consider whether the following will be classed as visitors under the Occupiers' Liability Act 1957:

1. George is a meter reader who has fallen down an unlit staircase in Bernard's cellar where the meter is located.
2. Trevor is the ten-year-old son of Malcolm's friends who have been invited to a party. Trevor has wandered into Malcolm's shed and cut himself on some broken glass lying on the floor.
3. Alison is a postwoman who has fallen down an uncovered trench in Horace's garden. After posting letters she had strayed from the path to smell some lavender growing in the garden.

EXTRACT ADAPTED FROM THE JUDGMENT IN *PHIPPS V ROCHESTER* CORPORATION [1955] 1 QB 450

A brother and sister aged five and seven respectively went on to land on which building was to take place. The boy was injured when he fell down a nine-foot deep trench. The council, as occupiers, were not liable for the boy's broken leg because they were entitled to suppose that children of such a tender age would be under some parental supervision.

DEVLIN J

The law recognises . . . a sharp difference between children and adults. But there might well, I think, be an equally marked distinction between 'big children' and 'little children'. When it comes to taking care of themselves, there is a greater difference between big and little children than there is between big children and adults, and much justification for putting little children into a separate category . . . the licensor is not entitled to assume that all children will, unless they are allured, behave like adults; but he is entitled to assume that normally little children will be accompanied by a responsible person and to discharge his duty of warning accordingly.

I think that it would be an unjustifiable restriction of the principle if one were to say that although the licensor may in determining the extent of his duty have regard to the fact that it is the habit, and also the duty, of prudent people to look after themselves, he may not in that determination have a similar regard to the fact that it is the habit, and also the duty, of prudent people to look after their little children.

No doubt there are places where little children go to play unaccompanied. If the licensor knows or ought to anticipate that, he may have to take steps accordingly. But the responsibility for the safety of little children must rest primarily upon the parents; it is their duty to see that such children are not allowed to wander about by themselves, or at the least to satisfy themselves that the places to which they do allow their children to go unaccompanied are safe for them to go. It would not be socially desirable if parents were, as a matter of course, able to shift the burden of looking after their children from their own shoulders to those persons who happen to have accessible bits of land.

EXTRACT ADAPTED FROM THE JUDGMENT IN *JOLLEY V LONDON BOROUGH OF SUTTON, NLJ REPORTS*, 19 JUNE 1998

A boat was left abandoned and rotting on council land for two years. A 14-year-old boy and his friend then decided to jack it up with a car jack and repair it. The boy suffered a spine injury and was left paraplegic when the boat fell on him. The judge considered the boat to be an 'allurement' and awarded damages, reducing them by 25 per cent for contributory negligence. The Court of Appeal held that there could be no liability since the damage was not a foreseeable consequence of the allurement.

LORD WOOLF MR

The council did not dispute they were negligent. The principle issue on the appeal was whether the council should have foreseen the accident which caused J's injuries.

It was common ground that the council owed to J, as a visitor, the 'common duty of care' as defined in s2 of the Occupiers' Liability Act 1957 which provided by s2(2)(a) that it had to 'be prepared for children to be less careful than adults'.

It was a combination of the attractiveness of the boat to the children and its dangerous condition that made it the duty of the council to have the boat removed. It failed to do that and in that respect it was negligent. However, those features were not established to be part of the causing of the accident. The immediate cause of the accident was that the two boys jacked and propped up the boat so that they could work underneath it and did so in a way that meant that the boat was unstable and could and did fall on J.

Even making full allowance for the unpredictability of children's behaviour, it was not reasonably foreseeable that an accident could occur as a result of the boys deciding to work under a propped-up boat. Nor could any similar accident have been foreseen. Ironically the state of the boat was so poor that it made it less likely that it would be repairable or that the boys would embark on doing the necessary repairs. In deciding whether the accident was foreseeable it was important not only to consider the precise accident which occurred but the class of accident.

An accident of the kind which J sustained could only occur because together with his friend, he behaved in a way which was not capable of being reasonably anticipated.

Questions

Read the two extracts above and answer the questions.

1. In what ways does the Occupiers' Liability Act 1957 suggest that children should be treated differently from adults?
2. For what reasons did the child's action fail in *Phipps v Rochester Corporation*?
3. Does this suggest that a different duty is owed to different children?
4. In the light of the case of *Jolley* what do you understand an 'allurement' to be, and what effect will this have on an occupier's duty to a child visitor?
5. What do you think that the judgment in *Jolley* tells us about the relationship between occupiers' liability and negligence?

Extract from the Occupiers' Liability Act 1984

1. Duty of occupier to persons other than his visitors

. . .

(3) An occupier of premises owes a duty to another (not being his visitor) in respect of any such risk as is referred to in subsection (1) above if—

(a) he is aware of the danger or has reasonable grounds to believe that it exists;

(b) he knows or has reasonable grounds to believe that the other is in the vicinity of the danger concerned or that he may come into the vicinity of the danger (in either case, whether the other has lawful authority for being in the vicinity or not); and

(c) the risk is one which, in all the circumstances of the case, he may be reasonably expected to offer the other some protection.

(4) Where by virtue of this section an occupier of premises owes a duty to another in respect of such a risk, the duty is to take such care as is reasonable in all the circumstances of the case to see that he does not suffer injury on the premises by reason of the danger concerned.

Questions

1. To whom in particular does the Occupiers' Liability Act 1984 apply?
2. Why do you think it was necessary to replace the common law with the 1984 Act?
3. What are the risks referred to in subsection (1) that the duty applies to?
4. What limitations then are in respect of people covered by the 1984 Act in comparison to those covered by the 1957 Act?

SECTION 12: LIABILITY FOR ANIMALS

Liability for animals now results from Act of Parliament, though there was always liability in common law. The Animals Act draws the distinction between domestic, or non-dangerous species, of animals and dangerous species, those not naturally residents of the UK. A person who keeps dangerous animals is always liable for the damage that they cause. On the other hand the 'keepers' of non-dangerous animals are only liable where those animals have unusual characteristics making them more dangerous than they normally would be and the keeper of the animal is aware of those characteristics.

EXTRACT FROM THE ANIMALS ACT 1971

2. Liability for damage done by dangerous animals

(1) Where any damage is caused by an animal which belongs to a dangerous species, any person who is a keeper of the animal is liable for the damage, except as otherwise provided by this Act.

(2) Where damage is caused by an animal which does not belong to a dangerous species, a keeper of the animal is liable for the damage, except as otherwise provided by this Act, if—

(a) the damage is of a kind which the animal, unless restrained, was likely to cause or which, if caused by the animal, was likely to be severe; and

(b) the likelihood of the damage or of its being severe was due to characteristics of the animal which are not normally found in animals of the same species or are not normally so found except at particular times or in particular circumstances; and

(c) those characteristics were known to that keeper or were at any time known to a person who at that time had charge of the animal as that keeper's servant or, where that keeper is the head of a household, were known to another keeper of the animal who is a member of that household and under the age of sixteen.

5. Exceptions from liability under sections 2 to 4

(1) A person is not liable under sections 2 to 4 of this Act for any damage which is due wholly to the fault of the person suffering it.

(2) A person is not liable under section 2 of this Act for any damage suffered by a person who has voluntarily accepted the risk thereof.

(3) A person is not liable under section 2 of this Act for any damage caused by an animal kept on any premises or structure to a person trespassing there, if it is proved either—

(a) that the animal was not kept there for the protection of persons or property; or

(b) (if the animal was kept there for the protection of persons or property) that keeping it there for that purpose was not unreasonable.

EXTRACT ADAPTED FROM THE JUDGMENT IN *CUMMINGS V GRAINGER* [1977] 1 QB 397

A woman entered a scrap yard one evening with her boyfriend who had permission to be there and had gone to recover some tools. The woman had no permission to enter the yard so was in effect a trespasser. An Alsatian dog that was used to guard the premises, and was left free to roam at night, attacked the woman and bit her cheek. A warning notice at the entrance to the yard read 'Beware of the dog'. The Alsatian was a normal dog, but, like other Alsatians, was likely to get excited and bite when being used as a guard dog, and the defendant knew this. The ingredients of s2(2)(b) and s2(2)(c) could therefore be made out. Since the bites of such a large dog were likely to be severe then s2(2)(a) could also be made out. The defendant was nevertheless able to rely on a defence under both s5(2) and s5(3) of the Act.

LORD DENNING MR

The statutory liability for a tame animal, like a dog, is defined in section 2(2) of the Act; subject to exceptions contained in section 5. . . . this is a case where the keeper of the dog is strictly liable unless he can bring himself within one of the exceptions . . . because the three requirements for strict liability are satisfied. Section 2(2)(a): this animal was a dog of the Alsatian breed; if it did bite anyone the damage was 'likely to be severe'. Section 2(2)(b): this animal was a guard dog kept so as to scare intruders and frighten them off. On the defendant's own evidence it used to bark and run round in circles . . . those characteristics are not normally found in Alsatian dogs, except in circumstances where they are used as guard dogs. Those circumstances are 'particular circumstances' within section 2(2)(b). It was due to those circumstances that the damage was likely to be severe if an intruder did enter on its territory. Section 2(2)(c): those characteristics were known to the defendant. It follows that the defendant is strictly liable unless he can bring himself within one of the exceptions in section 5. Obviously section 5(1) does not avail. The bite was not *wholly* due to the fault of the plaintiff, but only *partly* so.

Section 5(3) may, however, avail the keeper . . . If someone trespasses on property and is bitten or injured by a guard dog, the keeper . . . is exempt from liability if it is proved 'that keeping it there for that purpose was not unreasonable.' The judge held that the defendant was unreasonable in keeping it in this yard.

I take a different view. This was a yard in the East End of London where persons of the roughest type come and go. It was deserted at night and at weekends. If there was no protection, thieves would drive up in a lorry and remove the scrap with no one to see them or to stop them. The only reasonable way of protecting the place was to have a guard dog. True it was a fierce dog. But why not? A gentle dog would be no good. The thieves would soon make friends with him. . . . It was very reasonable—or at any rate, not unreasonable—for the defendant to keep this dog there.

Alternatively there is another defence provided by section 5(2). . . . a person is not liable 'for any damage suffered by a person who has voluntarily accepted the risk thereof'. The plaintiff certainly knew the animal was there. She worked next door. She knew all about it. She must have seen this huge notice on the door 'Beware of the dog.' Nevertheless she went in, following her man friend. In the circumstances she must be taken voluntarily to have incurred this risk.

Questions

Read the two extracts above and answer the questions.

1. The Animals Act distinguishes between animals of a dangerous species and those of a non-dangerous species. Why do you think that this should be the case?
2. In what ways is liability for a dangerous species more clear-cut than for non-dangerous species?
3. In what circumstances do you think that a keeper of a non-dangerous species of animal would be able to rely on s5(1) as a defence to damage caused by the animal?
4. How were all elements of s2(2) satisfied in the case of *Cummings v Grainger*?
5. Do you agree that the defences should have succeeded in the case?
6. Why is it vital that the keeper should know of the characteristics of the animal?

SECTION 13: TRESPASS TO THE PERSON

Trespass to the person is an ancient tort that covers all interferences with a person's bodily security. It includes assault which is the threat of some violence or threatening behaviour falling short of actual physical contact. One significant issue in assault is whether words on their own are sufficient to create liability. It also includes battery which in its simplest definition would include all unwanted touching. It is arguable whether the 'ordinary brushes of life' are actionable batteries. A more recent complication comes with the suggestion that 'hostility' is a necessary requirement. This would seem to contradict the position with regard to medical treatment where all intrusive treatment carried out without consent is theoretically at least a battery. The final type of action coming within the tort is false imprisonment. This involves the total bodily restraint of the victim. There must be no means of escape to succeed. Liability is possible even though the claimant is unaware of the restraint. Contractual agreements to the restraint may mean liability is avoided.

EXTRACT ADAPTED FROM THE JUDGMENT IN *READ V COKER* [1853] 13 CB 850, COURT OF COMMON PLEAS

The claimant was in arrears with his rent. One day the defendant told him to leave the premises. When he refused the defendant instructed his workmen to make him do so. They surrounded the claimant, rolled their sleeves up and threatened the claimant that if he did not leave they would break his neck. The claimant then alleged assault by the defendant and his workmen and succeeded.

BYLES SERJT

To constitute an assault there must be something more than a threat of violence. An assault is thus defined in Buller's *Nisi Prius*: 'An assault is an attempt or offer, by force or violence, to do a corporal hurt to another, as, by pointing a pitchfork at him, when standing within reach; presenting a gun at him; drawing a sword and waving it in a menacing manner. But no words can amount to an assault.'

So an assault is said to be 'an attempt or offer to beat another without touching him; as if one lifts up his cane or his fist in a threatening manner at another; or strikes at him but misses him; this is an assault, which Finch describes to be "an unlawful setting upon one's person".'

Questions

1. How does Byles describe and define an assault?
2. What was the assault in the case?
3. Do you think it is justifiable to say that 'no words can amount to an assault'?

EXTRACT ADAPTED FROM THE JUDGMENT IN *NASH V SHEEN*, THE TIMES, 13 MARCH 1953

A woman went to the hairdressers having asked for a 'permanent wave'. The hairdresser applied a 'tone rinse' instead. This caused the claimant's hair to change colour quite dramatically and also led to a painful rash not just on her head but all over her body. The plaintiff recovered damages for the battery.

HILBERY J

The first question to be considered was whether what was applied to the hair, which was called in the trade a 'tone-rinse,' was applied without the plaintiff's express consent and was a trespass. It was quite clear that she went to the salon for a permanent wave, and [the court] did not believe that Mrs Nash consented to the application of the colouring matter . . . that was a trespass. Even on the defendant's account it was plain that the plaintiff never gave consent to the application of any dye or colouring matter to her hair.

The plaintiff recovered £437 damages, including £50 for 'her appearance being altered in a way which was distressing to her.'

EXTRACT ADAPTED FROM THE JUDGMENT IN *WILSON V PRINGLE* [1987] QB 237, CA

Two schoolboys, both aged 13, were walking down a corridor at school. The one boy, as an act of horseplay, pulled on the bag that the other boy, the claimant, was carrying causing him to fall to the ground. The claimant's hip was injured in the fall. He sued successfully for battery following which the other boy appealed.

CROOM-JOHNSON LJ

In the action for negligence the physical contact is normally though by no means always unintended. In the action for trespass, to constitute a battery it is deliberate. Even so ... not every intended contact ... is tortious. Apart from special justifications (such as acting in self-defence) there are many examples in everyday life where an intended contact or touch is not actionable as a trespass.

Another ingredient ... is ... hostility. The references to anger sufficing to turn a touch into battery (*Cole v Turner*) and the lack of an intention to assault which prevents a gesture from being an assault are instances of these.

What then turns a friendly touching into an unfriendly one? A recent authority is *Collins v Wilcock.* [In] the judgment Robert Goff LJ said:

'We are here concerned primarily with battery. The fundamental principle, plain and incontestable, is that every person's body is inviolate. It has long been established that any touching of another person, however slight, may amount to a battery. So Holt CJ held in *Cole v Turner* that "the least touching of another in anger is a battery."

But so widely drawn a principle must inevitably be subject to exceptions. For example, children may be subjected to reasonable punishment; people may be subjected to the power of arrest; and reasonable force may be used in self-defence ... a broader exception has been created to allow for the exigencies of everyday life. Generally speaking, consent is a defence to battery; and most of the physical contacts of everyday life are not actionable because they are impliedly consented to by all who move in society and so expose themselves to the risk of bodily contact.'

In our view, the authorities lead one to the conclusion that in a battery there must be an intentional touching or contact in one form or another of the plaintiff by the defendant. That touching must be proved to be a hostile touching. That still leaves unanswered the question 'when is a touching to be called hostile?' Hostility cannot be equated with ill will or malevolence. It cannot be governed by the obvious intention shown in acts like punching, stabbing or shooting. It cannot be governed solely by an expressed intention. [It] must be a question of fact for the tribunal of fact.

Questions

Read the two extracts above and answer the questions.

1. What is the significant difference between an assault and a battery?
2. Why was there a battery in *Nash v Sheen*?
3. According to Croom-Johnson in *Wilson v Pringle*, when will touching not amount to a battery?
4. What does he suggest are the key ingredients of a battery?
5. If medical treatment in the absence of consent can be a battery do you think he is right in suggesting that a battery requires 'hostility' in the touching?

EXTRACT ADAPTED FROM THE JUDGMENT IN *BIRD V JONES* [1845] 7 QB 742, COURT OF QUEEN'S BENCH

The claimant was trying to cross Hammersmith Bridge. The defendants had cordoned off part of it and were charging spectators to watch a regatta. The claimant tried to pass through this area but was stopped by police, but was allowed to return back the way he had come. He sued unsuccessfully for false imprisonment. His free movement was not completely prevented, and so there was no trespass.

PATTESON J

I have no doubt that, in general, if one man compels another to stay in any given place against his will, he imprisons that other just as much as if he locked him up in a room: and ... it is not necessary, in order to constitute an imprisonment, that a man's person should be touched. I agree, also, that the compelling a man to go in a given direction against his will may amount to imprisonment. But I cannot bring my mind to the conclusion that, if one man merely obstructs the passage of another in a particular direction, whether by threat of physical violence or otherwise, leaving him at liberty to stay where he is or to go in any other direction if he pleases, he can be thereby said to imprison him. He does him wrong undoubtedly ... But imprisonment is, as I apprehend, a total restraint of the liberty of the person, for however short a time, and not a partial obstruction of his will, whatever inconvenience it may bring upon him.

EXTRACT ADAPTED FROM THE JUDGMENT IN *HERD V WEARDALE STEEL, COAL AND COKE CO* [1915] AC 67, HL

Close to the start of their shift, miners believed the work they were being asked to do was unsafe. As a result they asked to be taken to the surface but the employers refused. The miners were sued in the County Court for breach of their employment contract. They appealed arguing that they had been falsely imprisoned but their appeal was unsuccessful because the employer had a right to expect them to stay underground for the duration of their shift.

VISCOUNT HALDANE LC

By the law of this country no man can be restrained of his liberty without authority in law. [However] If a man chooses to go into a dangerous place at the bottom of a quarry or the bottom of a mine; from which by the nature of the physical circumstances he cannot escape, it does not follow that he can compel the owner to bring him up out of it.

There is another proposition which has to be borne in mind, and that is the application of the maxim volenti non fit injuria. If a man gets into an express train and the doors are locked pending its arrival at its destination, he is not entitled, merely because the train has been stopped by a signal, to call for the doors to be opened to let him out. He has entered the train on the terms that he is to be conveyed to a certain station without the opportunity of getting out before that, and he must abide by the terms on which he has entered the train. So when a man goes down a mine, from which access to the surface does not exist in the absence of special facilities given on the part of the owner of the mine, he is only entitled to the use of these facilities on the terms on which he has entered. It results from what was laid down in *Robinson v Balmain Ferry*. There there was a pier, and by the regulations a penny was to be paid by those who entered and a penny on getting out. The manager of the exit gate refused to allow a man who had gone in, having paid his penny, but having changed his mind, to come out without paying his penny. It was held that that was not a false imprisonment; volenti non fit injuria. So, it is not false imprisonment to hold a man to the conditions he has accepted when he goes down a mine.

Questions

Read the two extracts above and answer the questions.

1. What actions (or even lack of action) can amount to false imprisonment, according to Patteson J in *Bird v Jones*?
2. Why was there no false imprisonment in that case?
3. What defence does the *Herd* case suggest may be available to a claim of false imprisonment?
4. What everyday situations do you think that the tort of false imprisonment would be most appropriate to today?

SECTION 14: DEFAMATION

Defamation is a tort aimed at protecting a person's reputation. To be actionable it must involve false statements about the person that are published to at least one third party. Mere innuendo is often enough to attract liability. The tort seems to run at odds with general principles of freedom of expression and in particular with the freedom of the press to report matters of interest to the general public, although the defence of 'fair comment' is established. It is possible that, now that English law has incorporated the European Convention on Human Rights, that the law on defamation is likely to come into conflict with Article 10 of the Convention. The law on defamation is also seen to be discredited because it operates mostly for the rich and famous.

EXTRACT ADAPTED FROM THE JUDGMENT IN *CHARLESTON V NEWS GROUP NEWSPAPERS* [1995] 2 AC 65

A newspaper published a photograph with the heads of the two stars from the soap 'Neighbours' who played Madge and Harold Bishop superimposed on the naked bodies of two people engaged in a sexual act, with the caption: 'Strewth! What's Harold up to with our Madge?' Underneath was an article actually complaining about the use of these images in a computer game. The stars sued claiming that the suggestion that there was a suggestion that they had willingly sat for the pictures. Their case and subsequent appeal for defamation failed.

LORD BRIDGE

The theme of Mr Craig's argument runs out on the following lines. The techniques of modern tabloid journalism confront the courts with a novel situation with which the law has not hitherto had to grapple. It is plain that the eye-catching headline and the eye-catching photograph will first attract the reader's attention, precisely as they were intended to do, and equally plain that a significant number of readers will not trouble to read any further. This phenomenon must be well known to newspaper editors and publishers, who cannot, therefore, complain if they are held liable.

At first blush this argument has considerable attractions, but I believe it falls foul of two principles which are basic to the law of libel. The first is that, where no legal innuendo is alleged to arise from extrinsic circumstances known to some readers, the 'natural and ordinary meaning' to be ascribed to the words of an allegedly defamatory publication is the meaning which the words would convey to the minds of ordinary, reasonable, fair minded reader. The second is that, although a combination of words may in fact convey different meanings to the minds of different readers, the jury in a libel action, applying the criterion which the first principle dictates, is required to determine the single meaning which the publication conveyed to the notional reasonable reader and to base its verdict on the assumption that this was the one sense in which all readers would have understood it.

EXTRACT ADAPTED FROM 'EXPOSING THE FLAWS IN BRITAIN'S LIBEL LAWS', DAVID PANNICK, QC, *THE TIMES*, 20 APRIL 1999

Britain's libel laws may soon be tested—and found wanting—in the European Court of Human Rights. The challenge is expected to be brought after the Court of Appeal's recent decision to uphold many of the libel allegations in an action brought by the fast food chain McDonald's against two environmental campaigners, Dave Morris and Helen Street.

Their recent appeal resulted from a 314 day libel trial in 1997 which held that McDonald's had been libelled in a leaflet containing criticisms about the company's business practices.

The current state of the English law of defamation is impossible to reconcile with any developed concept of free speech. Defendants are liable even if they make statements that they reasonably believe to be true on matters of public interest; the plaintiff may receive substantial damages whether or not financial loss has been caused; and legal aid is unavailable.

London has long been the libel capital of the world. B-list celebrities, public figures with something discreditable to conceal, and companies oversensitive to criticism issue writs asserting that they have been 'lowered in the estimation of right thinking people' by a newspaper article . . . which would long ago have been forgotten but for the plaintiff's insistence on telling the world its contents. Our libel law assumes that damage to reputation is one of the most serious injuries that a person can suffer.

Article 10 of the European Convention on Human Rights guarantees the right to freedom of expression. Any interference must be necessary in a democratic society and proportionate. English law recognises the power of a writ to silence critics on matters of public importance and acknowledges that influential plaintiffs have other means to make their voice heard. For those reasons in 1993 the House of Lords held that a local authority could not sue Times Newspapers for libel.

Lord Keith explained that the difficulty of proving allegations by admissible evidence 'may prevent the publication of matters which it is very desirable to make public' in relation to a governmental body which 'should be open to uninhibited public criticism', and which has other means of defending its reputation.

The McDonald's case concerned matters of public importance . . . Some of the allegations were found to be true: that the company paid low wages, was cruel in the rearing of some of its animals, and exploited children in the targeting of its advertising. The Court of Appeal accepted that it was fair comment to say that McDonald's employees worldwide do badly in terms of pay and conditions, and there was justification for the allegation that too much McDonald's food provides the customer with a high-fat diet creating a real risk of heart disease.

The European Court is likely to conclude that English law fails adequately to control libel actions by companies.

Our law deters those who have something of value to add to the public debate on the standards adopted by companies such as McDonald's. That is especially so where there is a lack of equality of arms, with the plaintiff able to employ lawyers of its choice and the defendants unable to claim legal aid, however strong their case and however impecunious they may be. It is disproportionate to require such defendants to prove the truth of their allegations made in good faith in matters of public interest against an organisation with ample resources to answer criticisms and protect its reputation.

Questions

Read the three extracts above and answer the questions.

1. In the *Charleston* case what meaning does Lord Bridge say that can be given to the words or images in question does the jury have to concentrate on?
2. In the same case Lord Bridge uses the term 'innuendo'. What does this term mean in the context of defamation?
3. What serious defects in English libel law are identified in David Pannick's article on the McLibel case?

SECTION 15: VICARIOUS LIABILITY

Vicarious liability involves fixing one party with liability for the torts of another. Most usually this will mean an employer being liable for the acts of his/her employee. The employer will only be liable for torts that occur during the course of employment. It is a question of fact in each case what is in the course of employment. It is questionable to what extent an employer can be made liable for crimes committed by his/her employees or for other behaviour not amounting to a tort.

EXTRACT ADAPTED FROM THE JUDGMENT IN *CENTURY INSURANCE CO V NORTHERN IRELAND ROAD TRANSPORT BOARD* [1942] AC 509, HL

A tanker driver worked for the Board, but delivered petrol for another company. While delivering petrol, and having inserted the nozzle into the storage tank of the garage, he lit a cigarette and threw down the still lit match. This ignited material which caused a fire damaging the tanker, and surrounding property. The garage owner's insurance company paid off other claims and then sued the Board successfully. The employer's claims on appeal that, firstly the driver was not employed by them, and secondly was not acting in the course of his employment at the time he caused the fire, both failed.

VISCOUNT SIMON LC

On the second question, every judge who has had to consider the matter in Northern Ireland agrees with the learned arbitrator in holding that Davison's careless act which caused the conflagration and explosion was an act done in the course of employment. Admittedly, he was serving his master when he put the nozzle into the tank and turned on the tap ... would be serving his master when he turned off the tap and withdrew the nozzle from the tank. In the interval, spirit was flowing from the tanker to the tank, and this was the very delivery which the respondents were required under their contract to effect. Davison's duty was to watch over the delivery of the spirit into the tank to see that it did not overflow, and to turn off the tap when the proper quantity had passed from the tanker. In circumstances like these, 'they also serve who only stand and wait.' He was presumably close to the apparatus, and his negligence in starting smoking and in throwing away a lighted match at the moment is plainly negligence in the discharge of the duties on which he was employed by the respondents.

EXTRACT ADAPTED FROM '*TROTMAN V NORTH YORKSHIRE COUNTY COUNCIL* [1998] (CRTF 97/1273/3) THE LIMITS OF VICARIOUS LIABILITY', BRENDA BARRETT, (1999) *THE LAW TEACHER*, VOL 3, NO 1.

The Facts

The Council was defendant in an action by Simon Trotman in respect of allegations of sexual assaults on him by a deputy headmaster employed by the Council at the special school where the plaintiff was a pupil. The alleged incidents occurred during a school trip. Simon at the time needed nocturnal supervision because he suffered from fits. Thus he shared a bedroom with Stevens. Stevens was convicted for indecent assaults upon teenage boys other than Simon.

The appeal

... In his claim against the Council, Simon alleged 'The defendants are vicariously responsible for the indecent assaults by Stevens upon the plaintiff'. In the County Court Judge Spittle had found the Council liable on the basis 'that the acts of the deputy were so connected with his authorised responsibilities that they can be regarded as modes, albeit improper modes, of performing his authorised duties'.

The classic test

In the appeal, Lady Justice Butler-Sloss began by citing what she deemed the classic test for vicarious liability as stated by Salmond: '... A master, as opposed to employer of an independent contractor, is liable even for acts which he has not authorised provided they are so connected with acts he has authorised that they may rightly be regarded as modes—although improper modes—of doing them. In other words, a master is responsible not merely for what he authorises his servant to do but also for the way in which he does it ... On the other hand, if the unauthorised and wrongful act ... is not so connected with the authorised act as to be a mode of doing it, but is an independent act, the master is not responsible'.

The assault cases

... her Ladyship cited *Poland v Parr* where defendant employers were liable for injuries suffered by a boy whom their carter had struck. The Court of Appeal ... found the carter was acting in the course of his employment. On the other hand in *Warren v Henlys* a petrol pump attendant was deemed to be acting outside the course of employment when he assaulted a customer during an altercation about paying for petrol.

...

Discrimination cases

She noted that *Bracebridge v Darby* the EAT upheld the industrial tribunal's conclusion that sexual assault of a woman employee by male employees was something for which the employer should be liable. This case was cited in the Court of Appeal in *Jones v Tower Boot Co Ltd* where employers were found liable, under the Race Relations Act, for the verbal abuse and physical violence inflicted upon an employee by other employees.

Bailment cases

She then turned to the bailment cases. *Lloyd v Grace, Smith & Co* had dispelled the suggestion that the master could only be liable where the servant's fraud was committed for the benefit of the master.

The Council was not liable

... her Ladyship sought to apply the Salmond test to the case before her. Sharing a bedroom with the boy gave the master the opportunity to carry out the assaults. But availing himself of the opportunity seemed to her to be far removed from an unauthorised mode of carrying out a teacher's duties on behalf of his employer. It was the negation of the duty of the council to look after children for whom it was responsible. She concluded that the Council could not be liable.

Comment

There seems little doubt that the fraud cases can be regarded as a class apart. Liability is not *vicarious*: it is the *personal* liability of the employer and normally depends on the interpretation of express and implied contractual terms.

Arguably this case does no more than reiterate the ruling in *Jones*; ... that employer's liability under discrimination legislation is not confined within the straitjacket of the common law rules of vicarious liability. However, it serves to highlight some lack of consistency in the law and its protection of vulnerable categories of people.

This commentator always argues forcefully for the importance of the employer's personal responsibility for maintaining a safe system of operation. In her view investigation would have been likely to have disclosed that in both *Bracebridge* and *Jones* there was some fault on the part of the employer in permitting such conduct to occur on its premises. If that were so then liability might have been attached to those employers without resort to debate about the boundaries of vicarious liability.

Jones v Tower Boot Co Ltd seems likely to have determined beyond dispute that vicarious liability is to be interpreted broadly in cases which are bought under discrimination legislation. On the other hand it is equally likely that *Trotman* will not be viewed as the final statement of the limits of vicarious liability at common law even in the narrow context of child abuse.

Questions

Read the two extracts above and answer the questions.

1. Why is the employer liable in the *Century Insurance* case?
2. How does the judgment fit in with the 'classic test' as cited by Lady Justice Butler-Sloss in Brenda Barrett's article?
3. How does the case of *Trotman* compare to the 'assault cases' referred to in the article?
4. Why could vicarious liability not be imposed in the case of *Trotman*?
5. In the light of the discrimination cases that the author refers to, in what way is the law inconsistent as the author suggests?

SECTION 16: GENERAL DEFENCES

There are a number of defences open to a party accused of tortious behaviour. Some of them are specific to individual torts, as would, for example, be the case with the defences of qualified and absolute privilege in defamation. Other defences can be raised generally in answer to any torts.

Volenti non fit injuria (consent)

EXTRACT ADAPTED FROM THE JUDGMENT IN *SMITH V BAKER (CHARLES) & SONS* [1891] AC 325, HL

The appellant had been working at a drill in a railway cutting while fellow workers used a steam crane to remove stones from the cutting. The crane swung over his head and stones fell from it injuring him seriously. He sued his employers and succeeded in establishing liability on appeal despite the claim that he was consenting to the risk of harm.

LORD HALSBURY LC

The objection raised, and the only objection raised, to the plaintiff's right to recover was that he had voluntarily undertaken the risk. The facts upon which that question depends are given by the plaintiff himself in ... evidence. Speaking of the operation of slinging the stones over the heads of the workmen, he said ... that it was not safe, and that whenever he had sufficient warning, or saw it, he got out of the way. The plaintiff said he had been long enough at the work to know ... it was dangerous, and another fellow-workman in his hearing complained that it was a dangerous practice. Giving full effect to these admissions, upon which the whole case for the defendants depends, it appears ... that the utmost that they prove is that in the course of the work it did occasionally happen that stones were slung in this fashion over the workmen's heads, that the plaintiff knew this, and believed it to be dangerous, and whenever he could got out of the way. The question of law that seems to be in debate is whether upon these facts, and on an occasion when the very form of his employment prevented him from looking out for himself, he consented to undergo this particular risk, and so disentitled himself to recover when a stone was negligently slung over his head, or negligently permitted to fall on him and do him injury.

I am of the opinion that the application of the maxim volenti non fit injuria is not warranted by these facts. ... For my own part, I think that a person who relies on the maxim must show ... consent to the particular thing done. ...

Question

1. In *Smith v Baker* how does Lord Halsbury describe the defence of consent operating?

Necessity

EXTRACT ADAPTED FROM THE JUDGMENT IN *WATT V HERTFORDSHIRE COUNTY COUNCIL* [1954] 1 WLR 835, CA

A fireman was injured while transporting a heavy jack to a road traffic accident where a woman was trapped and needed emergency assistance. The jack was not secured as it normally should have been and fell on the fireman when the driver had to brake sharply. His action for damages against his employers failed, as did his appeal.

DENNING LJ

It is well settled that in measuring due care you must balance the risk against the measures necessary to eliminate the risk. To that proposition there ought to be added this: you must balance the risk against the end to be achieved. If this accident had occurred in a commercial enterprise without any emergency there could be no doubt that the servant would succeed. But the commercial end to make profit is very different from the human end to save life or limb. The saving of life or limb justifies taking considerable risk, and I am glad to say that there have never been wanting in this country men of courage ready to take those risks, notably in the fire service.

In this case the risk involved in sending out the lorry was not so great as to prohibit the attempt to save life. It is always a question of balancing the risk against the end.

Questions

1. How does Lord Denning consider that the defence of necessity should work?
2. What level of risk do you think there should be to justify a defendant's negligence?

Contributory negligence

EXTRACT FROM THE LAW REFORM (CONTRIBUTORY NEGLIGENCE) ACT 1945

1. Apportionment of liability in the case of contributory negligence

(1) Where any person suffers damage as the result partly of his own fault and partly the fault of any other person or persons, a claim in respect of that damage shall not be defeated by reason of the fault of the person suffering the damage, but the damages recoverable in respect thereof shall be reduced to such extent as the court thinks just and equitable having regard to the claimant's share in the responsibility for the damage.

EXTRACT ADAPTED FROM THE JUDGMENT IN *FROOM V BUTCHER* [1976] QB 286, CA

The claimant was injured in a car crash caused by the defendant's negligence. The injuries to his head and chest would not have occurred but for the fact that he failed to wear a seat belt. He was held to be contributorily negligent.

LORD DENNING

The accident is caused by the bad driving. The damage is caused in part by the bad driving of the defendant, and in part by the failure of the plaintiff to wear a seat belt. If the plaintiff was to blame for not wearing a seat belt, the damage is in part a result of his own fault. He must bear some share in the responsibility for the damage: and his damages fall to be reduced to such extent as the court thinks just and equitable.

Whenever there is an accident, the negligent driver must bear by far the greater share of responsibility. But in so far as the damage might have been avoided or lessened by wearing a seat belt, the injured person must bear some share.

Questions

1. Under the Act, against what measure will damages be reduced?
2. In what ways does Lord Denning's judgment in *Froom v Butcher* help to explain why the defence is available?

Novus actus interveniens

EXTRACT ADAPTED FROM THE JUDGMENT IN *MCKEW V HOLLAND & HANNEN & CUBITTS (SCOTLAND) LTD* [1969] 3 ALL ER 1621, HL

McKew suffered minor injuries to his leg at work, the fault of his employers. He then used a steep staircase with no handrails and when his leg gave way he jumped to avoid falling breaking his leg. He was unable to prove at trial or on appeal that the original injury was connected to the later one, and the employers were thus not liable for his broken leg.

LORD REID

The appellant's case is that the second accident was caused by the weakness of his left leg which in turn had been caused by the first accident. The main argument of the respondents is that the second accident was not the direct or natural and probable or foreseeable result of their fault in causing the first accident.

In my view the law is clear. If a man is injured in such a way that his leg may give way at any moment he must act reasonably and carefully. It is quite possible that in spite of all reasonable care his leg may give way in circumstances such that as a result he sustains further injury. Then that second injury was caused by his disability which in turn was caused by the defender's fault. But if the injured man acts unreasonably he cannot hold the defender liable for injury caused by his own unreasonable conduct. His unreasonable conduct is novus actus interveniens. The chain of causation has been broken and what follows may be regarded as caused by his own conduct and not by the defender's fault or the disability caused by it.

Questions

1. Why, according to the case, could the defendant who caused the original damage not be made liable for the second injury?
2. What in the claimant's own behaviour made him responsible for the second injury?
3. What does the defence have to do with causation?

CHAPTER 4

REVISION EXERCISES

CONTRACT CROSSWORD

Solve the clues below to answer the questions 1–13, and then discover the word that links them all inside the shaded box.

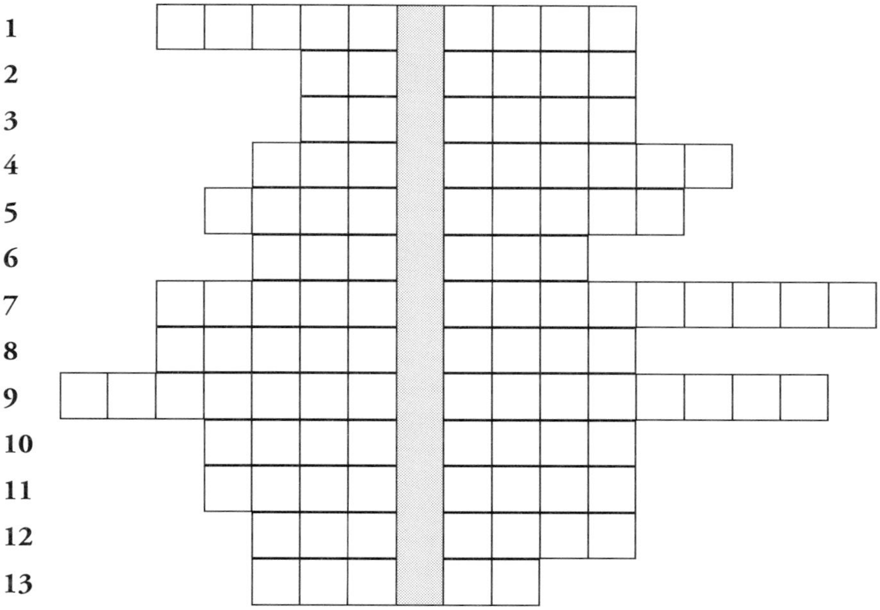

Clues

1 In law this is not the same as adequate.

2 I'll give you mine if you give me yours.

3 Roffey's got an extra one from Williams.

4 Did these brothers get more than they bargained for from the Constabulary?

5 Did they not like Mr and Mrs Rees?

6 He had no way of getting what he was owed from Atkinson.

7 Three chocolate bar wrappers is never enough. Or is it?

8 If you ground it would still have value.

9 Two Hong Kong gentlemen with a less than gentlemanly dispute.

10 A 'house' in Wimbledon with a famous place in contract law.

11 You would have to suffer this in return for getting 3.

12 Lord Denning's defence for 10.

13 No part payments allowed under this rule.

MULTIPLE CHOICE CASE LAW REVISION QUIZ

In each of the following lists of cases 1–7 one or more cases is fictitious. Identify which cases are real by placing a tick in the first box. Then identify from which area of law the case comes by placing a tick in the appropriate box under tort, contract or crime. You should also use the exercise to try to remember the significance of the specific case.

1		TORT	CONTRACT	CRIME
a Hyde v Wrench				
b Hyde v Spanner				
c Hyde v Jekyll				

2		TORT	CONTRACT	CRIME
a Jackson v Horizon Holidays				
b Michael v Jackson				
c Miller v Jackson				

3		TORT	CONTRACT	CRIME
a Anderson v Ryan				
b Anderton v Ryan				
c Anderton v Beckham				

4		TORT	CONTRACT	CRIME
a R v Stone & Dobinson				
b Bolton v Stone				
c Bolton v Barnsley				

5		TORT	CONTRACT	CRIME
a DPP v Smith				
b Smith v Stages				
c Smith v Eric S Bush				

6		TORT	CONTRACT	CRIME
a Junior Books v Veitchi				
b R v Junior				
c R v Senior				

7		TORT	CONTRACT	CRIME
a Victorian Railway Comm's v Coultas				
b Victoria Laundry v Newman Industries				
c Victoria v Adams				

10 CRIMINAL LAW CASES

Below is a table containing brief facts from 10 cases, numbered 1–10. Below this is a table of 10 case names, lettered A–J. Place the number of the appropriate facts in the column next to the case name the facts apply to. In the third column identify the area of criminal law from which the case comes, and briefly state the principle of law.

Case Facts

1	A doctor was convicted when he claimed money for an abortion that he had never carried out.
2	Two striking miners were convicted when they dropped a block of concrete off a bridge into the path of a taxi carrying a working miner and the taxi driver was killed.
3	A young boy killed an old man by hitting him on the head with a large frying man after the old man had buggered the boy and taunted him about it.
4	A taxi driver took £6 from a foreign student for a 50p taxi ride.
5	A man set fire to a hotel while he was drunk.
6	A man was convicted after he stabbed a Jehovah's Witness who then died having refused a blood transfusion.
7	A man walked behind the till area in a department store and opened the till to see if there was any money in it.
8	Sado-masochists consented to injuries they inflicted on each other.
9	A man burned down his house in order to be rehoused but his wife, girlfriend and children died in the fire and he was convicted.
10	A man was convicted after making repeated phone calls to women at night and remaining silent. Some of the women suffered psychiatric harm as a result.

10 Criminal Law Cases: Case Names

A	R v Goodfellow		
B	R v Walkington		
C	R v Ghosh		
D	R v Lawrence		
E	R v Hancock & Shankland		
F	Metropolitan Police Commissioner v Caldwell		
G	R v Ireland		
H	R v Blaue		
I	R v Brown and Others		
J	DPP v Camplin		

IDENTIFYING ANSWERS TO TORT PROBLEM QUESTIONS

Problem questions very often seem more difficult than essay questions because the first thing that you have to do is to identify what area of law the problem covers.

Doing this confidently is a skill which develops over time. However, getting used to examining the wording of problems for key words is a useful means of developing the skill.

Below are just some examples of key wording in tort problems:

Occupiers' Liability Act

- a key feature here will be someone visiting the premises of another person, e.g. *Gemma has been staying at the Crest Hotel*;
- remember, that premises can be a variety of things, e.g. *Richard was taking Valerie for a cruise down the river in his launch*;
- the occupier is the person in control of premises so there may also be clues as to who the potential defendant is, e.g. *Gareth has fallen and cut himself on broken glass in the Victoria Precinct. Westchester Corporation are responsible for cleaning the precinct*;
- since children are treated differently under the Act there will usually be some reference to a child also, e.g. *Terry, aged seven, went to fetch his ball from Gordon's garden and fell in a trench which Gordon had dug, injuring himself*;
- and remember also that trespassers are protected under the 1984 Act so somebody being on premises unlawfully is a straightforward clue, e.g. *Rod was stealing lettuces from George's allotment one night when he tripped over a barrow left unattended and injured himself.*

Nuisance

- here the obvious clue is that nuisance is indirect interference so it will involve things like smells, noises etc., e.g. *Des is building an extension. He drills and hammers often into the early hours of the morning. As a result Derek and Mavis, his neighbours, regularly lose sleep*;
- it also involves an unreasonable use of land, measured by things such as location, but what is a nuisance in one location may not be in another, e.g. *Stan is annoyed because his car is always dirty from dust from the quarry*;
- continuity is also a factor, so a one-off will not usually be a nuisance, e.g. *Sid and Ada had no sleep on the Friday night when the Rock Festival was held in the field behind their house*;
- malice is also a factor which can affect the outcome of an action, and therefore is commonly included in a problem, e.g. *Hattie became so annoyed by the constant crying of the baby next door that whenever it did cry she turned her stereo and her television up to full volume.*

Vicarious liability

- here the immediate clue is that the tortfeaser is doing work for someone else, e.g. *Ralph is repairing Sam's guttering. He leans too far on the ladder and falls onto a passer-by, Andrew, injuring him*;
- one point which will usually be in a question is whether the tortfeaser is an employee or an independent contractor, so a problem will include, e.g., *Horace makes his own tax and NI contributions, but is not allowed to accept work from anyone but Bodgitts Co*;
- the other key issue will be whether the employee commits the tort in the course of the employment or not, e.g. *Fred was injured when Dave gave him a lift home in the works van. Dave was taking an unofficial lunch break to go to see his wife.*

Nervous shock

- here the obvious clue is the type of injury suffered by the plaintiff, e.g. *since the car crash Gail has suffered a complete personality change, has regular flashbacks of the accident, and is too afraid to go out*;
- another common feature of such problems is distinguishing between primary victims and secondary victims so a question would include, e.g., *Harriet suffered shock when the racing car bounced off the barrier, flew into the air and came over the fence towards her*—compared with—*Raj was shocked when he was rushed to the hospital to find his daughter dead and still covered in blood*;
- rescuers are a class of claimant also commonly referred to in a problem, e.g. *Eric, a fireman, had struggled hard to release trapped people but had been forced to jump clear when the petrol tank exploded, and had suffered shock when the passengers burnt to death in front of him.*

10 CONTRACT LAW CASES

Below is a table containing brief facts from 10 cases, numbered 1–10. Below this is a table of 10 case names, lettered A–J. Place the number of the appropriate facts in the column next to the case name the facts apply to. In the third column identify the area of criminal law from which the case comes, and briefly state the principle of law.

Case Facts

1	An exclusion clause posted on the back of a hotel bedroom is invalid when a woman guest loses valuables left in the room.
2	A man offers land for £1,000. The buyer rejects this and offers to buy for £950. The seller refuses to sell. The buyer tries to sue for breach of contract.
3	A man part-exchanges his car at a garage and innocently gives the wrong age. The garage then allows him too much as a result.
4	Two parties contract for the sale and purchase of a cargo of grain which, unknown to either party, has already been sold because it is fermenting.
5	A company hiring out barges to deposit earth waste at sea state the wrong load that the barges can carry causing the other party contractual problems.
6	A body representing artistes want royalties from a confectionery company after it has given away records in return for three used chocolate bar wrappers.
7	No liability on employers when a security guard negligently burns down the factory he is guarding.
8	A music hall that has been hired to stage concerts burns down so that it is impossible for the concerts to go ahead.
9	A woman buys vending machines that she finds are defective. She cannot claim because she has signed a contract including an exclusion clause.
10	A man suffers a miserable holiday that is not how it was described in the contract. He claims damages for mental distress.

10 Contract Law Cases: Case Names

A	Chappell v Nestle		
B	Jarvis v Swan Tours		
C	Photo Productions v Securicor Transport		
D	Olley v Marlborough Court Hotel		
E	Oscar Chess v Williams		
F	Taylor v Caldwell		
G	Couturier v Hastie		
H	L'Estrange v Graucob		
I	Howard Marine & Dredging Co v Ogden		
J	Hyde v Wrench		

WORDSEARCH

Complete the Wordsearch below and you should find the five criminal law cases, five contract law cases, and five tort cases identified below.

The cases will be in a straight line but can be found running left to right or right to left, top to bottom or bottom to top, or diagonally up or down.

R	Y	L	A	N	N	R	T	U	R	O	B	L	C	C	H	V	G	N	I
P	O	S	A	I	N	K	I	O	V	O	I	E	E	D	C	K	I	N	H
T	E	E	R	Y	I	H	S	E	S	I	S	F	D	R	O	Y	G	I	C
E	G	N	O	S	N	E	V	E	T	S	V	E	U	H	G	O	N	O	D
N	I	Y	O	P	J	H	I	T	O	N	R	E	R	C	H	A	I	N	U
O	I	P	Y	O	H	S	S	V	N	I	O	M	I	M	M	A	N	T	Y
T	R	L	E	T	H	A	M	P	E	L	H	A	S	K	I	N	N	O	R
S	T	E	L	I	D	A	E	D	A	L	D	D	C	E	S	H	A	I	R
V	O	O	A	O	R	G	H	H	N	O	P	I	R	M	I	L	L	L	A
N	G	G	N	D	O	Y	S	E	D	C	D	D	L	A	E	E	V	O	B
O	P	E	E	T	V	W	O	O	D	V	S	C	A	R	T	H	R	E	V
T	I	N	T	T	E	L	V	I	O	R	H	M	T	Y	E	Z	E	O	N
L	E	F	F	E	B	R	Y	R	B	K	S	O	U	O	U	O	L	N	O
O	X	E	H	R	I	I	A	O	I	N	O	R	I	S	K	X	W	O	T
B	Y	T	S	A	R	P	H	E	N	C	G	S	T	R	I	O	O	G	L
R	D	E	O	N	A	P	I	T	S	S	G	H	H	I	R	A	F	I	E
I	N	N	H	C	H	T	S	T	O	N	O	L	E	B	R	A	M	F	P
A	S	T	G	T	H	H	H	C	N	E	R	W	V	E	D	Y	H	E	A
C	C	T	V	R	A	E	I	C	E	E	A	R	A	T	H	E	R	R	H
K	C	I	R	Y	I	M	V	K	L	I	T	S	P	P	A	T	T	I	C

The five criminal law cases are:

1 R v Collins

2 R v Woollin

3 R v Stone and Dobinson

4 R v Brown

5 R v Ghosh

The five contract law cases are:

1 Stilk v Myrick

2 Esso v Marden

3 Hyde v Wrench

4 Chapelton v Barry UDC

5 Wood v Scarth

The five tort cases are:

1 Donoghue v Stevenson

2 Caparo v Dickman

3 Fowler v Lanning

4 Bolton v Stone

5 Read v Lyons

10 TORT CASES

Below is a table containing brief facts from 10 cases, numbered 1–10. Below is a table of 10 case names, lettered A–J. Place the number of the appropriate facts in the column next to the case name the facts apply to. In the third column identify the area of criminal law from which the case comes, and briefly state the principle of law.

Case Facts

1	Relatives of people killed in the Hillsborough disaster unsuccessfully tried to sue the police.
2	An advertising company received a credit reference from the bank of a small company. The small company went into liquidation and the advertisers lost money.
3	A boy was injured while helping a milkman although the milkman had been told not to use young boys to help him.
4	A paying guest staying in the managers' quarters in a public house was killed falling down an unlit staircase.
5	A man went to the casualty department of a hospital complaining of stomach pains. He was told to see his own doctor but died of arsenic poisoning before he could.
6	A child died after eating poisonous berries in a public park that were not fenced off in any way.
7	There was no liability when the erection of a large building nearby interfered with people's TV reception.
8	A person was injured when a shell exploded in a munitions factory but there was no liability because there was no escape of the thing that caused the injury.
9	A man was questioned about theft in his employer's office and was unaware that two security men were stationed outside the office to prevent him leaving.
10	The caption to a picture of a couple in a newspaper wrongly stated that they were engaged.

10 Tort Cases: Case Names

A	Read v Lyons		
B	Rose v Plenty		
C	Wheat v Lacon		
D	Cassidy v The Daily Mirror		
E	Hedley Byrne v Heller & Partners		
F	Hunter v Canary Wharf		
G	Allcock v Chief Constable of South Yorkshire		
H	Meering v Graham-White Aviation Co Ltd		
I	Taylor v Glasgow Corporation		
J	Barnett v Chelsea & Kensington Hospital		

ELEMENTS OF OFFENCES IN CRIME

The following are the essential ingredients of crimes on the A Level courses. They may be a quicker revision aid than the sections of Acts or the common law definitions themselves.

Offences against the person

Murder

1. A sane person over the age of 10
2. Unlawfully kills
3. A living human being
4. Within the jurisdiction of the English courts
5. With intent:
   - A to kill; or
   - B to commit GBH

Constructive manslaughter

1. A sane person over 10
2. Intentionally or recklessly
3. Does an unlawful and dangerous act
4. Which causes the death of
5. A living human being
6. Within the jurisdiction of the courts

Gross negligence manslaughter

1. A sane person over the age of 10
2. Acting under a duty
3. Does an act or omission which is so negligent as to go beyond compensation and amount to a crime
4. That causes the death of
5. A living human being
6. Within the jurisdiction of the courts

Wounding with intent—contrary to s18 Offences Against the Person Act 1861

1. Unlawfully and
2. Maliciously
3. A wounds; or
   B causes GBH
4. To any person
5. With intent to

A cause GBH;
B resist lawful arrest

Unlawful wounding—contrary to s20 OAPA 1861

1. Unlawfully and
2. Maliciously
3. A wounds; or
   B inflicts GBH
4. On any person

Assault occasioning actual bodily harm—contrary to s47 OAPA 1861

1. Does an act (assault or battery)
2. That causes another
3. Actual bodily harm
4. With intent:
   A to cause apprehension of immediate and unlawful violence;
   B to cause GBH
5. Reckless as to whether:
   A apprehension of harm is caused;
   B actual bodily harm is caused

Offences against property

Theft—contrary to s1 Theft Act 1968

1. Dishonestly
2. Appropriates
3. Property
4. Belonging to another
5. With the intention to permanently deprive the other of it

Robbery—contrary to s8 Theft Act 1968

1. Steals (*actus reus* and *mens rea* of theft)
2. Immediately before or at the time of the theft
3. Uses force or puts in fear of force
4. For the purpose of stealing

Burglary with intent—contrary to s9(1)(a) Theft Act 1968

1. Enters
2. A building or part of a building
3. As a trespasser
4. With intent to
   A steal;
   B inflict GBH on a person therein;
   C rape a person therein;
   D cause criminal damage

Burglary—contrary to s9(1)(b) Theft Act 1968

1. Having entered
2. A building or part of a building
3. As a trespasser
4. A Steals;
   B Inflicts GBH;
   C Attempts either

Obtaining property by deception—contrary to s15 Theft Act 1968

1. By any deception
2. Dishonestly
3. Obtains
4. Property
5. Belonging to another
6. With the intention to permanently deprive the other of it

Evasion of liability—contrary to s2(1)(a) Theft Act 1978

1. By any deception
2. Dishonestly
3. Secures the remission of all or part of an existing debt
4. Owed by himself or by another

Evasion of liability—contrary to s2(1)(b) Theft Act 1978

1. By any deception
2. With intent to make permanent default
3. Induces a creditor to wait for payment or forego
4. A debt owed by himself or another

Evasion of liability—contrary to s2(1)(c) Theft Act 1978

1. By any deception
2. Dishonestly
3. Obtains exemption or abatement of a debt

Making off without payment—contrary to s3 Theft Act 1978

1. A person knowing payment on the spot is required
2. Dishonestly
3. Makes off without having paid as required or expected
4. Intending to avoid payment

Criminal damage—contrary to s1(1) Criminal Damage Act 1971

1. Without lawful excuse
2. Destroys or damages
3. Property
4. Belonging to another
5. A Intentionally;
   B recklessly

Inchoate offences

Attempt—contrary to s1 Criminal Attempts Act 1981

1. With intent to commit an offence
2. Does an act
3. More than merely preparatory to the commission of the offence

LATIN PHRASES QUIZ

Studying law inevitably means that you will have been introduced to a number of Latin phrases. In the following revision quiz 18 Latin phrases have been put in the left-hand column. In the middle column say whether the phrase applies in crime, contract or tort. In the right-hand column try to remember what the phrase means or what it is used for.

1	*res ipsa loquitur*		
2	*mens rea*		
3	*restitutio in integrum*		
4	*non est factum*		
5	*volenti non fit injuria*		
6	*contra preferentum*		
7	*novus actus interveniens*		
8	*actus reus*		
9	*quantum meruit*		
10	*res extincta*		
11	*ab initio*		
12	*ex turpi causa non oritur actio*		
13	*uberrimae fides*		
14	*consensus ad idem*		
15	*ultra vires*		
16	*doli incapax*		
17	*simplex commendatio non obligat*		
18	*res sua*		

MISSING LINKS: CRIME

In each of the following short statements fill in the missing words to complete the passages accurately.

1 …….. is the dishonest ………………. of property ………………… .. ………… with the ………….. of permanently depriving the other of it.

2 Manslaughter can occur in one of two ways. If ………. could be charged but the defendant can claim one of three partial defences identified in the ………….. Act 19…, then the charge may be reduced to manslaughter and a full range of ………… will be available rather than the mandatory 'life' as for murder. This is then known as ………… manslaughter. Three possible defences are ………….. ………….. under s2, ………….. under s3 and a …….. ………… ……. under s4.

3 A person is not guilty by reason of ……….. if he is labouring under a ………… …. ……….. caused by a ………….. of the mind so as not to know the ……….. of his act or if he did know he did not know that it was ………

MISSING LINKS: CONTRACT LAW

In each of the following short statements fill in the missing words to complete the passages accurately.

1 A contract is formed when there is an ………….. which is supported by ………….. and there is also an intention to create ……….. …………….. The ………… is reached when a valid ………….. follows a valid …………..

2 A ………. of …… clause is inserted in a contract to prevent the other party from doing something harmful to the party inserting the clause. Such clauses are …… …… void. They may be validated if seen to be ……….. as between the …… and in the ……. interest. The party inserting the clause is only able to protect legitimate interests such as ……. connection not to merely prevent …………

3 ………….. occurs where through an event which is not the fault of either party the contract becomes ………….. to ……… This could be because of the ……… of the subject-matter, through ………… …………….. of the contract, or through subsequent ……….

MISSING LINKS: TORT

In each of the following short statements fill in the missing words to complete the passages accurately.

1 Negligence is proved when it is shown that the defendant owes a …… of …… which he has ………. by falling below the appropriate ………….. This must then have caused ………… Which is not too ……….. a consequence of the defendant's ……….. of duty. The defendant may not be ……….. when there is a break in the ……… of …………..

2 …………… liability occurs when one person is liable for the torts of another. This would normally occur in an ……………… relationship. To be successful the claimant would first have to prove

that the tortfeaser was the .... Of the defendant and secondly that the tortfeaser was .... in the course of .... rather than being on a .... on his own

3 The tort of .... v .... involves .... things which escape. It is said to be a tort of .... The owner of land will be liable for things .... on to ...... and .... there which would cause .... if they did .... Besides this the thing brought onto the land must involve a .....-.......... use of the land. Since the case of *Cambridge Water* it is also clear that the damage must be ....

CHAPTER 5

EXAM TECHNIQUE

What follows is an indication of what is required in an examination question. It is not the answer, although it incorporates the elements of answering the question. It is rather a structure, a way of identifying what needs to be done in any question. In that sense the process can be repeated mentally or in very brief note form when breaking down any question prior to writing the actual answer.

ANSWERING A PROBLEM QUESTION IN TORT

Problem questions may seem hard at first because the first thing that you have to do is to decide what the problem is all about and what area of the law is being tested, unlike in an essay where you are told this.

As identified in Chapter 4 in the section 'Answering problems in tort' there is always certain information in any problem question that leads to the specific area of law.

There are always four essential ingredients to answering problem questions:

- First you must be able to identify the key facts in the problem, the ones on which any resolution of the problem will depend.
- Secondly you will need to identify which is the appropriate law which applies to the particular situation in the problem.
- The third task is to apply the law to the facts.
- Finally you will need to reach conclusions of some sort. If the question asks you to advise, then that is what you need to do. On the other hand if the problem says 'Discuss the legal consequences of . . .' then you know that you can be less positive in your conclusions.

Problem

Homer, his wife Marge and children Bart and Lisa go to the Springfield Holiday Camp for two weeks in August. In their holiday contract is the following clause: 'Neither the Springfield Holiday Camp nor their servants or agents will be liable for death or injury to visitors, howsoever caused.' A large notice to the same effect is placed at the entrance to the Camp. The camp is owned and managed by Springfield Leisure Co.

Late one night while returning to the holiday chalet, which is high up on a slope, Homer falls down the steep steps that lead to the chalet from the road below. There is no guard-rail to the steps and the steps are also unlit. Homer suffers severe head injuries in the fall.

Marge is electrocuted and badly burnt when she plugs in the kettle in the chalet's kitchenette. The socket has actually been left live due to the negligence of Shoddy Electric Co who recently rewired the chalet.

Bart cuts himself badly and wrecks his jacket with a sharp knife when he sneaks into the kitchen in the Camp Restaurant to make himself a sandwich. The door is not locked but a notice on the door of the kitchen reads: 'Danger. Staff only.'

Lisa suffers a very bad stomach when she eats berries on a bush growing by the chalet front door. The berries are poisonous.

Advise Homer, Marge, Bart and Lisa of any remedies that they might have for their injuries and against whom.

The facts

It is important to have a clear idea of what the principal facts are, particular as here where there a number of different people and different problems involved. The main facts seem to be:

1. Springfield Leisure Co own and manage the Springfield Holiday Camp.
2. Homer, Marge and their children Bart and Lisa contract for a holiday at the camp for two weeks in August.
3. The contract contains an exclusion of liability for death or injury, however caused.
4. A notice to the same effect is posted at the entrance to the camp.
5. Homer is injured when he falls at night down steep unlit steps to his chalet with no hand rail.
6. Marge is electrocuted and badly burnt when plugging in the kettle.
7. The socket is live due to the negligence of Shoddy Electric Co who rewired it.
8. Bart cuts himself on a knife in the restaurant kitchen.
9. A notice on the kitchen door reads: 'Danger. Staff only.'
10. Lisa is poisoned when she eats berries growing on a bush by the front door.
11. Bart and Lisa are both children.

The appropriate law

It is very important when answering problem questions that you use only the law that is relevant to the precise facts, if for no other reason that you are not getting any marks for using law that is irrelevant, and so you are wasting valuable writing time. By looking at the various facts we can say that the following law may be relevant in our problem here:

1. The area involved is the Occupiers' Liability Acts.
2. A the 1957 Act covers liability towards 'visitors'—those lawfully on the premises;
   B The 1984 Act concerns trespassers—and is appropriate only to personal injury, not property damage.
3. There are three key issues:
   A what counts as premises;
   B who is an 'occupier' and so who can be sued;
   C who can claim under the Acts and under which one;
4. There is no real definition of premises in either Act—the common law applies, and is widely defined (i.e. wide enough to include a ladder in *Wheeler v Copas*).
5. Occupier is again not defined in either Act—again the common law applies: an occupier is 'anybody who is in control of the premises'—*Wheat v Lacon.*
6. Under the 1957 Act a 'visitor' is anybody with a lawful right to be on the premises.
7. Under s2(1) a 'common duty of care' is owed to all visitors.
8. Under s2(2) the duty is to take all reasonable care to keep the visitor safe for the purposes for which (s)he has legitimately entered the premises.
9. The standard of care is as for negligence so the same sorts of principles apply:
10. A under s2(3) an occupier must be prepared for children to be less careful than adults would be;
    B the occupier must not do anything to 'allure' the child into danger—*Taylor v Glasgow Corporation*;
    C an occupier may be able to rely on the duty of parents to supervise very young children—*Phipps v Rochester Corporation.*
11. An occupier will not be liable for the harm caused by the work of independent contractors provided that:

A it is reasonable for the occupier to entrust the work to someone else—*Haseldine v Daw*;
B a competent contractor is hired—*Ferguson v Welsh*;
C The occupier carries out checks on the work if appropriate—*AMF v Magnet Bowling*.

12 An occupier may avoid liability under s2(1) in a number of ways:
A warning notices, provided they are effective—*Rae v Mars* (and nothing short of a barrier may possibly be sufficient for children);
B exclusion clauses in contracts—but these would be subject to the Unfair Contract Terms Act, and a clause excluding liability for death or injury caused by negligence is invalid under s2(1);
C the defences of contributory negligence and consent (not relevant here).

13 The 1984 Act applies by s1(1)(a) to persons other than visitors.

14 Under the 1984 Act an occupier is liable under s1(1) in respect of dangers 'due to the state of the premises or things done or omitted to be done on them'.

15 Under s1(3) the occupier will be liable if (a) he is aware of the danger, (b) knows that the trespasser may come into the vicinity of the danger, and (c) the risk is one against which the occupier might be expected to provide some protection.

Applying the law to the facts

1 We know that Springfield Leisure Co own and manage the holiday camp so we can feel that they 'control' the premises and are occupiers and therefore defendants under the Act.

2 We know also that Homer and his family have paid for their holiday and so will be 'visitors' and therefore may claim under the 1957 Act. The common duty of care applies to them all and they are entitled to expect the same standard of care.

3 'Premises' presents no problems here—the holiday camp clearly is.

4 It is easier past this point to take each individual in turn:

Homer:

- the question is whether not providing a handrail on the steep steps and not having them lit is a breach of Springfield's duty—it would certainly seem to fall below an appropriate standard of care, and the facts in any case seem to resemble those in *Wheat v Lacon*;
- the exclusion clause cannot apply because of s2(1) of UCTA;
- similarly the warning notice outside the camp would fail to relieve liability unless it covered specific risks—*Rae v Mars*.

Marge:

- leaving sockets 'live' clearly falls below an appropriate standard of care;
- the question here is whether it is Springfield or Shoddy who is responsible;
- it will obviously depend on whether Shoddy is a reliable contractor or not;
- clearly it is appropriate for Springfield to delegate that type of work, and they do not have the expertise to check it, they are relying on the contractors—*Haseldine v Daw*;
- the exclusion clause and warning notice would fail for the same reasons.

Lisa:

- Lisa is a child so under s2(3) is entitled to expect greater care than an adult;
- the bush appears to be a possible 'allurement', certainly if we compare it with the facts in *Taylor v Glasgow Corporation*;

- it would be hard to expect the parents to take full responsibility here where the bush is outside the front door, and so is unlikely that *Phipps v Rochester Corporation* could apply in the circumstances;
- again the exclusion clause cannot apply and the notice is even less appropriate here because Lisa is a child.

Bart:

- Bart has entered a part of the premises from which he is barred—this may make him a trespasser;
- Bart is a child and a kitchen may well be an allurement to a hungry child—Springfield may expect some risk of trespassers to such parts of the premises if they do not keep them locked up *Herrington v B R Board*;
- furthermore kitchen implements, sharp knives etc. are clearly dangerous if unattended;
- the notice on the door is unlikely to be sufficient warning since it is imprecise in respect of the risk and in any case Bart is a child;
- the 1984 Act applies only in respect of injuries so Bart may be unable to claim in respect of his damaged jacket.

Conclusions

We have shown how the law applies to each of our four central characters, and would be able to advise them to sue with confidence.

- Homer and Lisa could both sue Springfield for their injuries under the 1957 Act;
- Marge can sue for her injuries, but unless Shoddy are disreputable contractors whom Springfield should not have hired then her action will be against Shoddy rather than Springfield;
- Bart is a trespasser and will sue Springfield under the 1984 Act but for his injuries only, not for his other damage.

ANSWERING AN ESSAY QUESTION IN CONTRACT LAW

Essay questions may seem to be easy by comparison to problems but in fact they are not. In most cases you are told in the question what the specific area of law is that the examiner wishes you to write about. Nevertheless, if you are trying to gain good marks, finding out what the subject matter of the essay is provides only one part of actually answering it. It is very tempting to see that the essay is for instance about offer and then to dig deep into your memory of your lecture notes and to repeat everything on offer. However, as an experienced examiner I have never known a colleague to prepare an exam question entitled 'Write all you know about offer.' and I doubt that you have ever seen such a question either. The important thing is to try to answer the question set. So if the question asks you to 'Discuss the ways in which termination of an offer may take place' there is no point in discussing how an offer differs from an invitation to treat or a mere statement of price.

Many essay questions contain at least two elements:

- a requirement for you to display factual knowledge—here it is important for you to stick to the relevant details and not stray into the irrelevant. This merely makes the examiner think you are throwing in all of your knowledge on an area indiscriminately in order to impress with the breadth of your knowledge, while in fact it has the opposite effect. It is important here also not to assume knowledge on the part of the examiner, so define all your terminology. The factor that will distinguish your essay from that of someone who has not studied law is the extent to which it is supported by the case law and statute;
- a critical element—most essays are concerned with not merely testing your knowledge but also your appreciation of it. This is what words like 'discuss', 'analyse', 'critically evaluate' and

other similar terms are used for. This is often the crux of an essay question. The extent to which you appreciate how the law is inadequate, or why it is complicated or inconsistent is tested here. So you should at least try to respond to the particular question asked and direct the knowledge you are using towards that point. Again the most effective essay answers contain some sort of considered argument and reach some kind of conclusion.

Essay
Using cases in illustration critically discuss what is meant by the term 'offer'.

Knowledge

1. It is probably important to start by indicating that the offer is one part of the agreement necessary for formation of any contract, the other part being the acceptance of the offer.
2. The question is, however, asking specifically about offer so there is no requirement at all to consider acceptance beyond this basic point.
3. The essay is asking what an offer is so it is asking for a comparative definition with things that look like an offer but which are not.
4. Because of this it is probably not necessary to consider the various rules of offer in detail.
5. In this case it is necessary first to define an offer as a firm indication by the offeror of the terms by which he is prepared to be legally bound, and to state that the offer must be certain—*Guthing v Lynn.*
6. Then it is necessary to compare it with other things that though they may look at first glance to be similar to offer in fact operate in an entirely different way.
7. The first of these is an invitation to treat. It can be defined as an invitation to the other party to make an offer, usually an offer to buy. The contract is then formed by the agreement to sell which is the acceptance in this case.
8. You can use a variety of examples of invitation to treat and explain how the principle operates in each case:
   - A goods displayed on shelves in a self-service shop and *Pharmaceutical Society of GB v Boots Cash Chemists Ltd* (no contract is formed until the goods are selected from the shelves and taken to the cash desk, the offer, and the sale accepted by the assistant);
   - B goods on display in a shop window and *Fisher v Bell* (with similar conditions as to selecting the goods);
   - C goods or services advertised in a newspaper or magazine and *Partridge v Crittenden* (a party can respond to the advertisement by making an offer to buy the goods);
   - D tenders for services and *Spencer v Harding* (the request for tenders being the invitation to the other parties to make their offers by their tenders for the work and the party requesting the tenders can then accept whichever bid suits their best interests);
   - E an invitation to council tenants to buy their property and *Gibson v Manchester City Council*;
   - F lots at an auction and *British Car Auctions v Wright or Harris v Nickerson* (the lots are the invitation to the bidders to make offers to buy which they will do by making their bids, a contract is then only formed on the fall of the auctioneer's hammer).
9. It is also possible to compare an offer with the more passive situation represented by the mere stating of an acceptable price and *Harvey v Facey.*
10. Finally offer in its usual sense could be compared with the more complex type of offer in a unilateral contract and *Carlill v The Carbolic Smoke Ball Co* (this may be particularly appropriate in the case where rewards are offered for example when a pet is lost).

Critical comment

1. The essay is asking for a critical explanation of offer so some sort of commentary concerning the simple aspects of offer together with commentary on the complexities is required.
2. We have already looked at those areas that look like offer but are not in the section detailing knowledge above. Any sort of commentary on this basic point is valid, i.e.
   - A that offer as the starting point for a contract is a relatively simple concept: A asks B if B wants to buy specified goods in return for a specified price. If B is happy with the goods and the price (s)he accepts the offer and the contract is formed;
   - B that offer is not always as straightforward as it seems because there are so many contrasting circumstances which have very different consequences: invitation to treat, mere statements of price, unilateral offers etc. (and the explanation of why and how they are different).
3. The other significant critical element to pick up on are the range of situations that do not neatly conform to either the standard 'offer' situations or standard 'invitation to treat' situations:
   - A advertisements involving a unilateral offer and *Carlill v The Carbolic Smoke Ball Co* where there is no invitation to treat because a specific promise has been made to any party who conforms to the terms of the unilateral offer;
   - B a statement of price where an offer is also intended and *Biggs v Boyd Gibbins* where there was an offer rather than a mere invitation to treat because the negotiations indicated so;
   - C Competitive tendering and *Harvela Investments Ltd v Royal Trust Co of Canada* where the tender was not an invitation to treat but an offer because the parties had actually been told that the highest bidder would win the competition (the situation on referential bidding could also be considered here, and *Blackpool and Fylde Aero Club Ltd v Blackpool Borough Council* could also be considered with the added complication of all tenders in a competitive tendering situation having to be considered).

Conclusions

It is a good idea to draw all of this factual knowledge and critical comment to some form of conclusion. The logical one to make in this situation is that while, on the surface 'offer' seems a fairly straightforward concept it nevertheless has over the years been subjected to many complications. In this way any party contemplating entering negotiations towards a contract needs to be certain of their behaviour.

ANSWERING A DATA RESPONSE OR SOURCE-BASED QUESTION IN CRIMINAL LAW

Sources are not sufficient in themselves to answer the question, so you need to bring knowledge and understanding to the exam as well being given the source material.

However, like with problems, the source can provide a great deal of information necessary to answer the questions, and will lead you anyway to specific areas of law, and even specific problem areas to do with the law in the source material. You are given reading time with source based questions, even if without saying that a specific period of time is to be set aside. You should make use of this reading time to familiarise yourself with the source material. It is a good idea to get used to identifying important issues that crop up within the source. With practice of doing this you will find not only that there are elements in the source that can be used or referred to in your answers, but also that you are probably able to guess what types of questions are coming up even before you have read them, just by reading the source material.

It is in the nature of using source material that an examiner is able then to use the material to ask you a variety of different types of questions:

- you can be asked questions that specifically test your knowledge of a given area;
- you could be asked to consider a problem area identified in the source and thus to analyse, or to discuss, or to comment, or to evaluate, as you might have been called on to do in essay type questions;
- you might also be asked to apply material found in the source in some way, which is fairly similar to what you may come across in traditional problem questions.

You should be prepared to answer in all of these different ways. One advantage of this is that you get the opportunity to use the skills that you are good at as well as those where you may have less confidence.

Source material

EXTRACT ADAPTED FROM 'MANSLAUGHTER: *DALBY* REVISITED', STEPHEN O'DOHERTY, *JUSTICE OF THE PEACE*, VOL 163, 8 MAY 1999, PP 368–371

The offence of manslaughter can be divided into two limbs, voluntary and involuntary. The latter may itself be divided into two further categories: causing death by an unlawful and dangerous act and causing death by an act of gross negligence while a duty of care exists. This article concentrates upon the 'unlawful act' limb of the offence and its relationship to s23 Offences Against the Persons Act 1861.

The material parts of s23 provide that 'whosoever shall unlawfully and maliciously administer to, or cause to be administered to or taken by any other person any poison or other destructive or noxious thing, so as to endanger the life of such person ... shall be guilty of an offence.'

In *Cato,* the appellant went with friends back to the house they shared. One of them named Farmer produced a bag of heroin and syringes. Farmer and Cato each filled up the syringe with the amount of heroin he wished and then gave the syringe to the other to inject him. The strength of the mixture was determined by the person who was going to receive it. Farmer died and Cato was charged with manslaughter and administering a noxious thing contrary to s23.

The appeal centred on unlawful act manslaughter. Lord Widgery CJ dealt with the act of injecting the heroin. 'It may seem strange to most of us, although possession or supply of heroin is an offence, it is not an offence to take it or to administer it.' The fact that heroin was a noxious thing was sufficient to dismiss the appeal against the conviction for the s23 offence. In the view of the court the prohibition in that statute therefore made the injection of heroin into another an unlawful act for the purposes of the offence of manslaughter. In this case it would seem that the court was extending the accused's initial criminal act of possession and supply so that the entire incident, including the injection, thereby became unlawful.

In *Dalby* somewhat different circumstances arose. The defendant supplied *Diconal*, a class A drug, which he lawfully possessed, to the deceased, O'Such. Each prepared the tablets and then injected the drugs into himself. The following day O'Such was found dead from the effects of the drugs. Dalby pleaded guilty to supplying drugs and was convicted of manslaughter. The Court of Appeal quashed the manslaughter conviction, holding that the act of supplying a controlled drug was not an act which caused direct harm. The defendant had committed an unlawful act with supplying the drugs but the unlawful act had stopped with the supply. It had not caused O'Such's death. There was no s23 offence for the prosecution to rely on for the unlawful act because Dalby had not administered the drug.

In July 1998 the Court of Appeal had the opportunity to consider a case where the facts fell between those in *Cato* and *Dalby*. The deceased, Bosque, asked the accused for drugs. Kennedy agreed, prepared a syringe with a heroin mixture, handed the syringe to Bosque who immediately injected himself. A short time later Bosque stopped breathing and was subsequently pronounced dead. Kennedy was prosecuted for supplying heroin and for manslaughter based on the commission of an unlawful and dangerous act. In *Cato* the deceased determined the strength of the mixture but it was actually administered by the accused, hence the count under s23. In *Dalby*, the drugs were supplied by the defendant but it was the deceased who actually made up the mixture and injected himself. The principal distinction in *Kennedy* was the act of filling the syringe with the mixture. However the court declined to follow *Dalby* and applied *Cato*. Waller LJ stated: 'The injection of the heroin by Bosque was itself an unlawful act and if the appellant assisted in and wilfully encouraged that unlawful conduct he would himself be acting unlawfully.'

The basis of the decision therefore seems to be that the act of injection of a noxious thing by Bosque was itself unlawful and thereby Kennedy aided and abetted that unlawful act. The offence committed by Bosque was possession and that offence was completed at the moment he took the syringe from Kennedy. The act of injecting it added nothing to that offence. It is respectfully submitted that to infer that the self-injection itself was a separate criminal act is incorrect.

One aspect which has not yet been dealt with in detail is the central requirement that there must be an 'unlawful act'. Lord Widgery [in *Cato*] viewed the entire incident as a whole but it is necessary to be able to identify the precise unlawful act in order to ascertain if an act which might be unsavoury is an unlawful act for these purposes. As the actual *consumption* of heroin is not, of itself, illegal, is the act of injection an unlawful act? It seems clear from *Cato* that the court did not consider the act of injection illegal *per se* although it appears that the court in *Kennedy* came to a different conclusion.

It is submitted that on its own facts, the conviction of *Kennedy* can (just) be upheld. It was not the supply of the heroin which justified the conviction for manslaughter, but that Kennedy's actions caused Bosque to take the noxious substance which was responsible for his death.

Questions

1. Lines 1 and 2 of the source refer to 'voluntary manslaughter' and 'involuntary manslaughter. Briefly outline the differences between the two.

2. Using the source and decided cases critically discuss the offence of 'constructive' or 'unlawful act' manslaughter.

3. Giving reasons consider whether any of the following are likely to be prosecuted for constructive manslaughter in the light of the three cases in the source:
   (i) Amanda and Rachel went together to Rachel's house where Amanda produced a tin of solvent based glue. They put some glue in a carrier bag and both began sniffing the glue in turn. When Rachel was barely conscious she asked Amanda to put more glue in the bag and for Amanda to put the bag over her (Rachel's) nose. Some time later Rachel fell unconscious and died.

(ii) George asked Ronald, the landlord of a pub, to sell him two bottles of whisky to take home when it was after hours. Ronald sold George the whisky. Ronald drank both bottles in a short space of time when he got home and later died.

(iii) Jaz, who was depressed, asked Simon to supply him with amphetamines. While Simon was still with him Jaz took a fatal dose of the pills. Later after Simon had left Jaz died.

Before you answer any of the three questions you can identify certain things in the source itself:

1. There is reference to involuntary manslaughter.
2. In particular the source focuses on 'constructive' or 'unlawful act' manslaughter.
3. Much of the source material is considering what will and will not amount to an unlawful act for the purposes of a manslaughter charge.
4. Finally the source is also about deaths caused by using drugs and administering noxious substances.

Answering question 1

The first question is predominantly knowledge-based; some of it you can find from the source material as there is some information on what amounts to 'involuntary manslaughter' in the source itself. The details on voluntary manslaughter you will need to provide yourself.

Also you should remember that the question says 'briefly' so there is no need to give a blow-by-blow account of every last detail of every element of the offences.

So your answer could include that:

- all forms of manslaughter share the same *actus reus* as for murder: the unlawful killing of a living human being by a sane person over the age of ten within the jurisdiction of the English courts;
- voluntary manslaughter occurs where it is possible to show not only this actus reus but also the mens rea for murder: malice aforethought, whereas with involuntary manslaughter malice aforethought, the intent to kill or to cause grievous, that is serious, bodily harm, cannot be shown;
- with voluntary manslaughter the prosecution will therefore have brought a charge of murder whereas with involuntary manslaughter it may not;
- with voluntary manslaughter the defendant will ask for the court to accept one of three pleas from the Homicide Act 1957: diminished responsibility under s2, provocation under s3, or a failed suicide pact under s4, and will do so in order to reduce the charge and avoid a mandatory life sentence;
- in the case of involuntary manslaughter the defendant will be able to show insufficient *mens rea* for murder and the prosecution will either involve the commission of an unlawful act which is recognised as dangerous and which inadvertently causes death (constructive), or a death caused where the defendant, who owes a duty of care to the victim, falls so far below the appropriate standard that it goes beyond compensation and amounts to a crime, or indeed a death caused by recklessness, where an unjustified risk of harm has been recognised but nevertheless been taken.

Answering question 2

The question asks you to 'critically discuss' the offence, and also to use cases and the source—so you should use cases in illustration of your explanation of the offence, and also include some sort of critical comment.

Your factual ingredients might include:

- an explanation that unlawful act manslaughter involves an unlawful act, which is dangerous, and which causes the inadvertent death of the victim;

- that the *actus reus* will therefore be the same as for all homicides;
- that the *mens rea* will be the same as for the unlawful act;
- that the act must be unlawful rather than a lawful act carried out unlawfully, and use *Andrews v DPP*;
- that the act must such that all sober and reasonable people would recognise that it would subject the other to at least the risk of some harm and use cases such as *R v Church* and *DPP v Newbury and Jones*;
- that although according to *Dawson* traditionally the unlawful act had to be directed towards the victim, that following *Goodfellow* this no longer seems to be the case;
- that lawful justification for the act may mean that it is not unlawful, and mention *R v Scarlett*.

Your critical comments might include:

- that the offence is difficult to prove;
- that in some circumstances it can seem unfair that a person should be guilty of a homicide offence because they did an unlawful and dangerous act;
- the problem in *Cato* of what actually amounts to an unlawful act, and whether the definition of unlawful act is sometimes stretched too far;
- that the Law Commission has been critical of the offence in a number of ways:
  - —the uncertainty of circumstances where omission can lead to liability
  - —the sheer breadth of circumstances leading to the offence
  - —the difficulty of applying sentences
  - —that the offence is unprincipled because it 'requires only a foreseeable risk of some harm';

  and has suggested reform of the law in this area.

Answering question 3

You should be aware that when using application questions the examiner will try to use the source material to steer you towards the answers, so they will be based on the law that emerges from the source. Sometimes the scenarios that the examiner creates will be distinguishable from the cases in the source and sometimes not. Here you should be able to recognise that the three scenarios in question 3 are based in turn on each of the three cases in the source: *Cato, Dalby* and *Kennedy*:

A in the case of Amanda you would identify that as in *Cato* that it was the administering of the noxious thing, the glue, that can be classed as the unlawful act under s23, with the resultant death being manslaughter because of this;

B in the case of Ronald you will recognise that *Dalby* applies. Though Ronald has engaged in an unlawful act, the selling of the whiskey after hours, this in itself is not dangerous, and so cannot be the cause of the death;

C Simon's case seems to reproduce some of the complexities of *Kennedy*. His unlawful act is the supplying of an illegal drug but this has no connection with the death of Jaz. It is Simon's aiding and abetting of Jaz's offence that puts him in danger of a manslaughter charge. Since he handed the pills to Jaz, knew he was depressed and saw Jaz take so many of the pills this may amount to the 'wilful encouragement' identified in the article.

Answers to Revision Exercises

ANSWERS TO CONTRACT CROSSWORD

		s	u	f	f	i	c	i	e	n	t					
					p	r	o	m	i	s	e					
					b	e	n	e	f	i	t					
				G	l	a	s	s	b	r	o	o	k			
			D	C	B	u	i	l	d	e	r	s				
				T	w	e	d	d	l	e						
		C	h	a	p	p	e	l	l	v	N	e	s	t	l	e
		p	e	p	p	e	r	c	o	r	n					
P	a	o	O	n	v	L	a	u	Y	i	u	L	o	n	g	
			H	i	g	h	T	r	e	e	s					
			d	e	t	r	i	m	e	n	t					
				e	s	t	o	p	p	e	l					
				P	i	n	n	e	l							

ANSWERS TO THE MULTIPLE CHOICE CASE LAW REVISION QUIZ

1 A Contract

2 A Contract C Tort

3 B Crime

4 A Crime B Tort

5 A Crime B Tort C Tort

6 A Contract C Crime

7 A Tort B Contract

ANSWERS TO 10 CRIMINAL LAW CASES

1 C **2** E **3** J **4** D **5** F **6** H **7** B **8** I **9** A **10** G

ANSWERS TO 10 CONTRACT LAW CASES

1 D **2** J **3** E **4** G **5** I **6** A **7** C **8** F **9** H **10** B

ANSWERS TO THE WORDSEARCH

R	Y	L	A	N	N	R	T	U	R	O	B	L	C	C	H	V	G	N	I
P	O	S	A	I	N	K	I	O	V	O	I	E	E	D	C	K	I	N	H
T	E	E	R	Y	I	H	S	E	S	I	S	F	D	R	O	Y	G	I	C
E	G	N	O	S	N	E	V	E	T	S	V	E	U	H	G	O	N	O	D
N	I	Y	O	P	J	H	I	T	O	N	R	E	R	C	H	A	I	N	U
O	I	P	Y	O	H	S	S	V	N	I	O	M	I	M	M	A	N	T	Y
T	R	L	E	T	H	A	M	P	E	L	H	A	S	K	I	N	N	O	R
S	T	E	L	I	D	A	E	D	A	L	D	D	C	E	S	H	A	I	R
V	O	O	A	O	R	G	H	H	N	O	P	I	R	M	I	L	L	L	A
N	G	G	N	D	O	Y	S	E	D	C	D	D	L	A	E	E	V	O	B
O	P	E	E	T	V	W	O	O	D	V	S	C	A	R	T	H	R	E	V
T	I	N	T	T	E	L	V	I	O	R	H	M	T	Y	E	Z	E	O	N
L	E	F	F	E	B	R	Y	R	B	K	S	O	U	O	U	O	L	N	O
O	X	E	H	R	I	I	A	O	I	N	O	R	I	S	K	X	W	O	T
B	Y	T	S	A	R	P	H	E	N	C	G	S	T	R	I	O	O	G	L
R	D	E	O	N	A	P	I	T	S	S	G	H	H	I	R	A	F	I	E
I	N	N	H	C	H	T	S	T	O	N	O	L	E	B	R	A	M	F	P
A	S	T	G	T	H	H	H	C	N	E	R	W	V	E	D	Y	H	E	A
C	C	T	V	R	A	E	I	C	E	E	A	R	A	T	H	E	R	R	H
K	C	I	R	Y	I	M	V	K	L	I	T	S	P	P	A	T	T	I	C

ANSWERS TO 10 TORT CASES

1 G **2** E **3** B **4** C **5** J **6** I **7** F **8** A **9** H **10** D

ANSWERS TO THE LATIN PHRASES QUIZ

1 Tort. The thing speaks for itself. A means of making a negligence claim without the necessary proof of negligence.

2 Crime. The mental element in crime or criminal intent.

3 Contract. In rescission the remedy is lost unless it is possible to restore the parties to their actual pre-contract situation.

4 Contract. This is not my deed. A mistake relating to the signing of a document.

5 Tort. The defence of consent.

6. Contract. Rule that any ambiguity in a term operates against the party inserting it in the contract.
7. Tort. A new act intervenes. A break in the chain of causation that relieves the defendant of liability.
8. Crime. The guilty act. The conduct element in crime and its surrounding circumstances.
9. Contract. A remedy usually where the contract is silent on payment or a contract for services is incomplete. Payment for the work already done.
10. Contract. A mistake as to the existence of the subject matter of the contract.
11. Tort. From the beginning. Associated with trespass.
12. Tort. The defence that the other cannot claim because of his own illegality.
13. Contract. Utmost good faith. In contracts requiring fidelity e.g. insurance.
14. Contract. The mutuality of obligations between the parties representing the agreement made between them.
15. Contract. Beyond the powers of. As when a corporation acts outside the scope of its memorandum of association.
16. Crime. Below the age of ten a person is incapable of forming criminal intent.
17. Contract. Refers to the fact that 'trade puffs' create no contractual liability.
18. Contract. A mistake as to the ownership of the contract goods.

ANSWERS TO THE MISSING LINKS: CRIME

1. Theft—appropriation—belonging to another—intention.
2. murder—Homicide—57—sentence—voluntary—diminished responsibility—provocation—failed suicide pact
3. Insanity—defect of reason—disease—quality—wrong

ANSWERS TO THE MISSING LINKS: CONTRACT

1. agreement—consideration—legal relations—agreement—acceptance—offer
2. restraint—trade—*prima facie*—reasonable—parties—public—client—competition
3. Frustration—impossible—perform—destruction—commercial sterilisation—illegality

ANSWERS TO THE MISSING LINKS: TORT

1. duty—care—breached—standard—damage—remote—breach—liable—chain—causation
2. Vicarious—employment—employee—acting—employment—frolic
3. Rylands—Fletcher—dangerous—strict liability—brought—land—accumulated—damage—escape —non—natural—foreseeable

INDEX